Ext JS 3.0 Cookbook

109 great recipes for building impressive rich internet applications using the Ext JS JavaScript library

Jorge Ramon

BIRMINGHAM - MUMBAI

Ext JS 3.0 Cookbook

First published: October 2009

Production Reference: 1141009

Published by Packt Publishing Ltd.
32 Lincoln Road
Olton
Birmingham, B27 6PA, UK.

ISBN 978-1-847198-70-9

www.packtpub.com

Cover Image by Vinayak Chittar (vinayak.chittar@gmail.com)

Credits

Author

Jorge Ramon

Reviewer

Colin Ramsay

Acquisition Editor

David Barnes

Development Editor

Rakesh Shejwal

Technical Editors

Aditya Belpathak

Wilson D'souza

Copy Editor

Sneha Kulkarni

Editorial Team Leader

Abhijeet Deobhakta

Project Team Leader

Priya Mukherji

Project Coordinator

Ashwin Shetty

Proofreader

Andie Scothern

Indexer

Hemangini Bari

Production Coordinator

Dolly Dasilva

Cover Work

Dolly Dasilva

About the Author

Jorge Ramon is currently the Vice President of Development for Taladro Systems LLC, where he has led the design and development of a number of software products for the law industry.

Jorge has over 16 years of experience as a software developer and has also created web applications, search engines, and automatic-control software. He actively contributes to the software development community through his blog, MiamiCoder.com.

To my parents. They showed me the way.

Thanks to Kshipra Singh, Douglas Paterson, David Barnes, Abhijeet Deobhakta, Ashwin Shetty, Swapna V. Verlekar, Rakesh Shejwal, Wilson D'souza, Aditya Belpathak, and the rest of the team at Packt Publishing.

About the Reviewer

Colin Ramsay remembers the days when people tried to charge for web browsers, and marvels at how far we've come since then. He started his web career by hacking on ASP and PHP websites, and has now progressed to some of the more in-vogue technologies, such as ASP.NET MVC and Ruby on Rails. His JavaScript fascination has been constant throughout, and resulted in his co-authorship of 'Learning Ext JS'. He's a partner at Go Tripod Ltd, a UK development company, working with a range of interesting technologies to make exciting things for the Web!

Table of Contents

Preface

In the world of Rich Internet Applications (RIA) development, Ext JS stands out as a cross-browser JavaScript library that offers the applications developer a powerful toolset. With a set of customizable user interface widgets similar to those found in desktop operating systems, an effective data binding model, a comprehensive programming interface for manipulating the Document Object Model and communicating with the server, a committed development team, and an enthusiastic users' community, the Ext JS library is a great choice for today's web builders.

This book addresses many of the library's features, from the perspective of how they can be used to solve the real-world challenges faced by those that develop internet applications.

What this book covers

Chapter 1—The DOM and Data Types, the Ext JS way, covers the Ext JS facilities for working with different browsers, the Document Object Model (DOM), and the Ext JS data types. Its recipes will teach you how to detect browsers and platforms, manipulate the DOM, encode and decode JSON and URL data, and work with arrays, strings, numbers, and dates. In this chapter you will also learn how to augment the features of the Ext JS classes, as well as how to incorporate library features into your own JavaScript classes.

Chapter—Laying Out a Rich User Interface, will help you to learn how to use layouts to create user interfaces with the Ext JS widgets. This chapter explains the common uses of some of the library's native layouts, and teaches you how to combine and augment these layouts to build great-looking and functional interfaces.

Chapter 3—Load, Validate, and Submit Forms, focuses on forms processing. In this chapter you will find tips and techniques for effective field validation, details on how to load data into forms, as well as advice on how to use forms to upload files to the server. As in previous chapters, in Chapter 3 you will find examples of how to extend the library's classes, in particular, how to create custom form fields.

Chapter 4—Fun with Combo Boxes and Date Fields, is a continuation of the form fields recipes introduced in Chapter 3. Chapter 4 is loaded with examples of how to use the ComboBox and DateField form components. It will teach you how to take advantage of ComboBox features like paging and item templates, as well as how to safely capture master-details and dates range input.

Chapter 5—Using Grid Panels to Display and Edit Tabular Data, consists of recipes that encompass the display of data using Ext JS grid panels. They explain different approaches to loading, editing, and saving data, as well as looking at how to implement features like grouping and group summaries. Chapter 5 uses techniques introduced in Chapter 3 to teach you how the Ext JS GridPanel widget can be enhanced through the use of plugins.

Chapter 6—More Applications of Grid and List views, expands on Chapter 5's examples. It explains multiple ways to use the GridPanel widget to display master-details relationships, approaches to displaying tabular data more efficiently, and how to edit data with the new RowEditor class.

Chapter 7—Keeping Tabs on your Trees, explores the TabPanel and Treview widgets. Besides how to use their main features, in this chapter you will also learn how to take advantage of plugins to enhance these widgets. This chapter also teaches you how to implement usage scenarios involving drag-and-drop and master-details displays with tree views and panels.

Chapter 8—Making Progress with Menus and Toolbars, consists of recipes that examine the commonly-used menu items, as well as the different ways to set up toolbars and progress bars in your applications.

Chapter 9—Well Charted Territory, consists of recipes that explain the typical usage scenarios of the chart widget, as well as approaches to configuring and customizing the look of the slider widget.

Chapter 10—Patterns in Ext JS, provides examples of some important design patterns used to build robust and flexible applications. These examples cover techniques such as resource management using lazy instantiation, prototyping and encapsulating using code modules and pre-configured classes, dependency management with publish/subscribe models, and state preservation.

What you need for this book

The recipes in this book use the Ext JS 3.0 SDK, available from the Ext JS website at `http://www.extjs.com/products/extjs/download.php`. You will need to download and install the SDK in order to run the code for the recipes.

Some recipes use the Sakila sample database, provided by MySQL AB. The Sakila sample database is available from `http://dev.mysql.com/doc/`. Installation instructions are available at `http://dev.mysql.com/doc/sakila/en/sakila.html`.

It is recommended that you use a JavaScript debugger when running the code for the recipes.

Who this book is for

The Ext JS Cookbook is for Ext JS users who want a book of useful techniques, with explanations, that they can refer to and adapt to their purposes. Developers who are already familiar with Ext JS will find practical guidance and numerous examples covering most of the library's features and components that can be used as a solid foundation to build upon when creating rich internet applications.

Conventions

In this book, you will find a number of styles of text that distinguish between different kinds of information. Here are some examples of these styles, and an explanation of their meaning.

Code words in text are shown as follows: "Initialize the global QuickTips instance."

A block of code is set as follows:

```
var browser = "";
if (Ext.isChrome) {
    browser = "Hi! I'm the new kid on the block";
}
```

When we wish to draw your attention to a particular part of a code block, the relevant lines or items are set in bold:

```
{ xtype: 'textfield', id: 'login-pwd',
    fieldLabel: 'Password', inputType: 'password',
    allowBlank: false, minLength: 6, maxLength: 32,
    minLengthText: 'Password must be at least 6 characters long.'
}
```

New terms and **important words** are shown in bold. Words that you see on the screen, in menus or dialog boxes for example, appear in the text like this: "clicking the **Next** button moves you to the next screen".

Warnings or important notes appear in a box like this.

Tips and tricks appear like this.

Reader feedback

Feedback from our readers is always welcome. Let us know what you think about this book—what you liked or may have disliked. Reader feedback is important for us to develop titles that you really get the most out of.

To send us general feedback, simply drop an email to feedback@packtpub.com, and mention the book title in the subject of your message.

If there is a book that you need and would like to see us publish, please send us a note in the **SUGGEST A TITLE** form on www.packtpub.com or email suggest@packtpub.com.

If there is a topic that you have expertise in and you are interested in either writing or contributing to a book, see our author guide on www.packtpub.com/authors.

Customer support

Now that you are the proud owner of a Packt book, we have a number of things to help you to get the most from your purchase.

Downloading the example code for the book

Visit http://www.packtpub.com/files/code/8709_Code.zip to directly download the example code.

The downloadable files contain instructions on how to use them.

Errata

Although we have taken every care to ensure the accuracy of our contents, mistakes do happen. If you find a mistake in one of our books—maybe a mistake in text or code—we would be grateful if you would report this to us. By doing so, you can save other readers from frustration, and help us to improve subsequent versions of this book. If you find any errata, please report them by visiting http://www.packtpub.com/support, selecting your book, clicking on the **let us know** link, and entering the details of your errata. Once your errata are verified, your submission will be accepted and the errata added to any list of existing errata. Any existing errata can be viewed by selecting your title from http://www.packtpub.com/support.

Piracy

Piracy of copyright material on the Internet is an ongoing problem across all media. At Packt, we take the protection of our copyright and licenses very seriously. If you come across any illegal copies of our works in any form on the Internet, please provide us with the location address or website name immediately so that we can pursue a remedy.

Please contact us at copyright@packtpub.com with a link to the suspected pirated material.

We appreciate your help in protecting our authors, and our ability to bring you valuable content.

Questions

You can contact us at questions@packtpub.com if you are having a problem with any aspect of the book, and we will do our best to address it.

1

DOM and Data Types, the Ext JS Way

In this chapter, you will learn the following recipes:

- ▶ Detecting browsers and platforms used by clients
- ▶ Retrieving DOM nodes and elements
- ▶ Acquiring references to Ext JS components
- ▶ Running high-performance DOM queries
- ▶ Encoding and decoding JSON
- ▶ Encoding and decoding URL data
- ▶ Determining the object type and converting empty references to a default value
- ▶ Finding objects in an array and removing array items
- ▶ Manipulating strings à la Ext JS
- ▶ Effortless range checking for numbers
- ▶ Formatting, parsing, and manipulating dates
- ▶ Preventing naming conflicts and scoping non-global variables
- ▶ Extending JavaScript objects, the Ext JS way
- ▶ Adding features to the Ext JS classes
- ▶ Building custom JavaScript classes that inherit the functionality of Ext JS

Introduction

In this chapter, you will learn how to accomplish tasks related to working with different browsers, platforms, the Document Object Model (DOM), and the Ext JS data types. You will also take in how to create custom data types that extend the functionality of the native Ext JS types.

Detecting browsers and platforms used by clients

Although Ext JS is a cross-browser library, there are instances when your application needs to show a different behavior depending on the user's browser or platform. Browser and platform detection are very simple tasks with Ext JS, and this recipe shows how it's done.

How to do it...

You can detect various browsers and platforms used by your clients in the following way:

- You can use `Ext.isChrome` to find out if the detected browser is Chrome:

```
var browser = "";
if (Ext.isChrome) {
    browser = "Hi! I'm the new kid on the block";
}
```

- The browsers such as Mozilla and Firefox that use the Gecko rendering engine are detected with `Ext.isGecko`, `Ext.isGecko2`, and `Ext.isGecko3`:

```
if (Ext.isGecko) {
    browser = "Gecko";
}
if (Ext.isGecko2) {
    browser = "Gecko2";
}
if (Ext.isGecko3) {
    browser = "We like Firefox!";
}
```

- The Internet Explorer versions are flagged by `Ext.isIE`, `Ext.isIE6`, `Ext.isIE7`, and `Ext.isIE8`:

```
if (Ext.isIE) {
    browser = "IE";
}
if (Ext.isIE6) {
    browser = "Get a decent browser, now!";
}
if (Ext.isIE7) {
    browser = "IE7";
}
if (Ext.isIE8) {
    browser = "IE8";
```

```
}
```

- Opera is detected with `Ext.isOpera`:

```
if (Ext.isOpera) {
    browser = "Opera";
}
```

- And finally, Safari is detected with `Ext.isSafari`, `Ext.isSafari2`, `Ext.isSafari3`, and `Ext.isSafari4`:

```
if (Ext.isSafari) {
    browser = "Safari";
}
if (Ext.isSafari2) {
    browser = "Safari2";
}
if (Ext.isSafari3) {
    browser = "Safari3";
}
if (Ext.isSafari4) {
    browser = "Safari4";
}
```

- When it comes to platform detection, Adobe's Air is detected with `Ext.isAir`:

```
var platform = "";
if (Ext.isAir) {
    platform = "Air";
}
```

- Linux is detected with `Ext.isLinux`:

```
if (Ext.isLinux) {
    platform = "Linux";
}
```

- Mac OS is detected with `Ext.isMac`:

```
if (Ext.isMac) {
    platform = "Mac";
}
```

- Windows is detected with `Ext.isWindows`:

```
if (Ext.isWindows) {
    platform = "Windows ";
}
```

How it works...

As you can imagine, the values for Ext JS's browser and platform type flags are all obtained from parsing the value of the `userAgent` property of the JavaScript navigator object.

There's more...

Use this recipe when you need to alter the features or behavior of your application depending on the browser or platform being used. For example, depending on the platform used, you can provide Mac or Windows versions of a browser plugin; or you can account for rendering differences of various browsers when positioning DOM elements.

Retrieving DOM nodes and elements

Web development involves hefty doses of DOM manipulation. This recipe shows how you can use Ext JS to get a handle on any DOM element.

How to do it...

Using a div element as an example, you can get a handle to the div in the following way:

```
<html>
<head>
   <title></title>
   <link rel="stylesheet" type="text/css"
     href="../ext/css/ext-all.css"/>
   <script type="text/javascript" src="../ext/ext-base.js"></script>
   <script type="text/javascript"
     src="../ext/ext-all-debug.js"></script>
   <script type="text/javascript"> Ext.BLANK_IMAGE_URL = '../ext/
images/default/s.gif';
      Ext.onReady(function() {
         var firstDiv = Ext.get("div-1");
         Ext.Msg.alert('Using Ext.get(el)', firstDiv.id);
      });
   </script>
</head>
<body>
   <div id="div-1">This is the first div</div>
</body>
</html>
```

How it works...

The previous code uses `Ext.get(element)`, a shorthand for `Ext.Element.get(element)`, to acquire a reference to a div element in the document. You can use this function to retrieve references that encapsulate DOM elements.

There's more...

The `Ext.get(element)` function uses simple caching to consistently return the same object. Note that `Ext.get(element)` does not retrieve Ext JS components. This is can be accomplished using `Ext.getCmp()`, explained in the next recipe.

See also...

▶ The next recipe, *Acquiring references to Ext JS components*, explains how to obtain a reference to a previously created component.

▶ The *Running high performance DOM queries* recipe, which is covered later in this chapter, teaches you how to run queries against the DOM using Ext JS.

Acquiring references to Ext JS components

As Ext JS is all about working with components, it's essential to learn how to acquire a reference to any component in your code. For example, this recipe shows how easy it is to reference a `ComboBox` component.

How to do it...

You can reference a `ComboBox` component as shown in the following code:

```html
<html>
<head>
  <title></title>
  <link rel="stylesheet" type="text/css"
    href="../ext/css/ext-all.css"/>
  <script type="text/javascript" src="../ext/ext-base.js"></script>
  <script type="text/javascript"
    src="../ext/ext-all-debug.js"></script>
  <script type="text/javascript">
    Ext.BLANK_IMAGE_URL = '../ext/images/default/s.gif';
    Ext.onReady(function() {
        var colorsStore = new Ext.data.SimpleStore({
            fields: ['name'],
            data: [['Blue'],['Red'],['White']]
```

```
        });
        var combo = new Ext.form.ComboBox({
            store: colorsStore,
            displayField: 'name',
            typeAhead: true,
            mode: 'local',
            forceSelection: true,
            triggerAction: 'all',
            emptyText: 'Select a color...',
            selectOnFocus: true,
            applyTo: 'colors-combo',
            id: 'colors-combo'
        });
        // Get a reference to the combobox using Ext.getCmp(id).
        var combo = Ext.getCmp("colors-combo");
        // Using the reference to the combo, add a handler to the
        //'select' event.
        combo.on('select', function() {
        Ext.Msg.alert('Using Ext.getCmp(id)',
            The selected color is ' + combo.getValue();
        });
    });
    </script>
</head>
<body>
    <input type="text" id="colors-combo"/>
</body>
</html>
```

How it works...

References to components are obtained using the `Ext.getCmp(id)` function, where `id` is the ID of the component. Keeping track of components is possible, thanks to the `ComponentMgr` class. It provides for easy registration, un-registration and retrieval, as well as notifications when components are added or removed.

There's more...

This method is particularly useful when explicit component references do not already exist in your code, for example when components are defined as part of the items collection of a container. (Think of a tab panel and its tabs, or a border layout and its contained panels.)

There are other DOM and component utilities provided by Ext JS:

▸ `Ext.getBody()` returns the body of the document as an `Ext.Element`

▸ `Ext.getDoc()` returns the current HTML document as an `Ext.Element`

▸ `Ext.getDom(id)` returns the DOM node for the supplied ID, DOM node, or element

See also...

▸ The *Retrieving DOM nodes and elements* recipe, covered earlier in this chapter, explains how to get a handle on any DOM element.

▸ The next recipe, *Running high-performance DOM queries*, teaches you about running queries against the DOM.

Running high-performance DOM queries

Now you'll see how to run queries against the DOM using Ext JS—a must-have when you need to manipulate or perform actions on multiple, related DOM elements. The examples show how to reference all the div elements in a document, obtain all the elements with a CSS class name `msg`, and iterate over the options of a select element.

How to do it...

The following code snippets are examples of how to run high performance queries against the DOM using Ext JS:

▸ When you need to retrieve the elements that match the div selector to find the div elements in the document, use the following code snippet:

```
Ext.onReady(function() {
    // Get all the div elements.
    var nodes = Ext.query('div');
    Ext.each(nodes, function(item, index, allItems) {
        document.write(index + '<br/>');
    });
});
```

▸ When you need to reference the elements with the class name `msg`, use the following code snippet:

```
var msgLinks = Ext.query('.msg');
Ext.each(msgLinks, function(item,index) {
    // Do something with the element here.
});
```

▶ When you want to iterate over the options of a select element, use the following code snippet:

```
var select = Ext.get('countries-select');
Ext.each(select.options, function(item,index) {
    // Do something with the item here.
});
```

How it works...

The previous examples use `Ext.query(path, [root])`, a shorthand of `Ext.DomQuery.select(path, [root])`, to retrieve an array of DOM nodes that match a given selector.

There's more...

`DomQuery` provides high-performance selector/XPath processing by compiling queries into reusable functions. It works on HTML and XML documents, supports most of the CSS3 selector's specification as well as some custom selectors and basic XPath, and allows you to plug new pseudo classes and matchers.

See also...

▶ The *Retrieving DOM nodes and elements* recipe, covered earlier in this chapter, shows how you can use Ext JS to get a handle on any DOM element.

▶ The *Acquiring references to Ext JS components* recipe, covered earlier in this chapter, explains how to acquire a reference to any component in your code.

Encoding and decoding JSON

Converting JavaScript and Ext JS objects to JSON, and converting JSON data back to JavaScript objects is easily achievable with Ext JS. For example, here's how to JSON-encode an array and how to rebuild the array from its JSON representation:

JavaScript Object Notation (**JSON**) is a lightweight text format where an object is represented with an unordered set of name/value pairs and an array with an ordered collection of values.

JSON is completely language independent, easy for humans to read and write, and easy for machines to parse and generate. These properties make JSON an ideal data-interchange format.

Find out more about JSON at `www.json.org`.

How to do it...

Let's encode an array of colors using the following steps:

1. Create an array called `colorsArray`:

   ```
   var colorsArray = new Array();
   ```

2. Put some values in the array:

   ```
   colorsArray[0] = 'Blue';
   colorsArray[1] = 'Red';
   colorsArray[2] = 'White';
   ```

3. Now, convert to JSON:

   ```
   var colorsJson = Ext.encode(colorsArray);
   ```

   The value of the `colorsJson` variable should be the string
   `["Blue","Red","White"]` string.

4. Let's re-create the array based on its JSON string. Take the JSON representation of `colorsArray`:

   ```
   var colorsJson = '["Blue","Red","White"]';
   ```

5. Parse the JSON and rebuild the array:

   ```
   var colorsArray = Ext.decode(colorsJson);
   ```

After this, `colorsArray` contains the colors data: `colorsArray[0]` is 'Blue',
`colorsArray[1]` is 'Red', and `colorsArray[2]` is 'White'.

How it works...

To obtain a JSON representation of an array, object, or other value, pass the value to `Ext.util.JSON.encode(object)`. You can also use the shorthand, `Ext.encode(object)`.

You can parse a JSON string by using `Ext.util.JSON.decode(json)`, or its shorthand `Ext.decode(json)`.

While decoding JSON involves simply calling the JavaScript `eval(String)` function, the encoding process is more complicated and requires different implementations depending on the data type being encoded. Internally, the `encode(object)` function calls specialized encoding functions for arrays, dates, Boolean values, strings, and other types.

You can also set the `Ext.USE_NATIVE_JSON` property to true, which will cause calls to `encode(object)` and `decode(json)` to use the browser's native JSON handling features. This option is turned off by default. If you turn it on, beware that native JSON methods will not work on objects that have functions, and that property names should be quoted in order for the data to be correctly decoded.

There's more...

JSON encoding and decoding is a pillar of modern web development, given the role of JSON—a language-independent, data-interchange format—in facilitating communications between the client-side and server-side of web applications. For instance, you can expect to find JSON manipulation when your application needs to send data to the server, as well as when the application needs to dynamically create objects from server-supplied data.

See also...

▶ The next recipe, *Encoding and decoding URL data*, shows how to do two-way conversion between objects and URL data.

Encoding and decoding URL data

Two-way conversion between objects and URL data is a challenge that Ext JS can help with. Let's examine how a JavaScript object can be encoded for transmission through the URL query string, as well as how information contained in a URL can be used to build a JavaScript object.

How to do it...

The following steps will guide you through the process of encoding and decoding URL data:

1. Take a `selectedColors` object as the data to be passed in a URL:

```
var selectedColors = {color1:'Blue', color2:'Red',
  color3:'White'};
```

2. Convert the object to URL data like this:

```
var encodedUrl = Ext.urlEncode(selectedColors);
// encodedUrl is an encoded URL query string:
//color1=Blue&color2=Red&color3=White.
```

3. Now, a URL can be built using the data just created. For example, `http://MyGreatApp/SetSelectedColors?color1=Blue&color2=Red&color3=White`.

4. You can easily create objects from the encoded URL. Assuming we obtained the data from the URL we used above (`http://MyGreatApp/SetSelectedColors?color 1=Blue&color2=Red&color3=White`), obtain the URL data like this:

```
encodedUrl = location.search;
```

5. Re-create the `selectedColors` object as follows:

```
var selectedColors = Ext.urlDecode(encodedUrl);
  // Now the value of selectedColors' color1 property is 'Blue',
  // color2's value is 'Red' and color3's value is 'White'.
```

How it works...

`Ext.urlEncode(object)` and `Ext.urlDecode(string, overwrite)` provide object serialization to URL data and URL data deserialization to objects respectively. Encoding is accomplished by creating the URL query string's key-value pairs based on each object property, or array value passed to the encoding function. Decoding is accomplished by creating an object with a property for each key-value pair that exists in the URL's query string.

There's more...

You can use this recipe when your application needs to send information to the server via AJAX or standard HTTP requests, as well as when you need to use the URL's query string to feed the application data that can later be converted to JavaScript objects.

See also...

▸ The _Encoding and decoding JSON_ recipe, covered earlier in this chapter, explains how to convert JavaScript objects to JSON and how to convert JSON to JavaScript objects.

Determining the object type and converting empty references to a default value

This recipe teaches you how to determine the types of different objects using the facilities of Ext JS, as well as a simple method that can be used to initialize empty references with a default value.

How to do it...

You can determine the types of different objects in the following way:

1. Create some dummy data structures:

```
var colorsArray = new Array();
colorsArray[0] = 'Blue';
colorsArray[1] = 'Red';
colorsArray[2] = 'White';
var colorsObject = { color1: 'Blue', color2: 'Red', color3:
  'White' };
var aNumber = 1;
var aString = '1';
var sample;
var empty;
```

2. Check the types of our variables:

```
var colorsArrayType = Ext.type(colorsArray);
// colorsArrayType's value is "array".
var isArray = Ext.isArray(colorsArray);
// isArray is true
var colorsObjectType = Ext.type(colorsObject);
// colorsObjectType's value is "object".
var isArray = Ext.isArray(colorsObject);
// isArray is false
var number = Ext.num(aNumber, 0);
// number is 1.
number = Ext.num(aString, 0);
// Since aString is not numeric, the supplied
// default value (0) will be returned.
var defined = Ext.util.Format.undef(sample);
// defined is an empty string
sample = "sample is now defined";
defined = Ext.util.Format.undef(sample);
// defined is now "sample is now defined".
var notEmpty = Ext.value(empty, 'defaultValue', false);
// notEmpty is 'defaultValue'
```

How it works...

The `Ext.type(object)` function is capable of detecting elements, objects, text nodes, whitespaces, functions, arrays, regular expressions, numbers, and node lists.

As its name indicates, `Ext.isArray(object)` simply checks whether the passed object is a JavaScript array. `Ext.num(value, defaultValue)`, in turn, does a numeric type check on the passed value and returns the default value when the argument is not numeric.

`Ext.util.Format.undef(value)` is a very useful function when you need to test for undefined values. It returns either the supplied argument or an empty string if the argument is undefined.

`Ext.value(value, defaultValue, allowBlank)` also allows you to specify a default value when the value being tested is undefined.

Finding objects in an array and removing array items

The main task in this recipe is to find out whether an arbitrary object exists in an array. A way to remove objects from the array is also explored.

How to do it...

The following steps illustrate how you can perform object existence tests and object removal in an array:

1. Create a sample array as follows:

```
var colorsArray = new Array();
colorsArray[0] = 'Blue';
colorsArray[1] = 'Red';
colorsArray[2] = 'White';
```

2. Determine whether an object exists in an array by trying to find its position in the array:

```
var position = colorsArray.indexOf('White');
// postition is 2, the index of 'White' in the array.
position = colorsArray.indexOf('Brown');
// 'Brown' does not exist in the array,
// position is -1.
```

3. Remove one of the objects from the array:

```
colorsArray.remove('Blue');
position = colorsArray.indexOf('Blue');
// 'Blue' does not exist anymore,
// position is -1.
```

How it works...

Ext JS augments the native `Array` class with `Array.indexOf(object)` and `Array.remove(object)`. While `indexOf(object)` works by examining each array element until it finds one that matches the supplied argument, `remove(object)` uses the native `Array.splice(index, howmany, element1,....., elementX)` function to remove the supplied argument from the array.

Manipulating strings à la Ext JS

String manipulation has always been a challenging area in JavaScript. Here, you will learn how to escape special characters, trim, pad, format, truncate, and change the case of your strings with the help of the utilities of Ext JS.

How to do it...

You can manipulate strings as shown in the following steps:

1. Create your sample values as shown here:

```
var needsEscape = "ExtJS's String Class will escape this";
var needsTrimming = " Needs trimming ";
var cls = 'color-class'
var color = 'Blue';
var sort = 'ASC';
var sample = "some text";
var longText = "This text should be truncated, it's really long.";
var withScript = 'Some text<script type="text/javascript">var
  color = "Blue";<\/script>';
var longText = "Only a part of this text is needed.";
var multiLineText = "One line\nAnother line\nYet another line";
var money = 29.99;
var sample1 = '22';
var sample2 = '550';
var sample3 = '1500';
```

2. Now, let's use the string manipulation functions:

```
var escaped = String.escape(needsEscape);
document.write(escaped + '<br/>');
// The escaped string is "ExtJS\'s String Class will escape this".
var trimmed = needsTrimming.trim();
document.write(trimmed + '<br/>');
// the trimmed string is "Needs trimming"
var formatted = String.format('<span class="{0}">{1}</span>', cls,
  color);
document.write(formatted + '<br/>');
// formatted is '<div class="color-class">Color</div>'
sort = sort.toggle('ASC', 'DESC');
document.write(sort + '<br/>');
// instead of conditional logic:
//sort = (sort == 'ASC' ? 'DESC' : 'ASC');
var converted - Ext.util.Format.uppercase(sample);
document.write(converted + '<br/>');
// converted is now "SOME TEXT".
sample = "SOME TEXT";
converted = Ext.util.Format.lowercase(sample);
// converted is now "some text".
document.write(converted + '<br/>');
sample = "some text";
converted = Ext.util.Format.capitalize(sample);
document.write(converted + '<br/>');
// converted is now "Some text".
var truncated = Ext.util.Format.ellipsis(longText, 20);
document.write(truncated + '<br/>');
// truncated is "This text should ...".
// Removing script tags
var noScript = Ext.util.Format.stripScripts(withScript);
document.write(noScript + '<br/>');
// noScript is "Some text".
// Returning a portion of a string
var subString = Ext.util.Format.substr(longText, 0, 11);
document.write(subString + '<br/>');
// subString is "Only a part".
// Converting newline characters to the html tag <br/>
var html = Ext.util.Format.nl2br(multiLineText);
document.write(html + '<br/>');
// html is
```

```
// One line
// Another line
// Yet another line
var usCurrency = Ext.util.Format.usMoney(money);
document.write(usCurrency + '<br/>');
// usCurrency is $29.99
// Normalizing strings
var normalized1 = String.leftPad(sample1, 4, '0');
// normalized1 is '0022'
var normalized2 = String.leftPad(sample2, 4, '0');
// normalized3 is '0550';
var normalized3 = String.leftPad(sample3, 4, '0');
// normalized2 is '1500'
document.write(normalized1 + '<br/>');
document.write(normalized2 + '<br/>');
document.write(normalized3 + '<br/>');
```

How it works...

The useful functions `escape(string)`, `trim()`, `format(value, start, length)`, `toggle(value1, value2)`, and `leftPad(string, size, [char])` all belong to the `Ext.String` class, which is an extension of the JavaScript `String` object.

The rest of the functions mentioned in this recipe belong to the `Ext.util.Format` class. `Format` is a singleton class that contains reusable formatting functions. Other useful functions in `Format` are `htmlEncode(string)` and `htmlDecode(string)`.

Effortless range checking for numbers

Now, you'll see how to use Ext JS in order to guarantee that a number falls within a certain range.

How to do it...

The following steps illustrate how to perform range checking on numeric values:

1. Create your sample numbers:

   ```
   var number1 = 30;
   var number2 = 75;
   ```

2. Check whether your numbers are within a range:

```
var constrained = number1.constrain(25, 50);
// constrained is 30 because number1 is
// within the specified range
constrained = number2.constrain(25, 50);
// constrained is 50 because number2 is
// greater than the max. value in the range
```

How it works...

Ext.Number is a one-function extension of the JavaScript Number object. The only function of Ext.Number is constrain(min, max), which simply uses methods of the Math JavaScript object to accomplish the range checks on the given number.

```
constrain: function(min, max) {
    return Math.min(Math.max(this, min), max);
}
```

Formatting, parsing, and manipulating dates

Another area where the dynamic nature of JavaScript creates challenges is dates manipulation. This recipe covers formatting, conversion, and range checking for dates.

How to do it...

You can format, convert, and range check dates as show in the following steps:

1. Add the date patterns you will use to format dates in your code:

```
Date.patterns = {
    ISO8601Long: "Y-m-d H:i:s",
    ISO8601Short: "Y-m-d",
    ShortDate: "n/j/Y",
    LongDate: "l, F d, Y",
    FullDateTime: "l, F d, Y g:i:s A",
    MonthDay: "F d",
    ShortTime: "g:i A",
    LongTime: "g:i:s A",
    SortableDateTime: "Y-m-d\\TH:i:s",
    UniversalSortableDateTime: "Y-m-d H:i:sO",
    YearMonth: "F, Y"
};
```

2. Create a sample `Date` object:

    ```
    var now = new Date();
    ```

3. Format the date using the patterns:

    ```
    var ISO8601Long = now.format(Date.patterns.ISO8601Long);
    //ISO8601Long is similar to 2009-03-05 14:01:45
    var ISO8601Short = now.format(Date.patterns.ISO8601Short);
    //ISO8601Long is similar to 2009-03-05
    var ShortDate = now.format(Date.patterns.ShortDate);
    //ISO8601Long is similar to 3/5/2009
    var LongDate = now.format(Date.patterns.LongDate);
    //ISO8601Long is similar to Thursday, March 05, 2009
    var FullDateTime = now.format(Date.patterns.FullDateTime);
    //ISO8601Long is similar to Thursday, March 05, 2009 2:01:45 PM
    var MonthDay = now.format(Date.patterns.MonthDay);
    //ISO8601Long is similar to March 05
    var ShortTime = now.format(Date.patterns.ShortTime);
    //ISO8601Long is similar to 2:01 PM
    var LongTime = now.format(Date.patterns.LongTime);
    //ISO8601Long is similar to 2:01:45 PM
    var SortableDateTime = now.format(Date.patterns.SortableDateTime);
    //ISO8601Long is similar to 2009-03-05T14:01:45
    var UniversalSortableDateTime =
      now.format(Date.patterns.UniversalSortableDateTime);
    //ISO8601Long is similar to 2009-03-05 14:01:45-0500
    var YearMonth = now.format(Date.patterns.YearMonth);
    //ISO8601Long is similar to March, 2009
    ```

4. Create a variable to hold your parsed date:

    ```
    var aDate = new Date();
    ```

5. Convert a string to a date:

    ```
    aDate = Date.parseDate("March, 2009", Date.patterns.YearMonth);
    //aDate = Thu Mar 5 00:00:00 EST 2009
    aDate = Date.parseDate("2:01:45 PM", Date.patterns.LongTime);
    //aDate = Thu Mar 5 14:01:45 EST 2009
    aDate = Date.parseDate("2009-03-05", Date.patterns.ISO8601Short);
    //aDate = Thu Mar 5 00:00:00 EST 2009
    ```

6. For range checking, create range limits:

```
var low = Date.parseDate("July, 2008", Date.patterns.YearMonth);
var high = Date.parseDate("July, 2009", Date.patterns.YearMonth);
```

7. Check whether your date is in the range:

```
var now = new Date();
var inRange = now.between(low, high);
// inRange is true
```

How it works...

Ext JS enhances the JavaScript `Date` object with the `Ext.Date` class, which provides a number of properties and functions that simplify your work with dates.

Regarding date formats, although there isn't a central repository of format patterns in Ext JS, the Ext JS API documentation provides the ones used in the previous example. In order for these formats to become available on the `Date` object, they should be copied into any script that is included after `Date.js`.

There's more...

Besides the functions in the examples above, `Ext.Date` allows you to do things such as:

- Getting the numeric representation of the year
- Getting the number of days in the current month
- Determining the number of milliseconds between two dates
- Getting the date of the first day of the month in which a date resides
- Getting the first day of the current month
- Getting the offset from GMT of the current date
- Getting the date of the last day of the month in which a date resides
- Getting the last day of the current month
- Getting the month number for the given short/full month name
- Getting the short day name for a given day number
- Getting the short month name for a given month number
- Determining if a date is in a leap year

Preventing naming conflicts and scoping non-global variables

Naming conflicts and scoping problems increase as applications gain size, and you start to work with multiple code files and modules. In Ext JS, you can resolve these issues by creating namespaces where you can logically organize your code.

How to do it...

The following steps will show how to create a namespace and "hide" local variables in it. These variables will not collide with similarly-named variables that are stored in other namespaces or have global scope:

1. Define a namespace for the variables that are not global:

    ```
    Ext.namespace('ExtJSCookbook.Samples');
    ```

2. Create a local variable and a global variable with the same name:

    ```
    Ext JSCookbook.Samples.var1 = 'var1 (local)';
    // ExtJSCookbook.Samples.var1 is limited to the ExtJSCookbook.
    Samples namespace
    var var1 = 'var1 (global)';
    // var1 is a global variable
    ```

3. Prevent name collisions by putting any custom types inside the namespace you created:

    ```
    // A custom type inside the Ext JSCookbook.Samples namespace
    ExtJSCookbook.Samples.Person = function() {
        return {
            firstName: '',
            lastName: '',
            show: function() {
                alert(this.firstName + ' ' + this.lastName);
            }
        }
    }
    var person1 = new Ext JSCookbook.Samples.Person();
    person1.firstName = 'Jorge';
    person1.lastName = 'Ramon';
    person1.show();
    ```

How it works...

`Ext.namespace(namespace1, namespace2, namespace3,...)` and its shorthand `Ext.ns(...)` allow you to create an arbitrary number of namespaces that you can use to scope variables and classes that are not global. For example, have a look at the following piece of code:

```
Ext.namespace('MyApplication', 'MyApplication.UI',
  'MyApplication.Data', 'MyApplication.Services');
```

This namespace's definition above is equivalent to the following statements:

```
MyApplication = {};
MyApplication.UI = {};
MyApplication.Data = {};
MyApplication.Services = {};
```

Extending JavaScript objects, the Ext JS way

You can use Ext JS to enhance the native JavaScript classes by making your own functions appear as if they were members of those classes. This recipe uses the `Array` class as an example, explaining how to augment its features by adding a function that will allow an array to copy itself into another array.

How to do it...

Adding a new function to the `Array` class is shown in the following steps:

1. Use Ext JS to add a new function, `copyTo(array, startIndex)`, to the `Array` class's prototype:

```
Ext.applyIf(Array.prototype, {
    copyTo: function(dest, startIndex) {
        l = this.length;
        for (var i = 0; i < l; i++) {
            dest[startIndex + i] = this[i];
        }
    }
})
```

2. Create a `source` array and a `destination` array in order to test the new function:

```
var source = new Array();
var destination = new Array();
source[0] = '1';
source[1] = '2';
```

```
source[2] = '3';
destination[0] = '4';
destination[1] = '5';
destination[2] = '6';
destination[3] = '7';
destination[4] = '8';
destination[5] = '9';
```

3. Verify that the function is available in the `Array` class:

```
var serialized = destination.toString();
// serialized is "4,5,6,7,8,9"
// Copy the source array, starting at index 2 of the destination
source.copyTo(destination, 2);
serialized = destination.toString();
// serialized is "4,5,1,2,3,9"
```

How it works...

`Ext.applyIf(object1, object2)` copies all of the properties of `object2` to `object1`, if they do not already exist. This effectively allows you to add new functionality to `object1`.

There's more...

If you want to add or replace an object's current properties, you can use `Ext.apply(object1, object2)`. This function will copy the properties of `object2` to `object1`, replacing the ones that `object1` has already defined.

Adding features to the Ext JS classes

It is possible to add new functions to the Ext JS classes, as well as modify the behavior of the native functions. To illustrate this point, this recipe explains how you can modify the `MixedCollection` class so that it features a new function which allows items to be added only when they don't already exist in the collection.

How to do it...

The following example shows how to add a new function to the `MixedCollection` class:

1. Define the new `addUnique(key, object)` function within the `MixedCollection` class:

```
// Add a function to the MixedCollection Class.
Ext.override(Ext.util.MixedCollection, {
```

```
    addUnique: function(key, object) {
        if (this.indexOf(object) > -1) return;
        this.add(key, object);
    }
});
```

2. Now, we can use the new feature here:

```
Ext.onReady(function() {
    // Create our enhanced collection.
    var col = new Ext.util.MixedCollection();
    // Confirm that the same value cannot be added twice.
    col.add("key 1", "value 1");
    document.write("Original count: " + col.getCount() + "<br/>");
    // Use the added function to make sure duplicates are not
    //added.
    col.addUnique("key 2", "value 1");
    // Number of elements in the collection is still 1.
    document.write("Count after trying to add a duplicate: " +
        col.getCount() + "<br/>");
});
```

How it works...

The magic in this recipe is achieved through the use of Ext.override(originalClass, overrides). This function adds a list of functions to the prototype of an existing class, replacing any existing methods with the same name:

```
override: function(origclass, overrides) {
    if (overrides) {
        var p = origclass.prototype;
        Ext.apply(p, overrides);
        if (Ext.isIE && overrides.toString != origclass.toString) {
            p.toString = overrides.toString;
        }
    }
}
```

There's more...

Using Ext.override(originalClass, overrides), it is also possible to modify the behavior of a class's native functions.

Let's modify the add(key, object) function of the MixedCollection class so that only unique values can be added to the collection.

Use `Ext.override(originalClass, overrides)` to redefine the add function as shown in the following code:

```
Ext.override(Ext.util.MixedCollection, {
    // The new add function, with the unique value check.
    add: function(key, o) {
        // The unique value check.
        if (this.indexOf(o) > -1) return null;
        //From this point, the code is the add function's original
        //code.
        if (arguments.length == 1) {
            o = arguments[0];
            key = this.getKey(o);
        }
        if (typeof key == "undefined" || key === null) {
            this.length++;
            this.items.push(o);
            this.keys.push(null);
        } else {
            var old = this.map[key];
            if (old) {
                return this.replace(key, o);
            }
            this.length++;
            this.items.push(o);
            this.map[key] = o;
            this.keys.push(key);
        }
        this.fireEvent("add", this.length - 1, o, key);
        return o;
    }
});
```

Now, we can use the new behavior:

```
Ext.onReady(function() {
    // Create our enhanced collection.
    var col = new Ext.util.MixedCollection();
    // Confirm that the same value cannot be added twice.
    col.add("key 1", "value 1");
    document.write("Original count: " + col.getCount() + "<br/>");
    // Try to add a duplicate.
    col.add("key 2", "value 1");
    // Number of elements in the collection is still 1.
    document.write("Count after trying to add a duplicate: " +
        col.getCount() + "<br/>");
});
```

- The next recipe, *Building custom JavaScript classes that inherit the functionality of Ext JS*, explains how to incorporate Ext JS's features into your custom classes.

Building custom JavaScript classes that inherit the functionality of Ext JS

You can incorporate features of Ext JS into your own JavaScript classes. For example, the ObservableList class created in this recipe will use the features of the framework's Ext.util.Observable class to fire notifications when items are added, removed, or when the list is cleared. The list's interface will be as follows:

- add(object): A function that inserts an item in the list and returns the position into which the item was inserted
- insert(index, object) : A function that inserts an item to the List at the specified index
- item(index): A function that returns the element at the specified index
- remove(object): A function to remove the first occurrence of a specific object
- removeAt(index): A function in charge of removing the item at the specified index
- each(fn, scope): A method that executes the specified function once for every item in the list
- clear() : A function to remove all items from the list
- add: An event signaling that an element was added
- remove: An event notifying that an element was removed
- clear: An event signaling that the list was cleared

How to do it...

Let's proceed to build and test the ObservableList class as shown in the following steps:

1. Define the ObservableList class:

```
Ext.namespace("Samples");
Samples.ObservableList = function() {
    this.items = [];
    this.length = 0;
    // The events our custom class will expose.
    // The parent Class, Observable, will handle event publishing
```

```
        //for us.
        this.addEvents("add", "remove", "clear");
        Samples.ObservableList.superclass.constructor.call(this);
   };
```

2. Inherit the `Observable` class's functionality by establishing our class as an extension of `Observable`:

```
Ext.extend(Samples.ObservableList, Ext.util.Observable, {
   //Disable having functions as items.
   allowFunctions: false,
   //Our Class members go here...
});
```

3. Now, implement our class's interface:

```
Ext.extend(Samples.ObservableList, Ext.util.Observable, {
   allowFunctions: false,
   //Adds an item to the list and
   //returns the position into which the new element was inserted.
   add: function(o) {
      this.items.push(o);
      this.length++;
      // Fire the add event, returning the position
      // into which the new element was inserted.
      pos = this.length - 1;
      this.fireEvent("add", pos);
      return pos;
   },
   // Inserts an item to the List at the specified index.
   insert: function(index, o) {
      //If the index is outside the list, insert the element at
      // the end of the list.
      if (index >= this.length) {
         return this.add(o);
      }
      this.length++;
      this.items.splice(index, 0, o);
      this.fireEvent("add", index);
   },
   // Removes all items from the list.
   clear: function() {
      this.length = 0;
      this.items = [];
      this.fireEvent("clear");
   },
   // Determines the index of a specific item in the list.
   indexOf: function(o) {
      return this.items.indexOf(o);
```

```
    },
    // Determines whether the List contains a specific value.
    contains: function(o) {
        return this.indexOf(o) != -1;
    },
    // Our enumerator function. Executes the specified function
    //once for every element in the list.
    each: function(fn, scope) {
        var items = [].concat(this.items); for (var i = 0, len =
          items.length; i < len; i++) {
          if (fn.call(scope || items[i], items[i], i, len) ===
            false) {
            break;
          }
        }
    },
    // Removes the item at the specified index.
    removeAt: function(index) {
        if (index < this.length && index >= 0) {
            this.length--;
            var o = this.items[index];
            this.items.splice(index, 1);
            this.fireEvent("remove", o);
        }
    },
    // Removes the first occurrence of a specific object.
    remove: function(o) {
        this.removeAt(this.indexOf(o));
    },
    // Return the element at the specified index.
    item: function(index) {
        var item = this.items[index];
        return item;
    }
});
Samples.ObservableList.prototype.get =
    Samples.ObservableList.prototype.item;
```

4. It's time to test our class. Let's do it as follows:

```
Ext.onReady(function() {
    list = new Samples.ObservableList();
    for (var i = 0; i < 15; i++) {
        pos = list.add("test " + i);
    }
    // Add handlers for the list's events.
    list.on("remove", function(o) {
        alert("Removed: " + o);
```

```
        });
        list.on("add", function(index) {
            alert("Added at position: " + index);
        });
        list.on("clear", function() {
            alert("List length is: " + list.length);
        });
        document.write("List length is " + list.length + "<br/>");
        // Insert an additional element and
        //check that the add event fires.
        var index = 2;
        list.insert(index, "A new item");
        document.write("Just inserted: " + list.item(index) +
            "<br/>");
        document.write("List length is: " + list.length + "<br/>");
        // Remove an item an verify that the remove event fires.
        index = 5;
        document.write("Removing item at position" + index + "<br/>");
        list.removeAt(index);
        document.write("List length after removal: " + list.length +
            "<br/>");
        document.write("Clearing list...<br/>");
        // Remove all items and check that the clear event fires.
        list.clear();
        document.write("List length after clear: " + list.length +
            "<br/>");
    });
```

How it works...

A powerful mechanism for extending classes is provided by Ext JS with `Ext.extend(subclass, superclass, [overrides])`. This function allows you to extend one class with another class and, optionally, to override the superclass's members.

Our example first defines the custom `ObservableList` class and passes its events to the parent, `Ext.Observable`. It then uses `Ext.extend(subclass, superclass, [overrides])` not only to establish that the custom class implements `Ext.Observable`, but also to define the bulk of its own interface—the `add(object)`, `insert(index, object)`, `clear()`, `indexOf(object)`, `each(fn, scope)`, `removeAt(index)`, `remove(object)`, and `item(index)` functions.

Multiple versions of this approach are used by Ext JS to define its own class hierarchy. I encourage you to examine the source code of the library in order to get familiar with them.

See also...

- ▶ The *Adding features to the Ext JS classes* recipe, covered earlier in this chapter, explains how to add new functions to the Ext JS classes

- ▶ The *A custom column layout* recipe from Chapter 2 is an example of how to extend the native Ext JS layouts

- ▶ The *A three-panel application layout with one line of code* recipe from Chapter 2 shows how to build a reusable Ext JS component that encapsulates a three-panel layout

2

Laying Out a Rich User Interface

These are the recipes that you will learn in this chapter:

- ► Laying out items within a container using CSS style absolute positioning
- ► How form elements and other components maintain their proportions when their containers are resized
- ► Stacking items with an accordion layout
- ► Wizard style UI using a card layout
- ► Using a tabbed look
- ► Taking all the browser window's real estate
- ► Positioning components in multiple columns
- ► Using the table layout
- ► Creating a modern application layout with collapsible regions
- ► A custom column layout
- ► A three-panel application layout with a single line of code
- ► Creating a portal and a portlets catalog

Introduction

Components layout is one of the most important areas of the Ext JS library. This chapter teaches you how to create different layouts that the Ext JS library provides, and informs you about their most common uses. You will also be introduced to creating custom reusable layouts that can meet the most demanding requirements of your applications.

Laying out items within a container using CSS-style absolute positioning

Sometimes, you need to position components using the standard X and Y coordinates. In this recipe, I position two panels in the container using an absolute layout. The following screenshot shows how the end result will look like:

How to do it...

1. Create a couple of panels that will be absolute-positioned:

```
panel1=new Ext.Panel({
    title: 'Panel 2',
    // When using absolute layouts,
    // you need to specify the coordinates.
    x: 50,
    y: 50,
    width: 200,
    height:200,
    html: 'Positioned at x:50, y:50'

});
panel2=new Ext.Panel({
    title: 'Panel 2',
    x: 200,
    y: 200,
    width: 300,
    height: 150,
    html: 'Positioned at x:100, y:100'
});
```

2. Create a container for the panels:

```
var viewport=new Ext.Viewport({
    // Position items within this container using
    // CSS-style absolute positioning.
    layout:'absolute',
    items:[panel1, panel2]
});
```

How it works...

Locating items in specific positions is achieved by assigning an absolute layout for the `layout` configuration option of the container. Remember that when using absolute layouts, you need to specify the coordinates of the contained components.

Maintaining components' proportions when their containers are resized

Having components that maintain their proportions when their containers are resized is important, especially, when dealing with form elements.

In the following screenshot, there are three panels that resize themselves as their container is resized:

How to do it...

1. Create the panels that will be displayed:

```
panel1=new Ext.Panel({
    title: 'Panel 1',
    html: 'Width=container width\' - 50 px',
    // Width=container width' - 50 px.
    anchor: '-50'
});
panel2=new Ext.Panel({
    title: 'Panel 2',
    html: 'Width=75% of container',
    // Width=75% of container.
    anchor: '75%'
});
panel3=new Ext.Panel({
    title: 'Panel 3',
    html: 'Width=50% of container<br/>Height=container\'s - 150
    px',
    // Width=50% of container,
    // Height=container's - 150 px.
    anchor: '50%, -150'
});
```

2. Now, create the container window. When this window is resized, the panels will maintain their proportions:

```
var container=new Ext.Window({
    title: 'Anchor Layout',
    width: 600,
    height: 350,
    defaults: { bodyStyle: 'padding:10px' },
    // The anchored items will automatically resize
    // to maintain the same relative dimensions.
    layout: 'anchor',
    items: [panel1, panel2, panel3]
});
container.show();
```

How it works...

The relative anchoring is achieved by specifying an `AnchorLayout` for the layout configuration option of the container. If the container is resized, all anchored items are automatically rendered according to their anchor rules.

There's more...

The container using the `AnchorLayout` can supply an anchoring-specific `config` property, `anchorSize`. By default, `AnchorLayout` will calculate anchor measurements based on the size of the container itself. However, if `anchorSize` is specified, the layout will use it as a virtual container for the purposes of calculating anchor measurements based on it instead. This will allow the container to be sized independent of the anchoring logic if necessary.

It's also possible to supply the horizontal and vertical anchor values through the `anchor` config option. They can refer to the percentage an item should take up within its container, the offset from the right and bottom edges, or the container's sides. For example, `'-50 75%'` would render the width offset from the container's right edge by 50 pixels and 75% of the container's height.

Stacking items with an accordion layout

Countless applications use a layout where multiple panels are positioned in an expandable accordion style, such that only one panel can be open at any given time. This recipe is a sample that tries to borrow the look of popular email applications to explain how to configure and use an accordion layout.

How to do it...

1. Create the **Mail** panel:

```
panel1=new Ext.Panel({
    title: 'Mail',
    items: [{
        xtype: 'treepanel',
        id: 'inbox-tree',
        autoScroll: true,
        animate: true,
        enableDD: true,
        containerScroll: true,
        border: false,
        dataUrl: 'mail-folders.php',
        root: {
            nodeType: 'async',
            text: 'MailBox',
            draggable: false,
            id: 'mailbox'
        }
    }]
});
```

2. Create the **Calendar** panel:

```
panel2=new Ext.Panel({
    title: 'Calendar',
    bodyStyle: 'padding:10px',
    items: [{ xtype: 'datepicker',
        style: 'border:0'
    }]
});
```

3. Create the **Contacts** panel:

```
panel3=new Ext.Panel({
    title: 'Contacts',
    bodyStyle: 'padding:10px',
    items: [{ xtype: 'fieldset',
        title: 'Current View',
        autoHeight: true,
        bodyStyle: 'padding:3px',
        items: [
```

```
        { xtype: 'radio', boxLabel: 'Address Cards',
          hideLabel: true, name: 'contacts-view',
          checked: true },
        { xtype: 'radio', boxLabel: 'Phone List',
          hideLabel: true, name: 'contacts-view' },
        { xtype: 'radio', boxLabel: 'By Category',
          hideLabel: true, name: 'contacts-view' },
        { xtype: 'radio', boxLabel: 'By Location',
          hideLabel: true, name: 'contacts-view'}]
    }]
});
```

4. Now position the panels in a container and expand the tree's root node.

```
var container=new Ext.Panel({
    title: 'Accordion Layout',
    width: 200,
    height: 350,
    applyTo: 'accordion-panel',
    // Displays one item at a time in a stacked layout.
    layout: 'accordion',
    items: [panel1, panel2, panel3]
});
// Expand the root node of the tree.
Ext.getCmp('inbox-tree').getRootNode().expand();
```

How it works...

The trick to the stacked panels resides in specifying an `AccordionLayout` for the layout configuration option of the container.

There's more...

Together with `CardLayout`, `AccordionLayout`, is a popular layout choice when UI real estate is at a premium. This is because it allows you to keep visible the contents of just one panel at a time.

See also...

▶ The next recipe, *Wizard-style UI using a card layout,* explains how to create a wizard to lead the user through multiple steps

Wizard style UI using a card layout

The Wizard style UI is perfect when you need to lead the user through a series of steps in a specific sequence. Wizards are especially suited for complex or infrequently performed tasks, where the user is unfamiliar with the steps involved. In the following screenshot, you'll see what the Wizard style UI built in this recipe looks like:

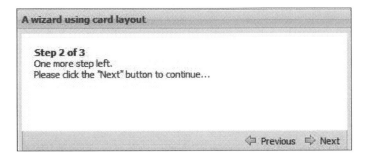

How to do it...

1. Create the wizard's cards or steps:

```
card0=new Ext.Panel({
    id: 'card-0',
    html: '<h1>Step 1 of 3</h1><p>Welcome to the wizard.
</p><p>Click the "Next" button to continue...</p>'
});
card1=new Ext.Panel({
    id: 'card-1',
    html: '<h1>Step 2 of 3</h1><p>One more step left.</p><p>Please
    click the "Next" button to continue...</p>'
});
card2=new Ext.Panel({
    id: 'card-2',
    html: '<h1>Step 3 of 3</h1><p>This is the last step. You made
    it!</p>'
});
```

2. You need a function to switch the steps:

```
var navigationHandler=function(increment) {
    var layout=Ext.getCmp('card-wizard').getLayout();
    var activeItemIdx=layout.activeItem.id.split('card-')[1];
    var next=parseInt(activeItemIdx) + increment;
    layout.setActiveItem(next);
    if (next==0) {
        Ext.getCmp('card-prev').setDisabled(true);
```

```
        } else {
            Ext.getCmp('card-prev').setDisabled(false);
        }
        if (next==2) {
            Ext.getCmp('card-next').setDisabled(true);
        } else {
            Ext.getCmp('card-next').setDisabled(false);
        }
    };
```

3. Now, put the steps together in a container:

```
var cardWizard=new Ext.Panel({
    id: 'card-wizard',
    title: 'A wizard using card layout',
    applyTo: 'card-panel',
    width: 400,
    height: 300,
    frame:true,
    layout: 'card',
    activeItem: 0,
    bodyStyle: 'padding:15px;background-color:#ffffff',
    defaults: { border: false },
    bbar: ['->', {
        id: 'card-prev',
        text: 'Previous',
        handler: navigationHandler.createDelegate(this, [-1]),
        disabled: true,
        iconCls: 'btn-arrow-left-green',
        cls:'x-btn-text-icon',
        minWidth:50
    }, {
        id: 'card-next',
        text: 'Next',
        handler: navigationHandler.createDelegate(this, [1]),
        iconCls: 'btn-arrow-right-green',
        cls: 'x-btn-text-icon',
        minWidth: 50,
        style:'text-align:left'
    }],
        items: [card0, card1, card2]
});
```

How it works...

A wizard is built by creating a number of panels that will function as wizard steps. The panels are hosted in a container that uses a `CardLayout`. This layout makes each panel fit to the container with only a single panel visible at any given time.

There's more...

The `CardLayout` does not provide a mechanism for handling navigation from one panel to the next. Therefore, this functionality must be provided by the developer. Since only one panel is displayed at a time, the navigation handler will achieve moving from one panel to the next by calling the layout's `setActiveItem` method and passing the ID or index of the next panel to display.

See also...

 ▸ The *Creating a modern application layout with collapsible regions* recipe (seen later in this chapter) explains how to create one of the most popular UI layouts

Using a tabbed look

A tabbed GUI is modeled on the traditional card tabs or card indexes. It makes your screens easier to understand and navigate, and gives the application a more natural look. This recipe helps you to build a panel with three tabs, as shown in the following screenshot:

First Tab	**Second Tab**	Third Tab

Content for the second tab

How to do it...

1. Create the tabs. Each tab is simply a `Ext.Component`, such as a panel:

```
var tab1={
    title: 'First Tab',
    html: 'Content for the first tab'
};
var tab2={
    title: 'Second Tab',
```

```
    html: 'Content for the second tab'
};
var tab3={
    title: 'Third Tab',
    html: 'Content for the third tab'
};
```

2. What's left is to put the tabs in their containers:

```
var tabPanel=new Ext.TabPanel({
    title: 'Tab Panels',
    width: 400,
    height: 300,
    applyTo: 'tab-panel',
    // Each tab is just a panel managed by the card layout.
    items: [tab1, tab2, tab3],
    activeItem: 0,
    defaults: {bodyStyle:'padding:5px'}
});
```

How it works...

After you build your tabs, use an Ext.TabPanel as their container. The TabPanel class displays one tab at a time using the CardLayout layout manager.

There's more...

When using TabPanel, each child component fires events that only exist for tabs: activate and deactivate.

Tab panels can also be rendered from pre-existing markup, either already structured as a TabPanel, or from different elements within the page by ID, regardless of page structure. For example, based on the following markup:

```
<div id="my-tabs" style="width:400px;margin:10px;"></div>
<div id="tab1" class="x-hide-display" style="height:200px">A simple
tab</div>
<div id="tab2" class="x-hide-display" style="height:200px">Another
one</div>
```

You need to add the following code to create a tab panel similar to the one in the next screenshot:

```
var tabPanel=new Ext.TabPanel({
    renderTo: 'my-tabs',
    activeTab: 0,
    items: [
    { contentEl: 'tab1', title: 'Tab 1' },
    { contentEl: 'tab2', title: 'Tab 2' }
    ]
});
```

See also...

▸ The previous recipe, *Wizard-style UI using a card layout,* explains how to create a Wizard to lead the user through multiple steps

Taking all the browser window's real estate

There are times when you want a component to automatically expand and fill its container. In the following screenshot, you'll see how a panel can be made to take up the whole browser window using a `FitLayout` layout manager:

How to do it...

1. Create the panel that will take all of its container's area:

```
greedyPanel={ title: 'Fit Layout',
    html: 'Panel using FitLayout'
}
```

2. The container is the one that lets its children fill the area:

```
var container=new Ext.Viewport({
    layout: 'fit',
    defaults: {
      bodyStyle: 'padding:10px'
    },
    items: [
        greedyPanel
    ]
});
```

How it works...

Note the use of the `layout:'fit'` configuration option. `FitLayout` automatically expands the panel to fill its container, the `Ext.ViewPort` instance. The `Viewport` renders itself to the document body and automatically resizes itself to the size of the browser's viewport.

There's more...

When using fit layouts, you should be aware that if the container has multiple panels, only the first one will be displayed. Also, the `Viewport` class does not provide scrolling. If child panels within the `Viewport` need scrolling, it should be enabled with the `autoScroll` configuration option. There may only be one `Viewport` created in a page.

Positioning components in multiple columns

Multicolumn layouts are pervasive today. They are a favorite choice when there is a need to display complex data, or to have an organized and easy-to-navigate GUI. This recipe explains how to set up this type of layout with Ext JS, as shown in the following screenshot:

Column 1	Column 2	Column 3
Width = 30%	Width = 50%	Width = 200px

How to do it...

1. Create the columns of your layout:

```
var column1={
    xtype:'panel',
    title: 'Column 1',
    columnWidth: .3,
    html: 'Width=30%'
}
var column2={
    xtype: 'panel',
    title: 'Column 2',
    columnWidth: .5,
    html: 'Width=50%'
}
var column3={
    xtype: 'panel',
    title: 'Column 3',
    width: 200,
    html: 'Width=200px'
}
```

2. Position the columns in a container that uses the column layout:

```
var container=new Ext.Viewport({
    layout: 'column',
    defaults: {
        bodyStyle: 'padding:10px'
    }, items: [column1, column2, column3]
});
```

How it works...

Building a column layout requires you to create the panels that will constitute the columns. These columns are then added to a container that uses `ColumnLayout`. (Note the use of the `layout:'column'` configuration option.)

There's more...

In a `column` layout, the width of each column can be specified as a percentage or fixed width, but the height is allowed to vary, based on the content. The percentage width is set via the `columnWidth` configuration property, which is included in the `config` object of any panel added to it.

The specific rules about setting column widths can be found in the Ext JS documentation at `http://extjs.com/deploy/dev/docs/?class=Ext.layout.ColumnLayout`.

 Note that the concept of rows is absent in this layout. If you need precise control over the horizontal alignment of components across columns, you need to consider using a table layout.

See also...

▸ The following recipe, *Using the table layout* illustrates how to lay out components in multiple rows or columns

Using the table layout

If you have remained faithful to HTML tables, then you are in luck! Ext JS provides a layout manager—`TableLayout`—whose basic building concept is conceptually similar to building an HTML table.

This is how you can create a complex table layout with cells that span multiple rows or columns. In the following screenshot, you'll see what the end result looks like:

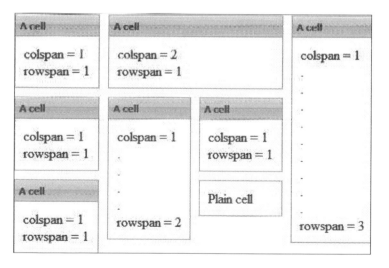

How to do it...

1. The table cells are built as follows:

```
c1={ title: 'A cell', html: '<p>colspan=1<br/>rowspan=1</p>' }
// This cell spans 2 columns.
c2={ title: 'A cell', html: '<p>colspan=2<br/>rowspan=1</p>',
          colspan: 2 }
// This cell spans 3 rows.
c3={ title: 'A cell', html: '<p>colspan=1<br/>.<br/>.<br/>.<br/>.
<br/>.<br/>.<br/>.<br/>.<br/>rowspan=3</p>', rowspan: 3 }
c4={ title: 'A cell', html: '<p>rowspan=3<p>' }
// This cell spans 2 rows.
c5={ title: 'A cell', html: 'colspan=1<br/>.<br/>.<br/>.<br/>
rowspan=2</p>', rowspan: 2 }
c6={ title: 'A cell', html: '<p>colspan=4<p>' }
c7={ title: 'A cell', html: '<p>colspan=4<p>' }
// This cell does not have the panel header.
c8={ html: 'Plain cell' }
```

2. The cells are added to their container. Notice the `layout:'table'` configuration option:

```
var container=new Ext.Viewport({
    layout: 'table',
    defaults: {
        bodyStyle: 'padding:10px'
    },
    layoutConfig: {
        columns: 4
    },
    items: [c1,c2,c3,c4,c5,c6,c7,c8]
});
```

How it works...

The code starts by creating the table cells, which are panel components. Note how you can use the `colspan` and `rowspan` configuration options of each cell to build a layout as complex as you need.

These cells are added to their container, which uses a table layout specified through the `layout` configuration option. Additionally, the number of columns is passed via the `layoutConfig` object.

There's more...

`TableLayout` is useful when you need a rich, grid-like structure for your components. This layout figures out how to position each panel within the table based on the column count, `rowspans`, and `colspans`. Be mindful that, as with the HTML tables, `rowspans` and `colspans` should add up correctly in the overall layout.

See also...

▶ The previous recipe, *Positioning components in multiple columns*, illustrates how to display complex data or have an organized and easy-to-navigate GUI using columns

Creating a modern application layout with collapsible regions

This layout is very popular in modern applications where the GUI consists of multiple nested panels with split bars and collapsible regions. Here's a sample that you can use as a foundation for your applications as seen below:

North Panel			
West Panel	Center Panel		East Panel
South Panel			

How to do it...

1. Set up the panels of the application:

```
northPanel={
    title: 'North Panel',
    region: 'north',
    height: 150,
    minSize: 75,
```

```
            maxSize: 250,
            cmargins: '0 0 5 0'
        }
        southPanel={
            title: 'South Panel',
            region: 'south',
            height: 150,
            minSize: 75,
            maxSize: 250,
            cmargins: '5 0 0 0'
        }
        westPanel={
            title: 'West Panel',
            region: 'west',
            margins: '0 0 0 0',
            cmargins: '0 5 0 0',
            width: 175,
            minSize: 100,
            maxSize: 250
        }
        eastPanel={
            title: 'East Panel',
            region: 'east',
            margins: '0 0 0 0',
            cmargins: '0 0 0 5',
            width: 175,
            minSize: 100,
            maxSize: 250
        }
        centerPanel={
            title: 'Center Panel',
            collapsible: false,
            region: 'center',
            margins: '0 0 0 0'
        }
```

2. Now, build the container and add the panels to it:

```
var container=new Ext.Viewport({
    layout: 'border',
    defaults: {
        collapsible: true,
        split: true,
        bodyStyle: 'padding:15px'
    },
    items: [northPanel, southPanel,
        westPanel, eastPanel, centerPanel
    ]
});
```

How it works...

When creating this complex layout, you first need to decide on the configuration for each of your panels: what region each panel will belong to, which panels will be collapsible, and what will be the panel margins when expanded and when collapsed.

When it comes to putting the panels in their container, the layout that you must use is `Ext.layout.BorderLayout`.

There's more...

The regions of a `BorderLayout` are fixed at render time. Thereafter, no regions may be removed or added. Be mindful that a `BorderLayout` must have a center region, which will always fill the space that is not used up by the other regions in the layout.

Border layouts are very popular in modern applications due to the efficient use of space that can be achieved in the GUI. They also contribute to having well-defined interface areas that encapsulate elements that work together to perform a piece of functionality.

Examine how you can use nested border layouts to divide the **West Panel** into two separate regions, as shown in the following screenshot:

Firstly, set up the two panels that will make up the two regions within the **West Panel**:

```
nestedPanel1={
    region: 'north',
    height: 150
}
nestedPanel2={
    region: 'center'
}
```

Observe how `nestedPanel2` is assigned to the center region, so it fills the space not used by `nestedPanel1`.

As the final step, modify the **West Panel** by adding the nested panels, and configure its layout as a `BorderLayout`:

```
westPanel={
    title: 'West Panel',
    region: 'west',
    margins: '0 0 0 0',
    cmargins: '0 5 0 0',
    width: 175,
    minSize: 100,
    maxSize: 250,
    bodyStyle:'border:0px',
    layout: 'border',
    defaults: {
        collapsible: true,
        split: true,
        bodyStyle: 'padding:15px'
    },
    items:[nestedPanel1,nestedPanel2]
}
```

See also...

▶ The recipe, *Wizard-style UI using a card layout* (seen previously in this chapter), illustrates how to create a Wizard to lead the user through multiple steps

▶ The previous recipe, *Using the table layout,* explains how to lay out components in multiple rows or columns

A custom column layout

Some applications have special layout requirements that cannot be met by the native Ext JS layouts. Luckily, you can extend these layouts and add the features that you need.

As an example, this recipe explains how to build a custom layout based on the `column` layout's features. This custom layout will allow you to separate each of the columns with a configurable distance. For example, a sample three-column `ColumnLayout` layout would look like this by default:

Column 1	Column 2	Column 3
Width = 30%	Width = 50%	Width = 200px

But when using this recipe's custom layout, the same sample allows for user-defined space between columns:

Column 1	Column 2	Column 3
Width = 30%	Width = 50%	Width = 200px

Getting ready...

Since this layout borrows heavily from `Ext.layout.ColumnLayout`, I recommend that you make yourself familiar with the source code of `Ext.layout.ColumnLayout` located in the `ColumnLayout.js` file of the library's SDK.

How to do it...

1. Create the namespace for your custom layout:

    ```
    Ext.namespace('Ext.ux.layout');
    ```

2. Define your custom layout as an extension of `Ext.layout.ContainerLayout`:

    ```
    Ext.ux.layout.ColumnLayout=Ext.extend(Ext.layout.ContainerLayout,
    {...
    ```

3. Define a configuration option for the separation between columns and use the native configuration options of `Ext.layout.ColumnLayout`:

    ```
    columnSpacing: 5,
    monitorResize: true,
    extraCls: 'x-column',
    scrollOffset: 0,
    ```

4. Use the `Ext.layout.ColumnLayout`'s `onLayout()` function and introduce the new behavior:

```
onLayout: function(ct, target) {
    var cs=ct.items.items, len=cs.length, c, i;
    if (!ct.columnSpacing) {
        var nc=[];
        for (i=0; i < len; i++) {
            nc[i * 2]=cs[i];
            nc[i * 2 + 1] = new Ext.BoxComponent({
    autoEl: {
                tag: 'img',
                src: Ext.BLANK_IMAGE_URL,
                width:this.columnSpacing,
                border:0
    }
});
        }
        nc.pop();
        ct.items.items=nc;
        ct.columnSpacing=this.columnSpacing;
    }
    if (!this.innerCt) {
        target.addClass('x-column-layout-ct');
        this.innerCt=target.createChild({ cls: 'x-column-inner'
});
        this.innerCt.createChild({ cls: 'x-clear' });
    }
    this.renderAll(ct, this.innerCt);
    var size=Ext.isIE && target.dom !=Ext.getBody().dom ?
target.getStyleSize() : target.getViewSize();
    if (size.width < 1 && size.height < 1) {
        return;
    }
    var w=size.width - target.getPadding('lr') -
this.scrollOffset,
        h=size.height - target.getPadding('tb'),
        pw=w;
    this.innerCt.setWidth(w);
    for (i=0; i < len; i++) {
        c=cs[i];
        if (!c.columnWidth) {
            pw -=(c.getSize().width + c.getEl().getMargins('lr'));
        }
    }
```

```
        pw=pw < 0 ? 0 : pw;
        for (i=0; i < len; i++) {
            c=cs[i];
            if (c.columnWidth) {
                c.setSize(Math.floor(c.columnWidth * pw) -
                c.getEl().getMargins('lr'));
            }
        }
    }
}
```

5. Add your custom layout to the list of available layouts:

```
Ext.Container.LAYOUTS['ux.column']=Ext.ux.layout.ColumnLayout;
```

6. Now, you can use the custom layout. Create some columns:

```
var column1={
    title: 'Column 1',
    columnWidth: .3,
    html: 'Width=30%'
}
var column2={
    title: 'Column 2',
    columnWidth: .5,
    html: 'Width=50%'
}
var column3={
    title: 'Column 3',
    width: 200,
    html: 'Width=200px'
}
```

7. Add the columns to a container that uses your layout:

```
Ext.onReady(function() {
    var container=new Ext.Viewport({
        layout: 'ux.column',
        defaults: {
            bodyStyle: 'padding:10px'
        },
        layoutConfig: {
            columnSpacing: 20
        },
        items: [column1, column2, column3]
    });
});
```

In the following screenshot, you'll see the custom column layout in action:

Column 1	Column 2	Column 3
Width = 30%	Width = 50%	Width = 200px

How it works...

This recipe used the functionality of `Ext.layout.ColumnLayout`. The important differences reside in the introduction of a new property, `columnSpacing`, which defines the separation between columns in the layout.

The implementation of the columns separation occurs in the following code, inside the `onLayout()` function:

```
if (!ct.columnSpacing) {
    var nc=[];
    for (i=0; i < len; i++) {
        nc[i * 2]=cs[i];
        nc[i * 2 + 1] = new Ext.BoxComponent({
autoEl: {
            tag: 'img',
            src: Ext.BLANK_IMAGE_URL,
            width:this.columnSpacing,
            border:0
}
});
        }
    nc.pop();
    ct.items.items=nc;
    ct.columnSpacing=this.columnSpacing;
}
```

The first time that a layout operation occurs, this code creates a new columns array using the layout's original columns array as the source, but inserting a borderless image between each of the columns. Note how the width of image is set to `columnSpacing`, effectively creating the desired column separation. The assignment `ct.columnSpacing = this.columnSpacing` and the check on `ct.columnSpacing` are performed to make sure that the addition of the spacer images occurs only once and not every time that the `onLayout()` function is called.

There's more...

I chose `Ext.ux.layout` as the namespace name because, it's customary to put user extensions—remember that you are extending `ContainerLayout`—in the `Ext.ux` namespace.

See also...

- ▸ The recipe, *Positioning components in multiple columns* (seen earlier in this chapter) illustrates how to display complex data, or have an organized and easy-to-navigate GUI using columns
- ▸ The next recipe, *A three-panel application layout with a single line of code* explains how to build a reusable Ext JS component that encapsulates a three-panel layout

A three-panel application layout with a single line of code

This recipe explains how you can build a reusable Ext JS component that encapsulates one of the most popular GUI styles—a three-panel layout. Using the component will produce a layout like the one shown in the following screenshot:

This layout consists of a **Navigation** panel, a **Master** panel, and a **Details** panel as shown in the following screenshot:

The **Master** panel has a toolbar with a button that switches the **Details** panel's location from bottom to right, or hides it altogether:

Besides being able to add components to any of the layout's panels via configuration objects, you can also reconfigure any of the panels by the same means.

How to do it...

1. Create the skeleton code of our component:

```
Ext.ns('Ext.ux');
Ext.ux.ThreePanelApp=function(conf) {
    // Master Panel
    // Details Panel
    // Nav Panel
    // MasterDetailsCnt
}
```

2. Create the **Master** panel:

```
MasterPanel=function(conf) {
config={ title: 'Master',

region: 'center',
```

```
tbar: [{
    split: true,
    text: 'Details Panel',
    id: 'details-panel-button',
    handler: this.toggleDetails.createDelegate(this, []),
    menu: {
        id: 'details-menu',
        cls: 'details-menu',
        width: 100,
        items: [{
            text: 'Bottom',
            checked: true,
            group: 'rp-group',
            checkHandler: this.toggleDetails,
            scope: this,
            iconCls: 'details-bottom'
        }, {
            text: 'Right',
            checked: false,
            group: 'rp-group',
            checkHandler: this.toggleDetails,
            scope: this,
            iconCls: 'details-right'
        }, {
            text: 'Hide',
            checked: false,
            group: 'rp-group',
            checkHandler: this.toggleDetails,
            scope: this,
            iconCls: 'details-hide'
        }]
    }
    }]
};
Ext.apply(config, conf || {});
MasterPanel.superclass.constructor.call(this, config);
}
```

3. Specify that the **Master** panel extends the Ext.Panel class and implements the
   toggleDetails() function:

```
Ext.extend(MasterPanel, Ext.Panel, {
    toggleDetails: function(m, pressed) {
        if (!m) {
            var readMenu=Ext.menu.MenuMgr.get('details-menu');
```

```
            readMenu.render();
            var items=readMenu.items.items;
            var b=items[0], r=items[1], h=items[2];
            if (b.checked) {
                r.setChecked(true);
            } else if (r.checked) {
                h.setChecked(true);
            } else if (h.checked) {
                b.setChecked(true);
            }
            return;
        }
        if (pressed) {
            var details=Ext.getCmp('details-panel');
            var right=Ext.getCmp('right-details');
            var bot=Ext.getCmp('bottom-details');
            switch (m.text) {
                case 'Bottom':
                    right.hide();
                    right.remove(details, false);
                    bot.add(details);
                    bot.show();
                    bot.ownerCt.doLayout();
                    break;
                case 'Right':
                    bot.hide();
                    bot.remove(details, false);
                    right.add(details);
                    right.show();
                    right.ownerCt.doLayout();
                    break;
                case 'Hide':
                    bot.hide();
                    right.hide();
                    right.remove(details, false);
                    bot.remove(details, false);
                    right.ownerCt.doLayout();
                    break;
            }
        }
    }
});
```

4. Check if a configuration object for the **Master** panel was specified and create the **Master** panel instance:

```
var masterPanelConf={};
if (conf && conf.masterPanelConf) {
    masterPanelConf=conf.masterPanelConf;
}
var masterPanel=new MasterPanel(masterPanelConf);
```

5. Similar to the **Master** panel, create the **Details** panel:

```
DetailsPanel=function(conf) {
    config={
        id: 'details-panel',
        layout: 'fit',
        title: 'Details',
        id: 'details-panel'
    };
    Ext.apply(config, conf || {});
    DetailsPanel.superclass.constructor.call(this, config);
}
Ext.extend(DetailsPanel, Ext.Panel);
var detailsPanelConf={};
if (conf && conf.detailsPanelConf) {
    detailsPanelConf=conf.detailsPanelConf;
}
var detailsPanel=new DetailsPanel(detailsPanelConf);
```

6. Repeat the process with the **Navigation** panel:

```
NavPanel=function(conf) {
    config={
        title: 'Navigation',
        region: 'west',
        margins: '5 0 5 5',
        cmargins: '5 5 5 5',
        width: 200,
        minSize: 100,
        maxSize: 300
    };
    Ext.apply(config, conf || {});
    NavPanel.superclass.constructor.call(this, config);
}
Ext.extend(NavPanel, Ext.Panel);
var navPanelConf={};
if (conf && conf.navPanelConf) {
    navPanelConf=conf.navPanelConf;
}
var navPanel=new NavPanel(navPanelConf);
```

7. Define a container for the **Master** and **Details** panels:

```
MasterDetailsCnt=function(conf) {
    config={
        layout: 'border',
        region: 'center',
        collapsible: false,
        border: false,
        margins: '5 5 5 0',
        id: 'main-view',
        hideMode: 'offsets',
        items: [masterPanel
              , {
                    id: 'bottom-details',
                    layout: 'fit',
                    height: 300,
                    split: true,
                    border: false,
                    region: 'south',
                    items: detailsPanel
              }, {
                    id: 'right-details',
                    layout: 'fit',
                    border: false,
                    region: 'east',
                    width: 350,
                    split: true,
                    hidden: true
}]
    };
    Ext.apply(config, conf || {});
    MasterDetailsCnt.superclass.constructor.call(this, config);
}
```

8. Check if a configuration object for the **Master/Details** container panel was specified, and create the object's instance:

```
Ext.extend(MasterDetailsCnt, Ext.Panel);
var masterDetailsCntConfig={};
if (conf && conf.masterDetailsCntConfig) {
    masterDetailsCntConfig=conf.masterDetailsCntConfig;
}
var masterDetailsCnt=new MasterDetailsCnt(masterDetailsCntConfig);
```

9. Now that the panels have been created, define the layout:

```
Ext.ux.ThreePanelApp=function(conf) {
    // Master Panel
    // Details Panel
    // Nav Panel
    // MasterDetailsCnt
    config={
        layout: 'border',
        defaults: {
            collapsible: true,
            split: true
        },
        items: [{ xtype: 'box', el: 'app-header', height: 40,
            region: 'north' },
                navPanel, masterDetailsCnt]
    };
    if (conf) {
        Ext.apply(config, conf);
    }
    Ext.ux.ThreePanelApp.superclass.constructor.call(this, config);
}
Ext.extend(Ext.ux.ThreePanelApp, Ext.Viewport)
```

10. Your ouctom layout is rcady to be used and you can create it with only one line of code:

```
Ext.onRcady(function() {
    var container=new Ext.ux.ThreePanelApp();
});
```

11. Add a tree view to the **Navigation** panel and change the panels' titles:

```
Ext.onReady(function() {
    var navPanel={ title: 'MyInbox',
        collapsible: true,
        layout: 'fit',
        items: {
            xtype: 'treepanel',
            id: 'inbox-tree',
            autoScroll: true,
            animate: true,
            enableDD: true,
            containerScroll: true,
            border: false,
            dataUrl: 'mail-folders.php',
            root: {
```

```
                         nodeType: 'async',
                         text: 'MailBox',
                         draggable: false,
                         id: 'mailbox'
                  }
            }
      }
      var detailsPanel={ title: 'Re: Join us for happy hour' }
      var masterPanel={ title: 'Messages List' }
      var container=new Ext.ux.ThreePanelApp({
            detailsPanelConf: detailsPanel,
            navPanelConf: navPanel,
            masterPanelConf: masterPanel
      });
});
```

In the following screenshot, you will see what the finished layout looks like:

Logo Here	
MyInbox «	**Messages List**
MailBox	Details Panel ▼
Drafts	
Inbox	
Junk E-mail	
Sent Items	
	Re: Join us for happy hour

How it works...

The `ThreePanelApp` layout is essentially a custom Ext JS component based on the `Ext.Viewport` class. Creating the layout starts with a basic code template. This template has placeholders for each of the panels in the layout.

```
Ext.ns('Ext.ux');
Ext.ux.ThreePanelApp=function(conf) {
    // Master panel
    // Details panel
    // Nav panel
    // MasterDetailsCnt panel
}
```

Notice that in addition to the placeholders for the **Navigation, Master,** and **Details** panels, there is a place for a fourth panel—MasterDetailsCnt. This panel will be a container for the **Master** panel and two additional panels that will host the **Details** panel when it is positioned below or to the right of the **Master** panel respectively. ThreePanelApp will use a border layout that will contain the **Navigation** panel (which will take the west region) and the MasterDetailsCnt panel (which will take the center region). MasterDetailsCnt will use a BorderLayout to position the **Master** and **Details** panels' hosts.

Moving on, the **Master** panel is an Ext.Panel extension that contains the cycle button for repositioning the **Details** panel:

```
tbar: [{
        handler: this.toggleDetails.createDelegate(this, []),
    }]
```

The **Master** Panel uses a default config object that gets overridden by the masterPanelConf object passed during the construction of a ThreePanelApp instance.

```
MasterPanel=function(conf) {
        Ext.apply(config, cont || {});
        MasterPanel.superclass.constructor.call(this, config);
}
```

This pattern of overriding the default configuration (also used with the rest of the panels), allows you to add your application's components to ThreePanelApp.

Another interesting area in the **Master** panel is the toggleDetails() function. This function achieves the repositioning of the **Details** panel by switching the panel's container or hiding it altogether as shown here:

```
toggleDetails: function(m, pressed) {
    var details=Ext.getCmp('details-panel');
    var right=Ext.getCmp('right-details');
    var bot=Ext.getCmp('bottom-details');
    switch (m.text) {
        case 'Bottom':
            right.hide();
            right.remove(details, false);
            bot.add(details);
            bot.show();
```

```
                bot.ownerCt.doLayout();
                break;
            case 'Right':
                bot.hide();
                bot.remove(details, false);
                right.add(details);
                right.show();
                right.ownerCt.doLayout();
                break;
            case 'Hide':
                bot.hide();
                right.hide();
                right.remove(details, false);
                bot.remove(details, false);
                right.ownerCt.doLayout();
                break;
        }
    }
```

After defining the **Master** panel, the layout creates a working instance of this panel and applies any supplied configuration for it.

```
var masterPanelConf={};
if (conf && conf.masterPanelConf) {
    masterPanelConf=conf.masterPanelConf;
}
var masterPanel=new MasterPanel
```

The **Details** and **Navigation** panels do not have any out-of-the-box extra functionality and hence their creation is less involved. As with the **Master** panel, you can add components to these panels when building the layout by overriding their default configurations.

MasterDetailsCnt is a container panel for the **Master** and **Details** panels hosts. Notice how one host uses the south region of the MasterDetailsCnt layout, whereas the other uses the east region:

```
MasterDetailsCnt=function(conf) {
    config={
            items: [
            masterPanel,
            {
                id: 'bottom-details',
                layout: 'fit',
                height: 300,
                split: true,
                border: false,
                region: 'south',
                items: detailsPanel
        }, {
                id: 'right-details',
                layout: 'fit',
                border: false,
                region: 'east',
                width: 350,
                split: true,
                hidden: true
        }]
    }
}
```

When all of the panels needed by the ThreePanelApp component are created, what's left is defining the custom layout for the component. Notice the inclusion of a north region where you can put a logo and other components:

```
Ext.ux.ThreePanelApp=function(conf) {
    config_{
        layout: 'border',
        defaults: {
            collapsible: true,
            split: true
        },
        items: [{ xtype: 'box', el: 'app-header', height: 40, region:
        'north' },
            navPanel, masterDetailsCnt]
    };
    if (conf) {
        Ext.apply(config, conf);
    }
    Ext.ux.ThreePanelApp.superclass.constructor.call(this, config);
}
```

Now the custom layout can be put into action:

```
var navPanel={ ... }
var detailsPanel={ ... }
var masterPanel={ ... }
var container=new Ext.ux.ThreePanelApp({
    detailsPanelConf: detailsPanel,
    navPanelConf: navPanel,
    masterPanelConf: masterPanel
});
```

There's more...

Use this layout when you need a simple three-panel GUI without having to worry about all its plumbing. More importantly, the extension model used in `ThreePanelApp` can be used as a reference for creating even more complex reusable layouts and custom components.

See also...

▶ The recipe, *Creating a modern application layout with collapsible region* (seen earlier in this chapter), explains how to create one of the most popular UI layouts

Creating a portal and a portlets catalog

Portals are one of the most efficient ways to present information from diverse sources. This is how you can create a dashboard-style GUI that consists of a portal region and a **Portlets Catalog**. Portlets in the catalog can be added to the portal via a context menu. Once in the catalog, a portlet can be re-positioned or removed from the portal and sent back to the catalog. In the following screenshot, you'll see how a portlet is added using a context menu:

In the following screenshot, you'll see how a portlet is removed:

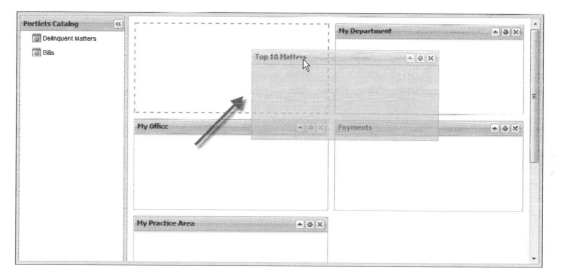

Portlets can also be re-positioned, as shown in the following screenshot:

How to do it...

The dashboard uses five main components:

- ▸ The `Portlet` class, which represents a portlet
- ▸ The `PortletsCatalog` class, which is a tree view where each node represents a portlet
- ▸ The `PortalColumn` class, which displays a number of portlets in a column layout

- ▶ The `Portal`, which contains two `PortalColumn` instances so that portlets are arranged into two columns
- ▶ A `DropZone`, which allows for portlet repositioning through drag-and-drop

The following steps will help you to examine the creation of each of these components and then build the dashboard.

1. Create the `Portlet` class:

```
Ext.ns('Dashboard');
Dashboard.Portlet=Ext.extend(Ext.Panel, {
    anchor: '100%',
    frame: true,
    collapsible: true,
    draggable: true,
    cls: 'x-portlet',
    height: 150,
    tools : [{
            id: 'gear',
            handler: function() {
                Ext.Msg.alert('Message', 'The Settings tool was
                clicked.');
            }
        }, {
            id: 'close',
            handler: function(e, target, panel) {
            panel.ownerCt.ownerCt.fireEvent('portletRemoved',
            panel);
            panel.ownerCt.remove(panel, true);
            }
    }]
});
Ext.reg('portlet', Dashboard.Portlet);
```

2. Create the `PortalColumn` class:

```
Dashboard.PortalColumn=Ext.extend(Ext.Container, {
    layout: 'anchor',
    autoEl: 'div',
    defaultType: 'portlet',
    cls: 'x-portal-column'
});
Ext.reg('portalcolumn', Dashboard.PortalColumn);
```

3. Create the `Portal` class:

```
Dashboard.Portal=function(config) {
    Dashboard.Portal.superclass.constructor.call(this, config);
    this.addEvents({portletRemoved:true});
}
Dashboard.Portal=Ext.extend(Ext.Panel, {
    layout: 'column',
    autoScroll: true,
    cls: 'x-portal',
    defaultType: 'portalcolumn',
    initComponent: function() {
        Dashboard.Portal.superclass.initComponent.call(this);
        this.addEvents({
            validatedrop: true,
            beforedragover: true,
            dragover: true,
            beforedrop: true,
            drop: true
        });
    },
    insertPortlet: function(id, text) {
        colIdx=0;
        if (this.items.itemAt(0).items.length > this.items.
        itemAt(1).items.length) {
            colIdx=1;
        }
        this.items.itemAt(colIdx).insert(0,{
            title: text, id: id
        });
        this.items.itemAt(colIdx).doLayout(true);
    },
    initEvents: function() {
        Dashboard.Portal.superclass.initEvents.call(this);
        this.dd=new Dashboard.Portal.DropZone(this,
        this.dropConfig);
    },
    beforeDestroy: function() {
        if (this.dd) {
            this.dd.unreg();
        }
```

```
                    Dashboard.Portal.superclass.beforeDestroy.call(this);
            }
    });
    Ext.reg('portal', Dashboard.Portal);
```

4. Define the portal's `DropZone`:

```
Dashboard.Portal.DropZone=function(portal, cfg) {
    this.portal=portal;
    Ext.dd.ScrollManager.register(portal.body);
    Dashboard.Portal.DropZone.superclass.constructor.call(this,
    portal.bwrap.dom, cfg);
    portal.body.ddScrollConfig=this.ddScrollConfig;
};
Ext.extend(Dashboard.Portal.DropZone, Ext.dd.DropTarget, {
    ddScrollConfig: {
        vthresh: 50,
        hthresh: -1,
        animate: true,
        increment: 200
    },
    createEvent: function(dd, e, data, col, c, pos) {
        return {
            portal: this.portal,
            panel: data.panel,
            columnIndex: col,
            column: c,
            position: pos,
            data: data,
            source: dd,
            rawEvent: e,
            status: this.dropAllowed
        };
    },
    notifyOver: function(dd, e, data) {
        var xy=e.getXY(), portal=this.portal, px=dd.proxy;
        if (!this.grid) {
            this.grid=this.getGrid();
        }
        var cw=portal.body.dom.clientWidth;
        if (!this.lastCW) {
            this.lastCW=cw;
```

```
} else if (this.lastCW !=cw) {
    this.lastCW=cw;
    portal.doLayout();
    this.grid=this.getGrid();
}
  var col=0, xs=this.grid.columnX, cmatch=false;
for (var len=xs.length; col < len; col++) {
    if (xy[0] < (xs[col].x + xs[col].w)) {
        cmatch=true;
        break;
    }
}
if (!cmatch) {
    col--;
}
var p, match=false, pos=0,
c=portal.items.itemAt(col),
items=c.items.items, overSelf=false;
for (var len=items.length; pos < len; pos++) {
    p=items[pos];
    var h=p.el.getHeight();
    if (h---0) {
        overSelf=true;
    }
    else if ((p.el.getY() + (h / 2)) > xy[1]) {
        match=true;
        break;
    }
}
pos=(match && p ? pos : c.items.getCount()) +
(overSelf ?
-1 : 0);
var overEvent=this.createEvent(dd, e, data, col, c, pos);
if (portal.fireEvent('validatedrop', overEvent) !==false
  &&
  portal.fireEvent('beforedragover', overEvent) !==false) {
    px.getProxy().setWidth('auto');
    if (p) {
        px.moveProxy(p.el.dom.parentNode, match ? p.el.dom
        : null);
    } else {
```

```
                    px.moveProxy(c.el.dom, null);
                }
                this.lastPos={ c: c, col: col, p: overSelf || (match
                && p) ? pos : false };
                this.scrollPos=portal.body.getScroll();
                portal.fireEvent('dragover', overEvent);
                return overEvent.status;
            } else {
                return overEvent.status;
            }
        },
        notifyOut: function() {
            delete this.grid;
        },
        notifyDrop: function(dd, e, data) {
            delete this.grid;
            if (!this.lastPos) {
                return;
            }
            var c=this.lastPos.c, col=this.lastPos.col, pos=this.
            lastPos.p;
            var dropEvent=this.createEvent(dd, e, data, col, c,
            pos !==false ? pos : c.items.getCount());
            if (this.portal.fireEvent('validatedrop', dropEvent)
            !==false &&
            this.portal.fireEvent('beforedrop', dropEvent) !==false) {
                dd.proxy.getProxy().remove();
                dd.panel.el.dom.parentNode.removeChild(dd.panel.
                el.dom);
                if (pos !==false) {
                    if (c==dd.panel.ownerCt && (c.items.items.
                    indexOf(dd.panel) <=pos)) {
                        pos++;
                    }
                    c.insert(pos, dd.panel);
                } else {
                    c.add(dd.panel);
                }
                c.doLayout();
                this.portal.fireEvent('drop', dropEvent);
                var st=this.scrollPos.top;
                if (st) {
                    var d=this.portal.body.dom;
                    setTimeout(function() {
                        d.scrollTop=st;
```

```
                }, 10);
            }
        }
        delete this.lastPos;
    },
    getGrid: function() {
        var box=this.portal.bwrap.getBox();
        box.columnX=[];
        this.portal.items.each(function(c) {
            box.columnX.push({ x: c.el.getX(), w: c.el.getWidth()
            });
        });
        return box;
    },
    unreg: function() {
        Dashboard.Portal.DropZone.superclass.unreg.call(this);
    }
});
```

5. Create the `PortletsCatalog` component:

```
Dashboard.PortletsCatalog=function() {
    Dashboard.PortletsCatalog.superclass.constructor.call(this, {
        root: new Ext.tree.TreeNode('Portlets'),
        region: 'west',
        id: 'portlets-catalog',
        title: 'Portlets Catalog',
        split: true,
        width: 200,
        minSize: 175,
        maxSize: 400,
        collapsible: true,
        rootVisible: false,
        lines: false,
        margins: '35 0 5 5',
        cmargins: '35 5 5 5',
        layoutConfig: {
            animate: true
        }
    });
    this.addEvents({insertPortletRequest:true});
}
Ext.extend(Dashboard.PortletsCatalog, Ext.tree.TreePanel, {
    addPortletNode: function(attrs, inactive, preventAnim) {
        var exists=this.getNodeById(attrs.id);
        if (exists) {
```

```
        if (!inactive) {
            exists.select();
            exists.ui.highlight();
        }
        return;
    }
    Ext.apply(attrs, {
        iconCls: 'x-portlet-node-icon',
        leaf: true,
        draggable: true
    });
    var node=new Ext.tree.TreeNode(attrs);
    this.root.appendChild(node);
    if (!inactive) {
        if (!preventAnim) {
            Ext.fly(node.ui.elNode).slideIn('l', {
                callback: node.select, scope: node, duration:.4
            });
        } else {
            node.select();
        }
    }
    return node;
},
contextMenu: new Ext.menu.Menu({
items: [{
                id: 'add-portlet',
                iconCls:'add-portlet-mnu',
                text: 'Add to Portal'
    }],
    listeners: {
    itemclick: function(item) {
            switch (item.id) {
            case 'add-portlet':
              var n=item.parentMenu.contextNode;
              if (n.parentNode) {
                n.getOwnerTree().fireEvent
        ('insertPortletRequest',{id:n.id,text:n.text});
                n.remove();
              }
              break;
    }
  }
}
```

```
    }),
    listeners: {
        contextmenu: function(node, e) {
        node.select();
        var c=node.getOwnerTree().contextMenu;
        c.contextNode=node;
        c.showAt(e.getXY());
        }
    }
    });
```

6. Create an instance of the `Portal` class:

```
var portalPanel=new Dashboard.Portal({
    id: 'portal',
    region: 'center',
    margins: '35 5 5 0',
    items: [{
        columnWidth: .5,
        style: 'padding:10px 0 10px 10px',
        items: [{
            title: 'Top 10 Clients',
            layout: 'fit',
            id: 'portlet1'
        }, {
            title: 'Bills',
            id: 'portlet3'
        }]
    }, {
            columnWidth: .5,
            style: 'padding:10px 10px 10px 10px',
            items: [{
                title: 'Top 10 Matters',
                id: 'portlet2'
            }, {
                title: 'Payments',
                id: 'portlet4'
            }]
    }]
});
```

7. Create an instance of the `PortletsCatalog` class:

```
var catalog=new Dashboard.PortletsCatalog();
```

8. Handle the portal's `portletRemoved` event:

```
portalPanel.on('portletRemoved', function(panel){
    catalog.addPortletNode({
        id: panel.id,
        text: panel.title
    }, true);
});
```

9. Handle the catalog's `insertPortletRequested` event:

```
catalog.on('insertPortletRequest', function(portletConfig){
    portalPanel.insertPortlet(portletConfig.id,
    portletConfig.text);
});
```

10. Create the layout:

```
var viewport=new Ext.Viewport({
    layout: 'border',
    items: [catalog, portalPanel]
});
```

11. Add some sample portlets to the catalog:

```
catalog.addPortletNode({
    id: 'portlet5',
    text: 'My Department'
}, true);
catalog.addPortletNode({
    id: 'portlet6',
    text: 'My Office'
}, true);
catalog.addPortletNode({
    id: 'portlet7',
    text: 'My Practice Area'
}, true);
catalog.addPortletNode({
    id: 'portlet8',
    text: 'Delinquent Matters'
}, true);
```

How it works...

Begin by defining the `Dashboard` namespace and creating the `Portlet` class. Portlet is an extension of `Ext.Panel` with default configuration options that include a handler for the close event. This handler will invoke the `portletRemoved` event in the `Portal` class.

```
{
    id: 'close',
    handler: function(e, target, panel) {
        panel.ownerCt.ownerCt.fireEvent('portletRemoved',panel);
        panel.ownerCt.remove(panel, true);
    }
}
```

The next step consists of defining a simple container for the portlets. This will be the `PortalColumn` class. The portal area will have two `PortalColumn` instances in order for the portlets to be arranged in two columns.

Besides containing two columns of portlets, the `Portal` class has three key features. They are as follows:

► The first key feature is the `insertPortlet(id,text)` function:

```
insertPortlet: function(id, text) {
    colIdx=0;
    if (this.items.itemAt(0).items.length >
    this.items.itemAt(1).items.length) {
        colIdx=1;
    }
    this.items.itemAt(colIdx).insert(0,{
        title: text, id: id
    });
    this.items.itemAt(colIdx).doLayout(true);
}
```

This function will be invoked when a portlet needs to be added to the portal. Since the portlets catalog does not actually contain portlets, `insertPortlet` creates a portlet based on the `id` and `text` properties of the selected node in the catalog's `Treeview`. (Remember that in the catalog's `Treeview`, each node represents a portlet.) Also, notice that the portlet is inserted in the portal's column that has fewer portlets.

▶ The second key feature in the portal is the `portletRemoved` event.

```
Dashboard.Portal=function(config) {
    Dashboard.Portal.superclass.constructor.call(this, config)
    this.addEvents({portletRemoved:true});
}
```

This event, which is invoked from inside a portlet when it is closed, will be used to notify the catalog that it needs to add a new node to represent the removed portlet.

▶ The last feature that deserves highlighting in the portal is the use of an extension of the `Ext.dd.DropTarget` class called `DropZone`. This class makes possible the drag-and-drop repositioning of portlets in the portal and its implementation was taken verbatim from the samples page of the Ext JS website.

Next comes the `PortletsCatalog` class. As already mentioned, the class is an `Ext.tree.Treeview` extension where each node represents a portlet.

When a portlet is removed from the portal and a new portlet node needs to be added to the catalog's tree, the `addPortletNode(...)` function is used.

```
addPortletNode: function(attrs, inactive, preventAnim) {
    var exists=this.getNodeById(attrs.id);
    if (exists) {
        if (!inactive) {
            exists.select();
            exists.ui.highlight();
        }
        return;
    }
    Ext.apply(attrs, {
        iconCls: 'x-portlet-node-icon',
        leaf: true,
        draggable: true
    });
    var node=new Ext.tree.TreeNode(attrs);
    this.root.appendChild(node);
    if (!inactive) {
        if (!preventAnim) {
            Ext.fly(node.ui.elNode).slideIn('l', {
                callback: node.select, scope: node, duration: .4
            });
        } else {
```

```
                    node.select();
            }
        }
        return node;
    }
```

When the `add-portlet` item of the `Treeview`'s context menu is clicked, the `insertPortletRequest` event in the `Treeview` is fired:

```
    itemclick: function(item) {
        switch (item.id) {
            case 'add-portlet':
                var n=item.parentMenu.contextNode;
                if (n.parentNode) {
                    n.getOwnerTree().fireEvent('insertPortletRequest',
                    {id:n.id,text:n.text});
                    n.remove();
                                }
            break;
        }
    }
```

After the classes that conform to the dashboard are defined, instances of both the portal and portlets catalog are created, along with a handler for the `portletRemoved` event of the portal. This handler takes care of adding the just-removed portlet back to the catalog by invoking the catalog's `addPortletNode(...)` function:

```
    portalPanel.on('portletRemoved', function(panel){
        catalog.addPortletNode({
            id: panel.id,
            text: panel.title
        }, true);
    });
```

A handler for the catalog's `insertPortletRequest` event takes care of the addition of portlets to the portal:

```
    catalog.on('insertPortletRequest', function(portletConfig){
        portalPanel.insertPortlet(portletConfig.id, portletConfig.text);
    });
```

What's left is to simply create the dashboard's layout and add a few sample portlets to the catalog.

There's more...

This modular portal implementation is easily adaptable to different needs. For example, with a few modifications to the configuration of the `Portal` class and the `insertPortlet()` function, the number of columns in the portal can be changed.

Another useful feature would involve using the `Ext.state.Manager` class to preserve the position of the portlets across application restarts.

See also...

> ▸ The previous recipe, *A three-panel application layout with a single line of code*, explains about building a re-usable Ext JS component that encapsulates a three-panel layout

> ▸ The recipe, *Creating a modern application layout with collapsible regions* (seen previously in this chapter), illustrates the creation of one of the most popular UI layouts

3
Load, Validate, and Submit Forms

You will learn the following recipes in this chapter:

- ▶ Specifying the required fields in a form
- ▶ Setting the minimum and maximum length allowed for a field's value
- ▶ Changing the location where validation errors are displayed
- ▶ Deferring field validation until form submission
- ▶ Creating validation functions for URLs, email addresses, and other types of data
- ▶ Confirming passwords and validating dates using relational field validation
- ▶ Rounding up your validation strategy with server-side validation of form fields
- ▶ Loading form data from the server
- ▶ Serving the XML data to a form
- ▶ Using forms for file uploads
- ▶ Building friendlier forms using text hints

Introduction

This chapter focuses on the topic of processing forms. The journey will include client-side and server-side field validation, form loading, submission, field customization, and layout techniques that will make it a breeze to build great-looking and friendly forms.

Specifying the required fields in a form

This recipe uses a login form as an example to explain how to create required fields in a form.

How to do it...

1. Initialize the global `QuickTips` instance:

```
Ext.QuickTips.init();
```

2. Create the login form:

```
var loginForm = { xtype: 'form',
    id: 'login-form',
    bodyStyle: 'padding:15px;background:transparent',
    border: false,
    url:'login.php',
    items: [{
        xtype: 'box',
        autoEl: { tag: 'div',
            html: '<div class="app-msg">
                <img src="img/magic-wand.png" class="app-img" />
                Log in to The Magic Forum</div>'}
    },
    { xtype: 'textfield', id: 'login-user',
        fieldLabel: 'Username',
        allowBlank: false
    },
    { xtype: 'textfield', id: 'login-pwd',
        fieldLabel: 'Password',
        inputType: 'password',allowBlank: false
```

```
    }],
    buttons: [{
        text: 'Login',
        handler: function() {
            Ext.getCmp('login-form').getForm().submit();
        }
    },
    {
        text: 'Cancel',
        handler: function() {
            win.hide();
        }
    }]
}
```

3. Create the window that will host the login form:

```
Ext.onReady(function() {
    win = new Ext.Window({
        layout: 'form',
        width: 340,
        autoHeight: true,
        closeAction: 'hide',
        items: [loginForm]
    });
    win.show();
});
```

How it works...

Initializing the QuickTips singleton allows the form's validation errors to be shown as tool tips. When the form is created, each required field needs to have the allowblank configuration option set to false:

```
{ xtype: 'textfield', id: 'login-user', fieldLabel: 'Username',
allowBlank: false
},
{ xtype: 'textfield', id: 'login-pwd', fieldLabel: 'Password',
inputType: 'password',allowBlank: false
}
```

Setting allowBlank to false activates a validation rule that requires the length of the field's value to be greater than zero.

There's more...

Use the `blankText` configuration option to change the error text when the blank validation fails. For example, the username field definition in the previous code snippet can be changed as shown here:

```
{ xtype: 'textfield', id: 'login-user', fieldLabel: 'Username',
        allowBlank: false, blankText:'Enter your username'
}
```

The resulting error is shown in the following figure:

Validation rules can be combined and even customized. Other recipes in this chapter explain how to range-check a field's length, as well as how to specify the valid format of the field's value.

See also...

- ▶ The next recipe titled *Setting the minimum and maximum length allowed for a field's value* explains how to restrict the number of characters entered in a field

- ▶ The *Changing the location where validation errors are displayed* recipe, covered later in this chapter, shows how to relocate a field's error icon

- ▶ Refer to the *Deferring field validation until form submission* recipe, covered later in this chapter, to learn how to validate all fields at once upon form submission, instead of using the default automatic field validation

- ▶ The *Creating validation functions for URLs, email addresses, and other types of data* recipe, covered later in this chapter, explains the validation functions available in Ext JS

▶ The *Confirming passwords and validating dates using relational field validation* recipe, covered later in this chapter, explains how to perform validation when the value of one field depends on the value of another field

▶ The *Rounding up your validation strategy with server-side validation of form fields* recipe, covered later in this chapter, explains how to perform server-side validation

Setting the minimum and maximum length allowed for a field's value

This recipe shows how to set the minimum and maximum number of characters allowed for a text field. The way to specify a custom error message for this type of validation is also explained.

The login form built in this recipe has username and password fields of a login form whose lengths are restricted:

How to do it...

1. The first thing is to initialize the `QuickTips` singleton:

   ```
   Ext.QuickTips.init();
   ```

2. Create the login form:

   ```
   var loginForm = { xtype: 'form',
       id: 'login-form',
       bodyStyle: 'padding:15px;background:transparent',
       border: false,
       url:'login.php',
       items: [
           { xtype: 'box', autoEl: { tag: 'div',
   ```

```
        html: '<div class="app-msg">
          <img src="img/magic-wand.png" class="app-img" />
          Log in to The Magic Forum</div>'
      }
    },
    { xtype: 'textfield', id: 'login-user',
      fieldLabel: 'Username',
      allowBlank: false, minLength: 3, maxLength: 32
    },
    { xtype: 'textfield', id: 'login-pwd',
      fieldLabel: 'Password', inputType: 'password',
      allowBlank: false, minLength: 6, maxLength: 32,
      minLengthText: 'Password must be at least 6 characters
        long.'
    }
  ],
  buttons: [{
    text: 'Login',
    handler: function() {
        Ext.getCmp('login-form').getForm().submit();
    }
  }, {
    text: 'Cancel',
    handler: function() {
        win.hide();
    }
  }]
}
```

3. Create the window that will host the login form:

```
Ext.onReady(function() {
  win = new Ext.Window({
    layout: 'form',
    width: 340,
    autoHeight: true,
    closeAction: 'hide',
    items: [loginForm]
  });
  win.show();
});
```

How it works...

After initializing the `QuickTips` singleton, which allows the form's validation errors to be shown as tool tips, the form is built.

The form is an instance of `Ext.form.FormPanel`. The username and password fields have their lengths restricted by the way of the `minLength` and `maxLength` configuration options:

```
{ xtype: 'textfield', id: 'login-user', fieldLabel: 'Username',
allowBlank: false, minLength: 3, maxLength: 32
},
{ xtype: 'textfield', id: 'login-pwd',
fieldLabel: 'Password', inputType: 'password',
allowBlank: false, minLength: 6, maxLength: 32,
minLengthText: 'Password must be at least 6 characters long.'
}
```

Notice how the `minLengthText` option is used to customize the error message that is displayed when the minimum length validation fails:

```
{ xtype: 'textfield', id: 'login-pwd',
    fieldLabel: 'Password', inputType: 'password',
    allowBlank: false, minLength: 6, maxLength: 32,
    minLengthText: 'Password must be at least 6 characters long.'
}
```

As a last step, the window that will host the form is created and displayed.

There's more...

You can also use the `maxLengthText` configuration option to specify the error message when the maximum length validation fails.

See also...

- ▸ The previous recipe, *Specifying the required fields in a form*, explains how to make some form fields required

- ▸ The next recipe, *Changing the location where validation errors are displayed*, shows how to relocate a field's error icon

- ▸ Refer to the *Deferring field validation until form submission* recipe (covered later in this chapter) to learn how to validate all fields at once upon form submission, instead of using the default automatic field validation

- ▸ Refer to the *Creating validation functions for URLs, email addresses, and other types of data* recipe (covered later in this chapter) for an explanation of the validation functions available in Ext JS

> ▶ The *Confirming passwords and validating dates using relational field validation* recipe (covered later in this chapter) explains how to perform validation when the value of one field depends on the value of another field

> ▶ The *Rounding up your validation strategy with server-side validation of form fields* recipe (covered later in this chapter) explains how to perform server-side validation

Changing the location where validation errors are displayed

A popular way to display validation errors is to place an error icon to the side of the invalid fields As shown in the next screenshot, this recipe uses a login form to explain how to implement this technique.

How to do it...

1. Initialize the `QuickTips` singleton:

```
Ext.QuickTips.init();
```

2. Create the login form:

```
var loginForm = { xtype: 'form',
    id: 'login-form',
    bodyStyle: 'padding:15px;background:transparent',
    border: false,
    url:'login.php',
    items: [
        { xtype: 'box',
          autoEl: { tag: 'div',
            html: '<div class="app-msg">
                <img src="img/magic-wand.png"
                class="app-img" />Log in to The Magic Forum</div>'
          }
        }
```

```
        },
        { xtype: 'textfield', id: 'login-user',
          fieldLabel: 'Username',
          allowBlank: false, minLength: 3, maxLength: 32,
          msgTarget:'side'
        },
        { xtype: 'textfield', id: 'login-pwd',
          fieldLabel: 'Password',
          inputType: 'password', allowBlank: false, minLength: 6,
          maxLength: 32, minLengthText: 'Password must be at least 6
            characters long.',
          msgTarget:'side'
        }
    ],
    buttons: [{
        text: 'Login',
        handler: function() {
            Ext.getCmp('login-form').getForm().submit();
        }
    },
    { text: 'Cancel',
      handler: function() {
          win.hide();
      }
    }]
}
```

3. Create the window that will host the login form:

```
Ext.onReady(function() {
    win = new Ext.Window({
        layout: 'form',
        width: 340,
        autoHeight: true,
        closeAction: 'hide',
        items: [loginForm]
    });
    win.show();
});
```

How it works...

First, initializing the QuickTips singleton allows the form's validation errors to be shown as tool tips.

Next, the form is built. To display error icons at the righthand side of the invalid fields, the `msgTarget` option is set to `side`:

```
{ xtype: 'textfield', id: 'login-user', fieldLabel: 'Username',
    allowBlank: false, minLength: 3, maxLength: 32,
    msgTarget:'side'
},
{ xtype: 'textfield', id: 'login-pwd', fieldLabel: 'Password',
inputType: 'password', allowBlank: false, minLength: 6,
maxLength: 32, minLengthText: 'Password must be at least 6
characters long.',
msgTarget:'side'
}
```

The last step consists of creating and displaying the window that hosts the form.

There's more...

The value of the `msgTarget` configuration option defaults to `qtip`, which displays a quick tip when the user hovers over the field. Besides `side`, used in this recipe, you can use these remaining values to change how the validation error displays:

- ▶ `title`: Displays a default browser title attribute pop up.
- ▶ `under`: Adds a block div beneath the field containing the error text.
- ▶ `[element id]`: Adds the error text directly to the `innerHTML` of the specified element.

See also...

- ▶ The *Specifying the required fields in a form* recipe, covered previously in this chapter, explains how to make some form fields required
- ▶ The previous recipe, *Setting the minimum and maximum length allowed for a field's value*, explains how to restrict the number of characters entered in a field
- ▶ The following recipe, *Deferring field validation until form submission*, explains how to validate all fields at once upon form submission, instead of using the default automatic field validation
- ▶ Refer to the *Creating validation functions for URLs, email addresses, and other types of data* recipe, covered later in this chapter, for an explanation of the validation functions available in Ext JS

▶ The *Confirming passwords and validating dates using relational field validation* recipe, covered later in this chapter, explains how to perform validation when the value of one field depends on the value of another field

▶ The *Rounding up your validation strategy with server-side validation of form fields* recipe, covered later in this chapter, explains how to perform server-side validation

Deferring field validation until form submission

Generally, a form field is validated on the client-side when the `keyup` event occurs, or when the field loses focus. Occasionally, you might prefer the validation to be performed just before the form is submitted.

In this recipe, a login form is built, with the validation deferred until the form is submitted. Focus changes or the keyup event will not trigger field validation, as shown in the following screenshot:

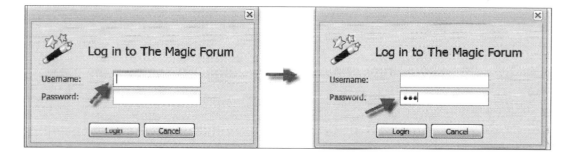

As shown in the next screenshot, submitting the form will trigger the validation:

How to do it...

1. Initialize the `QuickTips` singleton:

```
Ext.QuickTips.init();
```

2. Create the login form:

```
var loginForm = { xtype: 'form',
    id: 'login-form',
    bodyStyle: 'padding:15px;background:transparent',
    border: false,
    url:'login.php',
    items: [
        { xtype: 'box', autoEl: { tag: 'div',
          html: '<div class="app-msg">
            <img src="img/magic-wand.png" class="app-img" />
            Log in to The Magic Forum</div>'
          }
        },
        { xtype: 'textfield', id: 'login-user',
          fieldLabel: 'Username',
          allowBlank: false, minLength: 3, maxLength: 32,
          msgTarget:'side',validationEvent:false
        },
        { xtype: 'textfield', id: 'login-pwd',
          fieldLabel: 'Password', inputType: 'password',
          allowBlank: false, minLength: 6, maxLength: 32,
          minLengthText: 'Password must be at least 6 characters
            long.',
          msgTarget:'side',validationEvent:false
        }
    ],
    buttons: [{
        text: 'Login',
        handler: function() {
            Ext.getCmp('login-form').getForm().submit();
        }
    },
    {
        text: 'Cancel',
        handler: function() {
            win.hide();
```

```
        }
    }]
}
```

3. Create the window that will host the login form:

```
Ext.onReady(function() {
    win = new Ext.Window({
        layout: 'form',
        width: 340,
        autoHeight: true,
        closeAction: 'hide',
        items: [loginForm]
    });
    win.show();
```

How it works...

The first step consists of initializing the `QuickTips` singleton so that the form's validation errors can be shown as tool tips.

Next, the form is built. In order to disable automatic validation, the `validationEvent` configuration option is set to `false`:

```
{ xtype: 'textfield', id: 'login-user', fieldLabel: 'Username',
allowBlank: false, minLength: 3, maxLength: 32,
msgTarget:'side',validationEvent:false
},
{ xtype: 'textfield', id: 'login-pwd', fieldLabel: 'Password',
inputType: 'password',allowBlank: false,
minLength: 6, maxLength: 32,
minLengthText: 'Password must be at least 6 characters
long.',
msgTarget:'side',validationEvent:false
}
```

The `validationEvent` option indicates the event that should initiate field validation. The default value for this option is `keyup`. Like in the code above, when set to `false`, it simply disables automatic validation for the field.

The last step consists of creating and displaying the window that hosts the form.

There's more...

This recipe is a good solution in some data-intensive applications, where validating a field with every keystroke or focus change might become an annoyance for the user.

When you want to disable client-side field validation altogether and place on the server all of the responsibility for the validation, you can add the `clientValidation = false` configuration option to the `submit()` function call:

```
Ext.getCmp('login-form').getForm().submit({clientValidation:false});
```

See also...

▸ The *Specifying the required fields in a form* recipe, covered earlier in this chapter, explains how to make some form fields required

▸ The *Setting the minimum and maximum length allowed for a field's value* recipe, covered earlier in this chapter, explains how to restrict the number of characters entered in a field

▸ The previous recipe, *Changing the location where validation errors are displayed*, shows how to relocate a field's error icon

▸ Refer to the next recipe, *Creating validation functions for URLs, email addresses, and other types of data*, for an explanation of the validation functions available in Ext JS

▸ The *Confirming passwords and validating dates using relational field validation* recipe, covered later in this chapter, explains how to perform validation when the value of one field depends on the value of another field

▸ The *Rounding up your validation strategy with server-side validation of form fields* recipe, covered later in this chapter, explains how to perform server-side validation

Creating validation functions for URLs, email addresses, and other types of data

Ext JS has an extensive library of validation functions. This is how it can be used to validate URLs, email addresses, and other types of data.

The following screenshot shows email address validation in action:

Send your comments

Name:

Email: extjs   ⓘ

Web page:

Comments:

> ⓘ This field should be an e-mail address in the format "user@domain.com"

This screenshot displays URL validation in action:

Send your comments

Name:

Email:

Web page: extjs   ⓘ

Comments:

> ⓘ This field should be a URL in the format "http://www.domain.com"

How to do it...

1. Initialize the `QuickTips` singleton:

```
Ext.QuickTips.init();
```

2. Create a form with fields that accept specific data formats:

```
Ext.onReady(function() {
    var commentForm = new Ext.FormPanel({
        frame: true,
        title: 'Send your comments',
        bodyStyle: 'padding:5px',
        width: 550,
        layout: 'form',
        defaults: { msgTarget: 'side' },
        items: [
          { xtype: 'textfield',
            fieldLabel: 'Name',
            name: 'name',
            anchor: '95%',
```

```
            allowBlank: false
        }, {
            xtype: 'textfield',
            fieldLabel: 'Email',
            name: 'email',
            anchor: '95%',
            vtype: 'email'
        }, {
            xtype: 'textfield',
            fieldLabel: 'Web page',
            name: 'webPage',
            vtype: 'url',
            anchor: '95%'
        }, {
            xtype: 'textarea',
            fieldLabel: 'Comments',
            name: 'comments',
            anchor: '95%',
            height: 150,
            allowBlank: false
        }],
        buttons: [{
            text: 'Send'
        }, {
            text: 'Cancel'
        }]
    });
    commentForm.render(document.body);
});
```

How it works...

The vtype configuration option specifies which validation function will be applied to the field.

There's more...

Validation types in Ext JS include alphanumeric, numeric, URL, and email formats. You can extend this feature with custom validation functions, and virtually, any format can be validated. For example, the following code shows how you can add a validation type for JPG and PNG files:

```
Ext.apply(Ext.form.VTypes, {
    Picture:  function(v) {
        return /^.*\.(jpg|JPG|png|PNG)$/.test(v);
    },
    PictureText: 'Must be a JPG or PNG file';
});
```

If you need to replace the default error text provided by the validation type, you can do so by using the vtypeText configuration option:

```
{
    xtype: 'textfield',
    fieldLabel: 'Web page',
    name: 'webPage',
    vtype: 'url',
    vtypeText: 'I am afraid that you did not enter a URL',
    anchor: '95%'
}
```

See also...

- The *Specifying the required fields in a form* recipe, covered earlier in this chapter, explains how to make some form fields required.

- The *Setting the minimum and maximum length allowed for a field's value* recipe, covered earlier in this chapter, explains how to restrict the number of characters entered in a field.

- The *Changing the location where validation errors are displayed* recipe, covered earlier in this chapter, shows how to relocate a field's error icon.

- Refer to the previous recipe, *Deferring field validation until form submission*, to know how to validate all fields at once upon form submission, instead of using the default automatic field validation.

- The next recipe, *Confirming passwords and validating dates using relational field validation*, explains how to perform validation when the value of one field depends on the value of another field.

- The *Rounding up your validation strategy with server-side validation of form fields* recipe (covered later in this chapter) explains how to perform server-side validation.

Confirming passwords and validating dates using relational field validation

Frequently, you face scenarios where the values of two fields need to match, or the value of one field depends on the value of another field.

Let's examine how to build a registration form that requires the user to confirm his or her password when signing up.

How to do it...

1. Initialize the `QuickTips` singleton:

   ```
   Ext.QuickTips.init();
   ```

2. Create a custom `vtype` to handle the relational validation of the password:

   ```
   Ext.apply(Ext.form.VTypes, {
       password: function(val, field) {
           if (field.initialPassField) {
               var pwd = Ext.getCmp(field.initialPassField);
               return (val == pwd.getValue());
           }
           return true;
       },
       passwordText: 'What are you doing?<br/>The passwords entered
           do not match!'
   });
   ```

3. Create the signup form:

```
var signupForm = { xtype: 'form',
    id: 'register-form',
    labelWidth: 125,
    bodyStyle: 'padding:15px;background:transparent',
    border: false,
    url: 'signup.php',
    items: [
        { xtype: 'box',
          autoEl: { tag: 'div',
            html: '<div class="app-msg"><img src="img/businessman-
              add.png" class="app-img" />
              Register for The Magic Forum</div>'
          }
        },
        { xtype: 'textfield', id: 'email', fieldLabel: 'Email',
          allowBlank: false, minLength: 3,
          maxLength: 64,anchor:'90%', vtype:'email'
        },
        { xtype: 'textfield', id: 'pwd', fieldLabel: 'Password',
          inputType: 'password',allowBlank: false, minLength: 6,
          maxLength: 32,anchor:'90%',
          minLengthText: 'Password must be at least 6 characters
            long.'
        },
        { xtype: 'textfield', id: 'pwd-confirm',
          fieldLabel: 'Confirm Password', inputType: 'password',
          allowBlank: false, minLength: 6,
          maxLength: 32,anchor:'90%',
          minLengthText: 'Password must be at least 6 characters
            long.',
          vtype: 'password', initialPassField: 'pwd'
        }
    ],
    buttons: [{
        text: 'Register',
        handler: function() {
            Ext.getCmp('register-form').getForm().submit();
        }
    },
    {
```

```
        text: 'Cancel',
        handler: function() {
        win.hide();
        }
      }]
    }
```

4. Create the window that will host the signup form:

```
Ext.onReady(function() {
    win = new Ext.Window({
        layout: 'form',
        width: 340,
        autoHeight: true,
        closeAction: 'hide',
        items: [signupForm]
    });
    win.show();
```

How it works...

The first step is to initialize the QuickTips singleton. This allows the form's validation errors to show as tool tips.

Next, a custom vtype is created to support the relational validation of the password. A vtype consists of a validation function and the text to use when there is a validation error. The password validation function compares the values of the two password fields:

```
password: function(val, field) {
    if (field.initialPassField) {
        var pwd = Ext.getCmp(field.initialPassField);
        return (val == pwd.getValue());
    }
    return true;
}
```

When the validation fails, the error text is used:

```
passwordText: 'What are you doing?<br/>The passwords entered do
    not match!'
```

What follows is the creation and display of the signup form. Notice how the second password field has references to the custom `vtype` and the first password field. This allows the validation function in the custom `vtype` to work:

```
{ xtype: 'textfield', id: 'pwd-confirm',
  fieldLabel: 'Confirm Password', inputType: 'password',
  allowBlank: false, minLength: 6, maxLength: 32,anchor:'90%',
  minLengthText: 'Password must be at least 6 characters long.',
  vtype: 'password', initialPassField: 'pwd'
}
```

There's more...

You can also use this technique for validating date fields that act as a date range, where selecting an initial date in one field sets the minimum or maximum value for the other field.

Date Range	
Start Date:	
End Date:	

See also...

- ► The *Specifying the required fields in a form* recipe, covered earlier in this chapter, explains how to make some form fields required.

- ► The *Setting the minimum and maximum length allowed for a field's value* recipe (covered earlier in this chapter) explains how to restrict the number of characters entered in a field.

- ► The *Changing the location where validation errors are displayed* recipe, covered earlier in this chapter, shows how to relocate a field's error icon.

- ► Refer to the *Deferring field validation until form submission* recipe, covered earlier in this chapter, to know how to validate all fields at once upon form submission, instead of using the default automatic field validation.

- ► Refer to the previous recipe, *Creating validation functions for URLs, email addresses, and other types of data*, for an explanation of the validation functions available in Ext JS.

- ► The following recipe, *Rounding up your validation strategy with server-side validation of form fields*, explains how to perform server-side validation.

Rounding up your validation strategy with server-side validation of form fields

Server-side validation should be an important component of your validation strategy for any application. This recipe explains how to send validation codes and messages to a login form from the server-side code.

The login form built in this recipe performs client-side validation. Upon submission, the server returns an error code and a message, as shown in the next screenshot:

How to do it...

1. Initialize the `QuickTips` singleton so that we can have error messages as tool tips:

    ```
    Ext.QuickTips.init();
    ```

2. Define the login form:

    ```
    var loginForm = { xtype: 'form',
        id: 'login-form',
        bodyStyle: 'padding:15px;background:transparent',
        border: false,
        url:'login.php',
        items: [
            { xtype: 'box', autoEl: { tag: 'div',
              html: '<div class="app-msg">
                <img src="img/magic-wand.png" class="app-img" />
                Log in to The Magic Forum</div>'
              }
            },
            { xtype: 'textfield', id: 'login-user',
              fieldLabel: 'Username',allowBlank: false,
              minLength: 3, maxLength: 32
            },
            { xtype: 'textfield', id: 'login-pwd',
    ```

```
                  fieldLabel: 'Password', inputType: 'password',
                  allowBlank: false, minLength: 6, maxLength: 32,
                  minLengthText: 'Password must be at least 6 characters
                     long.'
              }
          ],
          buttons: [{
              text: 'Login',
              handler: function() {
                  Ext.getCmp('login-form').getForm().
                     submit({waitMsg: 'Please wait...' });
              }
          },
          {
              text: 'Cancel',
              handler: function() {
                  win.hide();
              }
          }]
      }
```

3. Create the window that will host the login form:

```
Ext.onReady(function() {
    win = new Ext.Window([
        layout: 'form',
        width: 340,
        autoHeight: true,
        closeAction: 'hide',
        items: [loginForm]
    });
    win.show();
```

4. Create the login.php server page:

```
<?php
echo "{success:false,errors:[{id:'login-pwd',msg:'Sorry, you have
  to type the magic word!'}]}";
?>
```

How it works...

The first step is to initialize the `QuickTips` singleton, so that we can show the form's validation errors as tool tips.

Next, the form and the window that serves as a host for the form are built. The form is set up to perform client-side validation as explained in the previous recipes in this chapter.

The interesting part of this recipe is the server page that handles the form submission. The PHP code here illustrates which elements are necessary to notify the form that one or more fields are invalid:

```
echo "{success:false,errors:[{id:'login-pwd',msg:'Sorry, you have to
    type the magic word!'}]}";
```

The server page returns the JSON representation of an object with two properties—`success` and `errors`. The `success` property is present both when there are problems with the validation (`success = false`), or when the submission was successful (`success = true`). `Errors` is an array containing one object for each invalid field. This object in turn contains the ID of the invalid field and the error message:

```
{id:'login-pwd',msg:'Sorry, you have to type the magic word!'}
```

There's more...

A comprehensive validation strategy is always recommended. Even though the client-side validation facilities in Ext JS are very powerful, do not skip server-side validation. Use it to add robustness and resiliency to your applications.

See also...

▶   The *Specifying required fields in a form* recipe, covered earlier in this chapter, explains how to make some form fields required.

▶   Refer to the *Deferring field validation until form submission* recipe, covered earlier in this chapter, to know how to validate all fields at once upon form submission, instead of using the default automatic field validation.

Loading form data from the server

An important part of working with forms is loading the data that a form will display. Here's how to create a sample contact form and populate it with data sent from the server.

How to do it...

1. Declare the name and company panel:

```
var nameAndCompany = { columnWidth: .5,
    layout: 'form',
    items: [
      { xtype: 'textfield',
        fieldLabel: 'First Name',
        name: 'firstName',
        anchor: '95%'
      },
      {
```

```
          xtype: 'textfield',
          fieldLabel: 'Last Name',
          name: 'lastName',
          anchor: '95%'
       },
       {
          xtype: 'textfield',
          fieldLabel: 'Company',
          name: 'company',
          anchor: '95%'
       },
       {

          xtype: 'textfield',
          fieldLabel: 'Title',
          name: 'title',
          anchor: '95%'
       }
    ]
 }
```

2. Declare the picture box panel:

```
var picBox = {
   columnWidth: .5,
   bodyStyle: 'padding:0px 0px 0px 40px',
   items: [
     { xtype: 'box',
       autoEl: { tag: 'div', style: 'padding-bottom:20px',
                 html: '<img id="pic"
                 src="' + Ext.BLANK_IMAGE_URL + '"
                 class="img-contact" />'
                }
     }, { xtype: 'button', text: 'Change Picture' }
   ]
}
```

3. Define the Internet panel:

```
var internet = { columnWidth: .5,
   layout: 'form',
   items: [
     { xtype: 'fieldset',
       title: 'Internet',
       autoHeight: true,
```

```
        defaultType: 'textfield',
        items: [{
            fieldLabel: 'Email',
            name: 'email',
            vtype: 'email',
            anchor: '95%'
        },
        { fieldLabel: 'Web page',
          name: 'webPage',
          vtype: 'url',
          anchor: '95%'
        },
        { fieldLabel: 'IM',
          name: 'imAddress',
          anchor: '95%'
        }]
    }]
}
```

4. Declare the phone panel:

```
var phones = { columnWidth: .5,
    layout: 'form',
    items: [{ xtype: 'fieldset',
        title: 'Phone Numbers',
        autoHeight: true,
        defaultType: 'textfield',
        items: [{
            fieldLabel: 'Home',
            name: 'homePhone',
            anchor: '95%'
        },
        {
            fieldLabel: 'Business',
            name: 'busPhone',
            anchor: '95%'
        },
        {
            fieldLabel: 'Mobile',
            name: 'mobPhone',
            anchor: '95%'
        },
```

```
            {
                fieldLabel: 'Fax',
                name: 'fax',
                anchor: '95%'
            }]
        }]
    }
```

5. Define the business address panel:

```
var busAddress = { columnWidth: .5,
    layout: 'form',
    labelAlign: 'top',
    defaultType: 'textarea',
    items: [{
        fieldLabel: 'Business',
        labelSeparator:'',
        name: 'bAddress',
        anchor: '95%'
    },
    {
        xtype: 'radio',
        boxLabel: 'Mailing Address',
        hideLabel: true,
        name: 'mailingAddress',
        value:'bAddress',
        id:'mailToBAddress'
    }]
}
```

6. Define the home address panel:

```
var homeAddress = { columnWidth: .5,
    layout: 'form',
    labelAlign: 'top',
    defaultType: 'textarea',
    items: [{
        fieldLabel: 'Home',
        labelSeparator:'',
        name: 'hAddress',
        anchor: '95%'
    },
    {
        xtype: 'radio',
```

```
        boxLabel: 'Mailing Address',
        hideLabel: true,
        name: 'mailingAddress',
        value:'hAddress',
        id:'mailToHAddress'
     }]
  }
```

7. Create the contact form:

```
var contactForm = new Ext.FormPanel({
   frame: true,
   title: 'TODO: Load title dynamically',
   bodyStyle: 'padding:5px',
   width: 650,
   items: [{
     bodyStyle: {
        margin: '0px 0px 15px 0px'
     },
     items: [{
       layout: 'column',
       items: [nameAndCompany, picBox]
     }]
   },
   {
     items: [{
        layout: 'column',
        items: [phones, internet]
     }]
   },
   {
     xtype: 'fieldset',
     title: 'Addresses',
     autoHeight: true,
     hideBorders: true,
     layout: 'column',
     items: [busAddress, homeAddress]
   }],
   buttons: [{
     text: 'Save'
   },
   {
```

```
            text: 'Cancel'
        }]
    });
```

8. Handle the form's `actioncomplete` event:

```
contactForm.on({
    actioncomplete: function(form, action){
        if(action.type == 'load'){
            var contact = action.result.data;
            Ext.getCmp(contact.mailingAddress).setValue(true);
            contactForm.setTitle(contact.firstName + ' ' +
              contact.lastName);
            Ext.getDom('pic').src = contact.pic;
        }
    }
});
```

9. Render the form:

```
contactForm.render(document.body);
```

10. Finally, load the form:

```
contactForm.getForm().load({ url: 'contact.php',
    params:{id:'contact1'},waitMsg: 'Loading'});
```

How it works...

The contact form's building sequence consists of defining each of the contained panels, and then defining a form panel that will serve as a host. The following screenshot shows the resulting form, with the placement of each of the panels pinpointed:

Moving on to how the form is populated, the JSON-encoded response to a request to provide form data has a structure similar to this:

```
{success:true,
    data:{Id:'1',firstName:'Jorge',lastName:'Ramon',
    company:'MiamiCoder',title:'Mr',pic:'img/jorger.jpg',
    email:'ramonj@miamicoder.net',webPage:'http://www.miamicoder.com',
    imAddress:'',homePhone:'',busPhone:'555 555-5555',
    mobPhone:'',fax:'',
    bAddress:'123 Acme Rd \#001\\nMiami, FL 33133',
    hAddress:'',mailingAddress:'mailToBAddress'}}
```

The `success` property indicates whether the request has succeeded or not. If the request succeeds, `success` is accompanied by a `data` property, which contains the contact's information. Although some fields are automatically populated after a call to `load()`, the form's title, the contact's picture, and the mailing address radio button require further processing. This can be done in the handler for the `actioncomplete` event:

```
contactForm.on({
    actioncomplete: function(form, action){
        if(action.type == 'load'){
        }
    }
});
```

As already mentioned, the contact's information arrives in the `data` property of the action's `result`:

```
var contact = action.result.data;
```

The default mailing address comes in the contact's `mailingAddress` property. Hence, the radio button for the default mailing address is set as shown in the following line of code:

```
Ext.getCmp(contact.mailingAddress).setValue(true);
```

The source for the contact's photo is the value of `contact.pic`:

```
Ext.getDom('pic').src = contact.pic;
```

And finally, the title of the form:

```
contactForm.setTitle(contact.firstName + ' ' + contact.lastName);
```

There's more...

Although this recipe's focus is on loading form data, you should also pay attention to the layout techniques used—multiple rows, multiple columns, fieldsets—that allow you to achieve rich and flexible user interfaces for your forms.

See also...

▶ The next recipe, *Serving the XML data to a form*, explains how to use a form to load the XML data sent from the server

Serving the XML data to a form

XML is an information interchange format that can be used to provide the data that a form will display. This recipe shows how to create a contact form that feeds off the XML data that is sent from the server. This is how the contact form looks like after receiving the XML data:

Jorge Ramon

First Name: Jorge

Last Name: Ramon

Company: MiamiCoder

Title: Mr

Change Picture

Phone Numbers

Home:

Business: 555 555-5555

Mobile:

Fax:

Internet

Email: ramonj@miamicoder.net

Web page: http://www.miamicoder.cc

IM:

Addresses

Business

123 Acme Rd #001
Miami, FL 33133

Home

◉ Mailing Address   ◯ Mailing Address

Save   Cancel

How to do it...

1. Build the name, company, picture box, internet, phone, business address, and home address panels as explained in the first six steps of the recipe *Loading form data from the server*.

2. Create the contact form and assign it an `XmlReader` as its data reader:

```
var contactForm = new Ext.FormPanel({
    frame: true,
    title: 'TODO: Load title dynamically',
    bodyStyle: 'padding:5px',
    width: 650,
    url: 'contact-xml.php',
```

```
        reader: new Ext.data.XmlReader({
          record: 'contact',
          success: '@success'
        },
        ['id', 'firstName', 'lastName', 'company', 'title',
          'pic','email', 'webPage', 'imAddress', 'homePhone',
          'busPhone','mobPhone', 'fax', 'bAddress', 'hAddress',
          'mailingAddress']
        ),
        items: [{
          bodyStyle: {
            margin: '0px 0px 15px 0px'
          },
          items: [{
            layout: 'column',
            items: [nameAndCompany, picBox]
          }]
        }, {
            items: [{
            layout: 'column',
            items: [phones, internet]
          }]
      }, {
          xtype: 'fieldset',
          title: 'Addresses',
          autoHeight: true,
          hideBorders: true,
          layout: 'column',
          items: [busAddress, homeAddress]
        }],
        buttons: [{
          text: 'Save'
        },
        {
          text: 'Cancel'
        }]
      });
```

3. Handle the form's `actioncomplete` event:

```
contactForm.on({
    actioncomplete: function(form, action){
        if(action.type == 'load'){
            var contact = action.result.data;
            Ext.getCmp(contact.mailingAddress).setValue(true);
            contactForm.setTitle(contact.firstName + ' ' +
              contact.lastName);
            Ext.getDom('pic').src = contact.pic;
        }
    }
});
```

4. Render the form:

```
contactForm.render(document.body);
```

5. Finally, load the form:

```
contactForm.getForm().load({ method:'get',
    params: { id: 'contact1' }, waitMsg: 'Loading' });
```

How it works...

The contact form's building sequence is similar to the one described in the recipe *Loading form data from the server*. This is the resulting form, with the placement of each of the panels pinpointed:

Although a real-world application will most likely do some processing to generate the XML information, for this example the server page will generate sample data as simply as this:

```php
<?php
header("content-type: text/xml");
echo "<?xml version=\"1.0\" encoding=\"utf-8\" ?>";
echo "<message success=\"true\">";
echo "  <contact>";
echo "    <id>contact1</id>";
echo "    <firstName>Jorge</firstName>";
echo "    <lastName>Ramon</lastName>";
echo "    <company>MiamiCoder</company>";
echo "    <title>Mr</title>";
echo "    <pic>img/jorger.jpg</pic>";
echo "    <email>ramonj@miamicoder.com</email>";
echo "    <webPage>http://www.miamicoder.com</webPage>";
echo "    <imAddress></imAddress>";
echo "    <homePhone></homePhone>";
echo "    <busPhone>555 555-5555</busPhone>";
echo "    <mobPhone></mobPhone>";
echo "    <fax></fax>";
echo "    <bAddress>123 Acme Rd #001 Miami, FL 33133</bAddress>";
echo "    <hAddress></hAddress>";
echo "    <mailingAddress>mailToBAddress</mailingAddress>";
echo "  </contact>";
echo "</message>";
?>
```

The data consists of a `message` entity with a `success` attribute, which signals whether the request succeeded, and a `contact` entity for the contact information.

This data can be read by the form, thanks to the use of an `XmlReader` instance:

```
reader: new Ext.data.XmlReader({
  record: 'contact',
  success: '@success'
}, ['id', 'firstName', 'lastName', 'company', 'title', 'pic','email',
    'webPage', 'imAddress', 'homePhone', 'busPhone','mobPhone',
    'fax', 'bAddress', 'hAddress', 'mailingAddress']
)
```

The handler for the `actioncomplete` event is used to process the results of the `load` or `submit` actions:

```
contactForm.on({
    actioncomplete: function(form, action){
```

```
    if(action.type == 'load'){
        .
        .
        .

    }
    if(action.type == 'submit'){
        .
        .
        .

    }
  }
});
```

When the handler processes the `load` action, it sets the default mailing address, the form's title, and the contact's picture.

As mentioned, the contact's information arrives in the `data` property of the action's `result`:

```
var contact = action.result.data;
```

The default mailing address comes in the contact's `mailingAddress` property, and the radio button for the default mailing address is set as shown in the following code:

```
Ext.getCmp(contact.mailingAddress).setValue(true);
```

The source for the contact's photo is the value of `contact.pic`:

```
Ext.getDom('pic').src = contact.pic;
```

And finally, the title of the form:

```
contactForm.setTitle(contact.firstName + ' ' + contact.lastName);
```

There's more...

XML is powerful and popular, and it is likely that you will encounter situations where it's appropriate to create forms that are able to read XML data. As you saw, this can be accomplished by using an `XmlReader` through the `reader` configuration option, instead of using the form's built-in support for processing JSON.

See also...

▶ The previous recipe, *Loading form data from the server*, explains how to populate a form with data sent from the server

Using forms for file uploads

The **Change Picture** form is a great example of how to implement file uploads in your Ext JS application. This form is also a complement to the contact form examined in the *Loading form data from the server* and *Serving XML data to a form* recipes.

Let's see how it's done.

How to do it...

1. Create the component that will display the contact's picture:

```
var picBox = {
    columnWidth: '100 px',
    bodyStyle: 'padding:10px',
    items: [
        { xtype: 'box',
          autoEl: { tag: 'div',
          html: '<img id="pic" src="' + Ext.BLANK_IMAGE_URL + '"
            class="img-contact" />'
            }
        }
    ]
}
```

2. Create a panel with text boxes that show the file names for the current picture and the picture to be uploaded:

```
var picFiles = {
    columnWidth: .65,
    layout: 'form',
```

```
            labelAlign:'top',
            items: [{
               xtype: 'textfield',
               fieldLabel: 'Current',
               labelSeparator: '',
               name: 'currPic',
               id:'currPic',
               readOnly: true,
               disabled:true,
               anchor:'100%'
            },
            {
               xtype: 'textfield',
               fieldLabel: 'New (JPG or PNG only)',
               labelSeparator: '',
               name: 'newPic',
               id:'newPic',
               style:'width: 300px',
               inputType: 'file',
               allowBlank: false
            }]
      }
```

3. Define a custom validation function that will be used to validate that the file to upload is either a JPG or PNG file:

```
function validateFileExtension(fileName) {
    var exp = /^.*\.(jpg|JPG|png|PNG)$/;
    return exp.test(fileName);
}
```

4. Now, create the form and define a handler for the **Upload Picture** button:

```
var pictUploadForm = new Ext.FormPanel({
    frame: true,
    title: 'Change Picture',
    bodyStyle: 'padding:5px',
    width: 420,
    layout: 'column',
    url: 'contact-picture.aspx',
    method: 'POST',
    fileUpload: true,
    items: [picBox, picFiles],
    buttons: [{
```

```
                text: 'Upload Picture',
                handler: function() {
                    var theForm = pictUploadForm.getForm();
                    if (!theForm.isValid()) {
                        Ext.MessageBox.alert('Change Picture',
                          'Please select a picture');
                            return;
                    }
                    if (!validateFileExtension(Ext.getDom('newPic').value)) {
                        Ext.MessageBox.alert('Change Picture',
                          'Only JPG or PNG, please.');
                            return;
                    }
                    theForm.submit({
                        params: { act: 'setPicture', id: 'contact1' },
                        waitMsg: 'Uploading picture'
                    })
                }
            },
            {
                text: 'Cancel'
            }]
        });
```

5. Define a handler for the `actioncomplete` event:

```
pictUploadForm.on({
    actioncomplete: function(form, action) {
        if (action.type == 'load') {
            var pic = action.result.data;
            Ext.getDom('pic').src = pic.file;
            Ext.getCmp('currPic').setValue(pic.file);
        }
        if (action.type == 'submit') {
            var pic = action.result.data;
            Ext.getDom('pic').src = pic.file;
            Ext.getCmp('currPic').setValue(pic.file);
            Ext.getDom('newPic').value = '';
        }
    }
});
```

6. Render the form and load the existing picture for the contact:

```
pictUploadForm.render(document.body);
pictUploadForm.getForm().load({ params: { act: 'getPicture',
    id: 'contact1' }, waitMsg: 'Loading' });
```

How it works...

The component that will display the contact's picture is created first, followed by the text boxes that show the filenames for the current and new picture. To provide the ability to browse for the appropriate file, the new picture text box uses the `inputType = 'file'` config option, which creates the equivalent HTML element consisting of a text box and a **Browse** button.

A first layer of validation is provided by the `validateFileExtensions` function. This function uses a regular expression test in order to make sure the selected file has a PNG or JPG extension:

```
function validateFileExtension(fileName) {
    var exp = /^.*\.(jpg|JPG|png|PNG|txt|TXT)$/;
    return (exp.test(fileName));
}
```

I recommend that you complement this function with server-side validation. This will guarantee that the uploaded file is actually a picture.

Carrying out the validation, as well as the submission, is the responsibility of the `click` handler for the **Upload picture** button. Notice the use of a request parameter (`act: 'setPicture'`) to signal the server page that a new picture is being uploaded:

```
buttons: [{
    text: 'Upload Picture',
    handler: function() {
        var theForm = pictUploadForm.getForm();
        if (!theForm.isValid()) {
            Ext.MessageBox.alert('Change Picture',
                'Please select a picture');
            return;
        }
        if (!validateFileExtension(Ext.getDom('newPic').value)) {
            Ext.MessageBox.alert('Change Picture',
                'Only JPG or PNG, please.');
            return;
        }
        theForm.submit({
            params: { act: 'setPicture', id: 'contact1' },
            waitMsg: 'Uploading picture'
        })
    }
}
```

The `actioncomplete` handler is in charge of displaying the contact's picture. Upon a form load, the contact's current picture is displayed. After the form is submitted, the just-uploaded picture is shown:

```
if (action.type == 'load') {
    var pic = action.result.data;
    Ext.getDom('pic').src = pic.file;
    Ext.getCmp('currPic').setValue(pic.file);
}
if (action.type == 'submit') {
    var pic = action.result.data;
    Ext.getDom('pic').src = pic.file;
    Ext.getCmp('currPic').setValue(pic.file);
    Ext.getDom('newPic').value = '';
}
```

Notice that after a successful upload, the JSON-encoded response will have the following structure:

```
"{success:true,data:{contactId:'contact id',file:'[picture path]'}}
```

There's more...

This approach is a good foundation for implementing file uploading code in Ext JS. You can easily modify it to accomplish multiple file uploads as well. More complex implementations are also possible through the use of plugins or extensions.

See also...

> ▶ File upload panel at `http://filetree.extjs.eu`

Building friendlier forms using text hints

Great usability is often attained with simple UI modifications. This recipe explains how you can make your forms easier to use by adding text hints to their contained fields. The next screenshot shows a form that contains text hints:

Send your comments	
Name:	Your name here
Email:	
Comments:	Enter your comments

[Send] [Cancel]

How to do it...

Create a form and use the `emptyText` configuration option to add text hints to the fields:

```
Ext.onReady(function() {
    var commentForm = new Ext.FormPanel({
        frame: true,
        title: 'Send your comments',
        bodyStyle: 'padding:5px',
        width: 550,
        layout: 'form',
        items: [{
            xtype: 'textfield',
            fieldLabel: 'Name',
            name: 'name',
            anchor: '98%',
            allowBlank:false,
            emptyText:'Your name here'
        },
        {
            xtype: 'textfield',
            fieldLabel: 'Email',
            name: 'email',
            anchor: '98%',
            vtype:'email'
        },
        {
            xtype: 'textarea',
            fieldLabel: 'Comments',
            name: 'comments',
```

```
            anchor: '98%',
            height:200,
            allowBlank: false,
            emptyText: 'Enter your comments'
        }],
        buttons: [{
            text: 'Send'
        },
        {
            text: 'Cancel'
        }]
    });
commentForm.render(document.body);
```

There's more...

When using `emptyText` to specify the default text to place into an empty field, be aware that this value will be submitted to the server if the field is enabled and configured with a name.

See also...

▶ The *Specifying required fields in a form* recipe, covered earlier in this chapter, explains how to make some form fields required

▶ The recipe titled *Setting the minimum and maximum length allowed for a field's value*, covered earlier in this chapter, explains how to restrict the number of characters entered in a field

▶ The *Changing the location where validation errors are displayed* recipe, covered earlier in this chapter, shows how to relocate a field's error icon

4

Fun with Combo Boxes and Date Fields

This chapter teaches you the following recipes:

▸ Using the combo box with local data

▸ Displaying remote data with a combo box

▸ Combo box with autocomplete

▸ How the combo box helps you to type

▸ Converting an HTML drop down list into an Ext combo box

▸ Cascading combo boxes

▸ Using templates to change the look of combo box items

▸ Using paging to handle a large number of combo box items

▸ The different ways to set up disabled dates in a date field

▸ The date range selector

Introduction

Combo boxes and date fields are combinations of the edit and list fields. They support safe data input and save space in your user interface. The recipes in this chapter explore the advantages of these widgets as well as their efficiency trade-offs.

Using the combo box with local data

This recipe explains how to populate the **Make** combo box with data from a local array.

In the following screenshot, you'll see what the combo box looks like:

How to do it...

1. Create the local data:

```
var makes=[['Acura'],
    ['Aston Martin'],
    ['Audi'],
    ['BMW'],
    ['Buick'],
    ['Cadillac'],
    ['Chevrolet'],
    ['Chrysler'],
    ['Dodge'],
    ['Ferrari'],
    ['Ford'],
```

```
        ['GMC'],
        ['Honda'],
        ['HUMMER'],
        ['Hyundai'],
        ['Infiniti'],
        ['Isuzu'],
        ['Jaguar']
    ]
```

2. Create the data store:

```
var makesStore=new Ext.data.SimpleStore({
    fields:['name'],
    data:makes
});
```

3. Define the combo box:

```
var makesCombo={
    xtype:'combo',
    store: makesStore,
    displayField: 'name',
    valueField: 'name',
    editable: false,
    mode: 'local',
    forceSelection: true,
    triggerAction: 'all',
    fieldLabel: 'Make'',
    emptyText: 'Select a make...',
    selectOnFocus: true
}
```

4. Create a form to host the combo box:

```
Ext.onReady(function() {
    var newCarForm=new Ext.FormPanel({
        frame: true,
        title: 'Get a quote',
        bodyStyle: 'padding:5px',
        width: 420,
        id: 'make-selector-frm',
        url: 'new-car.php',
        items: [makesCombo],
        buttons: [{
        text: 'Go',
```

```
                    handler: function() {
                    Ext.getCmp('make-selector-frm').getForm().submit();
                        }
                    }, {
                        text: 'Cancel'
                    }]
                });
                newCarForm.render(document.body);
            });
```

How it works...

After creating the array with the sample `makes` data, the data store is defined.
A `SimpleStore` instance is usually enough, if you are working with local data that will not
need much manipulation.

The use of the `mode='local'` configuration option in the combo box indicates that the data is
local. The default is `mode='remote'`, which means that the data will be loaded from the server.

There's more...

Typically, you would want to use the `local` mode when working with data that is not dynamic
in nature, that is not defined at runtime, or has little or no dependencies on application state
variables such as user, time, or preferences, and so on. The size of the data is also a factor to
take into account. Local mode is best suited for small numbers of items.

See also...

▶ The next recipe, *Displaying remote data with a combo box,* explains how to populate a
    combo box with data supplied by the server

▶ The *Combo box with autocomplete* recipe (covered later in this chapter) explains how
    to implement the autocomplete feature of a combo box

▶ The *How the combo box helps you type* recipe explains the type-ahead feature of
    a combo box

▶ The *Convert an HTML drop-down list into an Ext combo box* recipe explains how to
    make a combo box from an HTML drop-down list

Displaying remote data with a combo box

This recipe explains how to populate the **Make** combo box with data from the server, as seen in the following screenshot:

How to do it...

1. Create the data store:

```
var makesStore=new Ext.data.JsonStore({
    url: 'cars-makes.php',
    baseParams:{cmd:'makes'},
    root: 'makes',
    fields: ['id', 'name']
});
```

2. Declare the combo box:

```
var MakeCombo={
    xtype: 'combo',
    store: makesStore,
    displayField: 'name',
    valueField: 'id',
    editable: false,
    mode: 'remote',
```

```
                forceSelection: true,
                triggerAction: 'all',
                fieldLabel: 'Make'',
                emptyText: 'Select a make...',
                selectOnFocus: true
        }
```

3. Create a form to host the combo box:

```
    Ext.onReady(function() {
        var newCarForm=new Ext.FormPanel({
            frame: true,
            title: 'Get a quote',
            bodyStyle: 'padding:5px',
            width: 420,
            id: 'make-selector-frm',
            url: 'new-car.php',
            items: [
            MakeCombo
            ],
            buttons: [{
                text: 'Go',
                handler: function() {
                Ext.getCmp('make-selector-frm').getForm().submit();
                }
            }, {
                text: 'Cancel'
            }]
        });
        newCarForm.render(document.body);
    });
```

How it works...

The data store (a `JsonStore`) references the server page with the `url` configuration option:

```
    url: 'cars-makes.php',
```

In the combo box, the default `remote` mode is used to load remote data:

```
    mode: 'remote',
```

There's more...

The `remote` mode is most useful when the data in question is large, time sensitive, or dependent on application state variables.

See also...

- ► The *Using the combo box with local data* (seen previously in this chapter) recipe explains how to populate a combo box with data from a local array

- ► The next recipe, *Combo box with autocomplete*, will teach you how to implement the autocomplete feature of a combo box

- ► The *How the combo box helps you type* (covered later in this chapter) recipe explains the type-ahead feature of a combo box

- ► The *Converting an HTML drop-down list into an Ext combo box* (to be seen further along in this chapter) recipe explains how to make a combo box from an HTML drop-down list

Combo box with autocomplete

This recipe teaches you how to use a combo box to implement the autocomplete or autosuggest feature. The `Actor Name` textbox shows a list of suggestions as you type:

Actors Search	
Actor Name:	joh
	JOHNNY LOLLOBRIGIDA
	MATTHEW JOHANSSON
	JOHNNY CAGE
	RAY JOHANSSON
	ALBERT JOHANSSON
	JOHN SUVARI

Getting ready...

This recipe uses sample data from the Sakila sample database. You can obtain the Sakila database as well as installation instructions at the MySQL website (`http://dev.mysql.com/doc`).

How to do it...

1. Create the data store:

```
var actorsDs=new Ext.data.JsonStore({
    url: 'actors.php',
    baseParams: { cmd: 'movies' },
    root: 'actors',
    totalProperty: 'count',
    id: 'actor_id',
    fields: [{name:'id',mapping: 'actor_id'}, { name: 'name',
mapping: 'name' }
    ]
});
```

2. Define the actors combo box:

```
var actorSearch={
    xtype: 'combo',
    fieldLabel: 'Actor Name',
    store: actorsDs,
    valueField: 'id',
    displayField: 'name',
    typeAhead: false,
    loadingText: 'Searching...',
    emptyText: 'Type the first characters of the name',
    minChars: 3,
    anchor: '100%',
    pageSize: 0,
    hideTrigger: true,
    editable: true,
    triggerAction: 'all'
}
```

3. Create a container for the combo box:

```
Ext.onReady(function() {
    var movieBrowser=new Ext.FormPanel({
        iconCls:'panel-icon',
        frame: true,
        id: 'actors-form',
        title: 'Actors Search',
        bodyStyle: 'padding:5px',
        width: 450,
```

```
      items: [actorSearch
      ]
    });
    movieBrowser.render(document.body);
  });
```

How it works...

The `editable` and `minChars` configuration options are used in the combo box to activate the `autocomplete` feature:

```
editable: true,
minChars: 3,
```

While `editable` must be `true` for the autocomplete feature to work, `minChars` is the minimum number of characters that must be typed before autocomplete gets activated. It defaults to 4 if the data is remote, or to 0 if the data is local.

 Be mindful that if your list contains over 100 items, a single starting character may not be enough to take the user close to the item that he is looking for.

As shown in the following screenshot, you'll see how `hideTrigger` is set to `true` in order to hide the trigger element and display only the base text field:

Actors Search	
Actor Name:	Type first characters the name

There's more...

Some users do not realize that they can actually type values in the combo box. Hiding the trigger helps to alleviate this problem.

The type-ahead feature of combo box (examined in the *How the combo box helps you type* recipe) populates and selects the remainder of the text that is typed after a configurable delay.

See also...

- ▶ The *Using the combo box with local data recipe* (seen earlier in this chapter), explains how to populate a combo box with data from a local array

- ▶ The next recipe, *How the combo box helps you type,* shows the type-ahead feature of the combo box

- ▶ The *Converting an HTML drop-down list into an Ext combo box* (covered later in this chapter) recipe, explains how to make a combo box from an HTML drop-down list

- ▶ The *Displaying remote data with a combo box* (seen previously in this chapter) recipe, explains how to populate a combo box with data supplied by the server

How the combo box helps you type

Type-ahead is a popular feature of the ComboBox class. In this recipe's example, after typing the first characters of the car make in the **Make** combo box, the component completes the word and shows a number of suggestions, as shown below:

How to do it...

1. Create the local data:

```
var makes=[['Acura'],
    ['Aston Martin'],
    ['Audi'],
    ['BMW'],
    ['Buick'],
    ['Cadillac'],
    ['Chevrolet'],
    ['Chrysler'],
    ['Dodge'],
```

```
    ['Ferrari'],
    ['Ford'],
    ['GMC'],
    ['Honda'],
    ['HUMMER'],
    ['Hyundai'],
    ['Infiniti'],
    ['Isuzu'],
    ['Jaguar']
]
```

2. Create the data store:

```
var makesStore=new Ext.data.SimpleStore({
    fields: ['name'],
    data:makes
});
```

3. Declare the combo box:

```
var makesCombo={
    xtype:'combo',
    store: makesStore,
    displayField: 'name',
    valueField: 'name',
    typeAhead: true,
    editable: true,
    mode: 'local',
    forceSelection: true,
    triggerAction: 'all',
    fieldLabel: 'Make',
    emptyText: 'Select a make...',
    selectOnFocus: true
}
```

4. Create a form to host the combo box:

```
Ext.onReady(function() {
    var newCarForm=new Ext.FormPanel({
        frame: true,
        title: 'Get a quote',
        bodyStyle: 'padding:5px',
        width: 420,
```

```
                id: 'make-selector-frm',
                url: 'new-car.php',
                items: [
                   makesCombo
                      ],
                buttons: [{
                      text: 'Go',
                      handler: function() {
                      Ext.getCmp('make-selector-frm').getForm().submit();
                      }
                }, {
                      text: 'Cancel'
                }]
        });
        newCarForm.render(document.body);
});
```

How it works...

Type-ahead is accomplished with the use of the `typeAhead` configuration option for the combo box:

```
typeAhead: true
```

The `typeAhead` feature populates and selects the remainder of the text being typed after a configurable delay. This delay is settable through the `typeAheadDelay` option.

See also...

▸ The *Using the combo box with local data* (seen previously in this chapter) recipe, explains how to populate a combo box with data from a local array

▸ The next recipe, *Converting an HTML drop-down list into an Ext combo box,* explains how to create a combo box from an HTML drop-down list

▸ The *Displaying remote data with a combo box* (seen earlier in this chapter) recipe, shows how to populate a combo box with data supplied by the server

▸ The *Combo box with autocomplete* (seen earlier in this chapter) recipe, shows how to implement the autocomplete feature of the combo box

Converting an HTML drop-down list into an Ext combo box

This recipe explains how you can convert an HTML drop-down list into a combo box, as shown in the following screenshot:

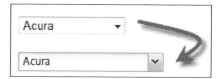

How to do it...

1. Create the HTML `select` element that will be converted:

```
<select name="makes-transformed" id="makes-transformed">
<option value="Acura">Acura</option>
<option value="Aston Martin">Aston Martin</option>
<option value="Audi">Audi</option>
<option value="BMW">BMW</option>
<option value="Buick">Buick</option>
<option value="Cadillac">Cadillac</option>
<option value="Chevrolet">Chevrolet</option>
<option value="Chrysler">Chrysler</option>
<option value="Dodge">Dodge</option>
<option value="Ferrari">Ferrari</option>
<option value="Ford">Ford</option>
<option value="GMC">GMC</option>
<option value="Honda">Honda</option>
</select>
```

2. Define the combo box:

```
Ext.onReady(function() {
    var makesCombo=new Ext.form.ComboBox({
        transform: 'makes-transformed',
        forceSelection: true,
        triggerAction: 'all',
        selectOnFocus: true
    });
});
```

How it works...

The combo box can be applied to an existing HTML `select` element through the use of the `transform` configuration option. The value for `transform` should be the ID, DOM node, or an element of the HTML `select` to be converted.

Note that if the converted combo box is going to be in an `Ext.form.BasicForm` or `Ext.form.FormPanel`, you must also set `lazyRender=true`.

See also...

▸ The *Using the combo box with local data* (seen earlier in this chapter) recipe, explains how to populate a combo box with data from a local array

▸ The *Displaying remote data with a combo box* (seen earlier in this chapter) recipe, explains how to populate a combo box with data supplied by the server

Cascading combo boxes

Sometimes, you need to present your users with two or more combo boxes, where the selection of an option in one combo box determines the available options in the others.

The **Car Reviews** form built in this recipe contains a **Make** combo box and a **Model** combo box, as seen below:

Selecting a make enables the **Model** combo box, which displays the models for the selected make, as seen in the following screenshot:

How to do it...

1. Create the makes data store:

```
var makesStore=new Ext.data.JsonStore({
    url: 'cars-makes-models.php',
    baseParams:{cmd:'makes'},
    root: 'makes',
    fields: ['id', 'name']
});
```

2. Create the models data store:

```
var modelsStore=new Ext.data.JsonStore({
    url: 'cars-makes-models.php',
    baseParams: { cmd:'models'},
    root: 'models',
    fields: ['id', 'name']
});
```

3. Define the **Make** combo box:

```
var MakeCombo={
    xtype: 'combo',
    store: makestore,
    displayField: 'name',
    valueField: 'id',
    typeAhead: true,
    editable: false,
    mode: 'remote',
    forceSelection: true,
    triggerAction: 'all',
    fieldLabel: 'Make',
    emptyText: 'Select a make...',
    selectOnFocus: true,
    anchor:'95%',
    listeners: {
        'select': function(cmb, rec, idx) {
            modelsCbx=Ext.getCmp('models-combo');
            modelsCbx.clearValue();
            modelsCbx.store.load({
                params: { 'makeId': this.getValue() }
            });
            modelsCbx.enable();
        }
    }
}
```

4. Define the **Model** combo box:

```
var ModelCombo={
    xtype: 'combo',
    id:'models-combo',
    store: modelsStore,
    displayField: 'name',
    valueField: 'id',
    typeAhead: true,
    editable: false,
    mode: 'local',
    forceSelection: true,
    triggerAction: 'all',
    fieldLabel: 'Model',
    emptyText: 'Select a model...',
    selectOnFocus: true,
    disabled: true,
    anchor: '95%'
}
```

5. Create a form to host both combo box instances:

```
Ext.onReady(function() {
    var newCarForm=new Ext.FormPanel({
        frame: true,
        title: 'Car Reviews',
        bodyStyle: 'padding:5px',
        width: 420,
        id: 'make-selector-frm',
        url: 'new-car.php',
        items: [
        MakeCombo, ModelCombo
        ],
        buttons: [{
            text: 'Go',
            handler: function() {
                Ext.getCmp('car-selector-frm').getForm().submit();
            }
        }, {
            text: 'Cancel',
            handler: function() {
                            }
        }]
    });
    newCarForm.render(document.body);
});
```

How it works...

Depending on the requested data, the server-side code creates a JSON representation of an array with the makes or models data store.

The `makesStore` uses the `url` and `baseParams` configuration options to request the make's data.

```
url: 'cars-makes-models.php',
baseParams:{cmd:'makes'},
```

The `modelsStore`, in turn, requests the model's data.

```
url: 'cars-makes-models.php',
baseParams: { cmd:'models'},
```

The `MakeCombo` and `ModelCombo` are configured as a master-slave pair, where the `MakeCombo` will control both, `makesStore` and `modelsStore`.

Selecting an item of the `MakeCombo` will enable the `ModelCombo` and load its data. This is implemented in a handler for the `select` event. Notice how the selected make is passed as the value for the `makeId` parameter of the `ModelCombo`. This tells the server page to return the model's data for the selected make:

```
listeners: {
        'select': function(cmb, rec, idx) {
            modelsCbx=Ext.getCmp('models-combo');
            modelsCbx.clearValue();
            modelsCbx.store.load({
                params: { 'makeId': this.getValue() }
            });
            modelsCbx.enable();
        }
    }
```

There's more...

Besides their benefits, there are also drawbacks in the use of cascading combo boxes. They multiply the number of steps a user must take to complete a task, which involves clicking repeatedly or dragging the thumb to arrive at a selection.

See also...

- ▶ The *Using the combo box with local data* (seen earlier in this chapter) recipe, explains how to populate a combo box with data from a local array

- ▶ The *Displaying remote data with a combo box* (seen earlier in this chapter) recipe explains how to populate a combo box with data supplied by the server

Using templates to change the look of combo box items

A combo box allows you to control the look of its items. In this recipe, the **Movies Browser** uses a ComboBox instance to display movie titles, as shown in the following screenshot:

Movies Browser	
Title:	CROWDS TELEMARK
Release Year:	2006
Rating:	R
Description:	A Intrepid Documentary of a Astronaut And a Forensic Psychologist who must Find a Frisbee in An Abandoned Fun House
Special Features:	Trailers,Behind the Scenes

The user experience can be enhanced by displaying not just the title, the year, the rating, but also the description of the movie as shown in the following screenshot:

Movies Browser	
Title:	cro
Release Year:	A Beautiful Documentary of a Dog And a Robot Rating: R
	who must Redeem a Womanizer in Berlin
Rating:	
Description:	**CROSSROADS CASUALTIES** Year: 2006
	A Intrepid Documentary of a Sumo Wrestler Rating: G
	And a Astronaut who must Battle a Composer in
	The Outback
Special Features:	
	CROW GREASE Year: 2006
	A Awe-Inspiring Documentary of a Woman And Rating: PG
	a Husband who must Sink a Database
	Administrator in The First Manned Space Station
	CROWDS TELEMARK Year: 2006
	A Intrepid Documentary of a Astronaut And a Rating: R
	Forensic Psychologist who must Find a Frisbee in
	An Abandoned Fun House

How to do it...

1. Create the styles needed for the combo's items:

```
<style type="text/css">
    .movie-item {
```

```
        font: normal 12px tahoma, arial, helvetica, sans-serif;
        line-height:150%;
        padding:5px 20px 5px 10px;
        border:1px solid #fff;
        border-bottom:1px solid #eeeeee;
        white-space: normal;
        color:#555;
    }
    .movie-item h2 {
        display: block;
        font: inherit;
        font-weight: bold;
        color:#336699;
    }
    .movie-item h2 span {
        float: right;
        font-weight: normal;
        color:#555;
        margin:0 0 5px 5px;
        width:100px;
        display: block;
        clear: none;
    }
    .panel-icon
    {
        background: url(img/folder-movie.png) 0 no-repeat
!important;
    }
</style>
```

2. Create the movies data store:

```
var moviesDataStore=new Ext.data.JsonStore({
    url: 'movies.php',
    baseParams: { cmd: 'movies' },
    root: 'movies',
    totalProperty: 'count',
    id: 'film_id',
    fields: [{ name: 'title', mapping: 'title' },
        { name: 'description', mapping: 'description' },
        { name: 'released', mapping: 'release_year' },
        { name: 'rating', mapping: 'rating' },
        { name: 'sFeatures', mapping: 'special_features' }
```

```
    ]
});
```

3. Create the template for the combo box items:

```
var movieTpl=new Ext.XTemplate(
    '<tpl for="."><div class="movie-item">',
        '<h2><span>Year: {released}<br />Rating: {rating}</
span>{title}</h2>',
        '{description}',
    '</div></tpl>'
);
```

4. Define the combo box:

```
var titleSearch={
    xtype: 'combo',
    fieldLabel: 'Title',
    store: moviesDataStore,
    displayField: 'description',
    typeAhead: false,
    loadingText: 'Searching...',
    emptyText: 'Type three or more letters of the title',
    minChars: 3,
    anchor: '100%',
    pageSize: 0,
    triggerAction: 'all',
    tpl: movieTpl,
    itemSelector: 'div.movie-item',
    onSelect: function(record) {
        this.setValue(record.data.title);
        this.collapse();
        Ext.getCmp('movies-form').getForm().loadRecord(record);
    }
}
```

5. Create the combo box's container:

```
Ext.onReady(function() {
    var movieBrowser=new Ext.FormPanel({
        iconCls:'panel-icon',
        frame: true,
        id: 'movies-form',
        title: 'Movies Browser',
        bodyStyle: 'padding:5px',
        width: 550,
        items: [titleSearch,
```

```
            { xtype: 'textfield', name: 'released', anchor: '35%',
            fieldLabel: 'Release Year', readOnly: true },
                { columnWidth: .5, xtype: 'textfield', name: 'rating',
                anchor: '35%', fieldLabel: 'Rating', readOnly: true },
            { xtype: 'textarea', name: 'description', anchor:
            '100%', fieldLabel: 'Description', readOnly: true },
                { xtype: 'textarea', name: 'sFeatures', anchor: '100%',
                fieldLabel: 'Special Features', readOnly: true }
            ]
        });
        movieBrowser.render(document.body);
    });
```

How it works...

Overriding the default combo box item template allows you to create custom UI layouts for items in the list. While the default template for a combo box item looks like this:

```
<tpl for="."><div class="x-combo-list-item">{' + this.displayField +
'}</div></tpl>
```

movieTpl is an Ext.XTemplate instance that is used to give each item a richer look:

```
var movieTpl=new Ext.XTemplate(
    '<tpl for="."><div class="movie-item">',
        '<h2><span>Year: {released}<br />Rating: {rating}</
span>{title}</h2>',
        '{description}',
    '</div></tpl>'
);
```

The above template's output is shown in the following screenshot:

In the template, the {title}, {description}, {released}, and {rating} substitution parameters create a one-way data binding mechanism. These parameters map to the properties of the provided data objects in the moviesDataStore data store:

```
var moviesDataStore=new Ext.data.JsonStore({
    url: 'movies.php',
    baseParams: { cmd: 'movies' },
    root: 'movies',
```

```
        totalProperty: 'count',
        id: 'film_id',
        fields: [{ name: 'title', mapping: 'title' },
            { name: 'description', mapping: 'description' },
            { name: 'released', mapping: 'release_year' },
            { name: 'rating', mapping: 'rating' },
            { name: 'sFeatures', mapping: 'special_features' }
        ]
});
```

Note that the use of the `itemSelector` configuration option is required when the custom item template uses a class other than the default `x-combo-list-item`.

```
itemSelector: 'div.movie-item'
```

See also...

 ▶ The *Using the combo box with local data* (seen earlier in this chapter) recipe, explains how to populate a combo box with data from a local array

 ▶ The *Displaying remote data with a combo box* (seen earlier in this chapter) recipe, explains how to populate a combo box with data supplied by the server

 ▶ The next recipe, *Using paging to handle a large number of combo box items*, explains how to display combo box items in fixed-length pages

Using paging to handle a large number of combo box items

The **Movies Browser** panel in this recipe, uses a combo box instance to display movie titles, as seen in the following screenshot:

When the list of items is large, it helps to display the items in fixed-length pages, as shown in the following screenshot:

How to do it...

1. Create the styles needed for the combo's items:

```
<style type="text/css">
    .movie-item {
        font: normal 12px tahoma, arial, helvetica, sans-serif;
        line-height:150%;
        padding:5px 20px 5px 10px;
        border:1px solid #fff;
        border-bottom:1px solid #eeeeee;
        white-space: normal;
        color:#555;
    }
    .movie-item h2 {
        display: block;
        font: inherit;
        font-weight: bold;
        color:#336699;
    }
    .movie-item h2 span {
        float: right;
        font-weight: normal;
```

```
        color:#555;
        margin:0 0 5px 5px;
        width:100px;
        display: block;
        clear: none;
    }
    .panel-icon
    {
        background: url(img/folder-movie.png) 0 no-repeat
!important;
    }
</style>
```

2. Create the movies data store:

```
var moviesDataStore=new Ext.data.JsonStore({
    url: 'movies.php',
    baseParams: { cmd: 'movies' },
    root: 'movies',
    totalProperty: 'count',
    id: 'film_id',
    fields: [{ name: 'title', mapping: 'title' },
        { name: 'description', mapping: 'description' },
        { name: 'released', mapping: 'release_year' },
        { name: 'rating', mapping: 'rating' },
        { name: 'sFeatures', mapping: 'special_features' }
    ]
});
```

3. Define the template for the combo box items:

```
var movieTpl=new Ext.XTemplate(
    '<tpl for="."><div class="movie-item">',
        '<h2><span>Year: {released}<br />Rating: {rating}</
span>{title}</h2>',
        '{description}',
    '</div></tpl>'
);
```

4. Create the combo box:

```
var titleSearch={
    xtype: 'combo',
    fieldLabel: 'Title',
    store: moviesDataStore,
    displayField: 'description',
    typeAhead: false,
    loadingText: 'Searching...',
    emptyText: 'Type three or more letters of the title',
    minChars: 3,
    anchor: '100%',
    pageSize: 15,
```

```
        triggerAction: 'all',
        tpl: movieTpl,
        itemSelector: 'div.movie-item',
        onSelect: function(record) {
            this.setValue(record.data.title);
            this.collapse();
            Ext.getCmp('movies-form').getForm().loadRecord(record);
        }
    }
```

5. Define a container for the combo box:

```
Ext.onReady(function() {
    var movieBrowser=new Ext.FormPanel({
        iconCls: 'panel-icon',
        frame: true,
        id: 'movies-form',
        title: 'Movies Browser',
        bodyStyle: 'padding:5px',
        width: 550,
        items: [titleSearch,
            { xtype: 'textfield', name: 'released', anchor: '35%',
            fieldLabel: 'Release Year', readOnly: true },
            { columnWidth: .5, xtype: 'textfield', name: 'rating',
            anchor: '35%', fieldLabel: 'Rating', readOnly: true },
            { xtype: 'textarea', name: 'description', anchor:
            '100%', fieldLabel: 'Description', readOnly: true },
            { xtype: 'textarea', name: 'sFeatures', anchor: '100%',
            fieldLabel: 'Special Features', readOnly: true }
        ]
    });
    movieBrowser.render(document.body);
});
```

How it works...

As in the previous recipe, *Using templates to change the look of combo box items,* the movieTpl is an Ext.XTemplate instance that is used to give each item a richer look.

Including a pageSize configuration option with a value greater than 0 displays an Ext. PagingToolbar in the footer of the drop-down list. In this case, the filter queries for the combo box will execute with the page start and page limit parameters. However, note that this applies only when the combo box is in a remote mode.

There's more...

Using paging is advisable when the number of items to display is large. However, paging multiplies the number of steps a user must take to make their selection in the combo box.

See also...

  ▸ The *Using the combo box with local data* recipe (seen earlier in this chapter), explains how to populate a combo box with data from a local array

  ▸ The *Displaying remote data with a combo box* recipe (seen earlier in this chapter), explains how to populate a combo box with data supplied by the server

  ▸ The *Using templates to change the look of combo box items* recipe (seen earlier in this chapter), explains how to enhance the look of the combo box items using templates

The different ways to set up disabled dates in a date field

With date fields, sometimes you need to disable specific dates or days, so that they cannot be selected.

The date field built in this recipe, with specific dates disabled, is shown in the following screenshot:

Specific days can also be disabled, as shown in the following screenshot:

DateField Examples

| Disabled dates example: | 04/18/2009 |
| Disabled days example: | |

	April 2009 ▼					
S	M	T	W	T	F	S
29	30	31	1	2	3	4
5	6	7	8	9	10	11
12	13	14	15	16	17	18
19	20	21	22	23	24	25
26	27	28	29	30	1	2
		4	5	6	7	8	9

Today

How to do it...

1. Declare a DateField with some disabled dates:

```
var disabledDatesField={
    xtype: 'datefield',
fieldLabel: 'Disabled dates example',
    disabledDates: ['4/15', '04/20/2009'],
    disabledDatesText: 'Office closed'
};
```

2. Declare a DateField with some disabled days:

```
var disabledDaysField={
    xtype: 'datefield',
fieldLabel: 'Disabled days example',
    disabledDays: ['2', '5'],
    disabledDaysText: 'Office Closed'
};
```

3. Create a container for the date fields:

```
Ext.onReady(function() {
    var panel=new Ext.Panel({
        frame: true,
        title: 'DateField Examples',
```

```
            layout:'form',
            bodyStyle: 'padding:5px',
            width: 300,
            labelWidth:170,
            renderTo:Ext.getBody(),
            items: [disabledDatesField,disabledDaysField]
        });
    });
```

How it works...

Specific dates can be disabled using the `disabledDates` configuration option. This option accepts an array representing the dates to be disabled. The `disabledDatesText` option is the tool tip text to display the disabled dates.

Similarly, `disabledDays` is used to specify the days to disable. The tool tip text for the disabled days can be set with `disabledDaysText`.

There's more...

The `disabledDates` option accepts regular expressions that allow you to go beyond disabling specific dates:

```
// disable these days for every year:
disabledDates: ["04/09", "08/11"]
// Match the beginning:
disabledDates: ["^04/09"]
// disable every day in April 2009:
disabledDates: ["04/../2009"]
// disable every day in every April:
disabledDates: ["^04"]
```

See also...

▶ The next recipe, *The date range selector*, explains how to use date fields to capture date ranges

The date range selector

When selecting date ranges, the **From** date and the **To** date need to work in sync, so that the selected range is valid.

The **Schedule Alerts** panel built in this recipe, shows how to perform this type of validation. Selecting a **From** date constrains the **To** date values, as seen in the following screenshot:

Similarly, selecting a **To** date constrains the **From** date values, as seen in the following screenshot:

How to do it...

1. Create a validation type for date ranges:

```
Ext.apply(Ext.form.VTypes, {
    daterange: function(val, field) {
        var date=field.parseDate(val);
        if (!date) {
            return;
        }
        if (field.startDateField && (!this.dateRangeMax || (date.
getTime()!=this.dateRangeMax.getTime()))) {
            var start=Ext.getCmp(field.startDateField);
            start.setMaxValue(date);
            start.validate();
            this.dateRangeMax=date;
        }
        else if (field.endDateField && (!this.dateRangeMin ||
(date.getTime()!=this.dateRangeMin.getTime()))) {
            var end=Ext.getCmp(field.endDateField);
            end.setMinValue(date);
            end.validate();
            this.dateRangeMin=date;
        }
        return true;
    }
});
```

2. Define the `StartDateField`:

```
var startDateFld={
    xtype: 'datefield',
    fieldLabel: 'From',
    name: 'start-date',
    id: 'start-date',
    vtype: 'daterange',
    endDateField: 'end-date'
};
```

3. Define the `EndDateField`:

```
var endDateFld={
    xtype:'datefield',
    fieldLabel: 'To',
    name: 'end-date',
    id: 'end-date',
```

```
    vtype: 'daterange',
    startDateField: 'start-date'
};
```

4. Define a container panel for the fields:

```
Ext.onReady(function() {
    var dr=new Ext.FormPanel({
        labelWidth: 125,
        frame: true,
        title: 'Schedule Alerts',
        bodyStyle: 'padding:5px',
        width: 325,
        defaults: { width: 160 },
        defaultType: 'datefield',
        items: [startDateFld, endDateFld]
    });
    dr.render(Ext.getBody());
});
```

How it works...

In the date range selector, the **From** date cannot be greater than the **To** date. The daterange () function is added to the Ext.form.VTypes using Ext.apply(). This results in making daterange() available as a field validation function. Daterange() performs the validation by adjusting the dateRangeMin and dateRangeMax properties of each date field, based on the current selections.

See also...

- ▸ The previous recipe, *The different ways to set up disabled dates in a date field*, shows how to disable specific dates or days in a date field

- ▸ The *How to confirm passwords and validate dates using relational field validation* recipe in Chapter 3, explains how to perform validation when the value of one field depends on the value of another field

5
Using Grid Panels to Display and Edit Tabular Data

The following recipes will be covered in this chapter:

- ▶ Displaying XML data sent by the server
- ▶ Displaying JSON data generated by the server
- ▶ Creating a grid that uses server-side sorting
- ▶ Implementing data paging
- ▶ Data grouping with live group summaries
- ▶ Creating data previews
- ▶ Creating a grid panel with expandable rows
- ▶ Using checkboxes to select grid rows
- ▶ Numbering rows in a grid panel
- ▶ Changing grid panel data using cell editors
- ▶ Automatic uploading of data edited with a grid
- ▶ Performing batch uploads of data edited with a grid
- ▶ Changing a grid's data store and columns at runtime

Introduction

This chapter focuses on how data is displayed using Ext JS grid panels. It examines data paging and grouping, implementation of live summaries and previews, in-place editing of data, and different approaches to sending data back to the server.

In this chapter you will also learn how to augment the grid panel's features using different plugins.

Displaying XML data sent by the server

This recipe explains how to populate the **Movies** grid with the XML data retrieved from the server. This is how the loaded grid will look:

Movies		
Title	Rating	Year
ACADEMY DINOSAUR	PG	2006
ACE GOLDFINGER	G	2006
ADAPTATION HOLES	NC-17	2006
AFFAIR PREJUDICE	G	2006
AFRICAN EGG	G	2006
AGENT TRUMAN	PG	2006
AIRPLANE SIERRA	PG-13	2006
AIRPORT POLLOCK	R	2006
ALABAMA DEVIL	PG-13	2006
ALADDIN CALENDAR	NC-17	2006
ALAMO VIDEOTAPE	G	2006

Getting ready...

The sample data used in this chapter's recipes comes from the Sakila sample database.

 You can obtain the Sakila database, as well as the installation instructions, at `http://dev.mysql.com/doc`.

How to do it...

1. Create a data store:

```
var store = new Ext.data.XmlStore({
    url: 'grid-xml-remote.php',
    record: 'movie',
    idPath: 'id',
    fields: ['id', 'title', 'year', 'rating']
})
```

2. Define a grid panel and retrieve the data:

```
Ext.onReady(function() {
    var grid = new Ext.grid.GridPanel({
        title: 'Movies',
        store: store,
        columns: [
            { header: "ID", width: 30, dataIndex: 'id',
              sortable: true, hidden:true },
            { id: 'title-col', header: "Title", width: 180,
              dataIndex: 'title', sortable: true },
            { header: "Rating", width: 75, dataIndex: 'rating',
              sortable: true },
            { header: "Year", width: 75, dataIndex: 'year',
              sortable: true, align: 'center' }
        ],
        autoExpandColumn: 'title-col',
        renderTo: Ext.getBody(),
        width: 600,
        height: 300,
        loadMask: true
    });
    store.load();
});
```

How it works...

First, the data store is created. The XmlStore store is automatically configured with an XmlReader in order to process the XML data. The XML data will look like this:

```
<?xml version="1.0" encoding="UTF-8" ?>
<movies>
  <movie>
    <id>1</id>
```

```
      <title>ACADEMY DINOSAUR</title>
      <year>2006</year>
      <rating>PG</rating>
    </movie>
    <movie>
      <id>2</id>
      <title>ACE GOLDFINGER</title>
      <year>2006</year>
      <rating>G</rating>
    </movie>
    <movie>
      <id>3</id>
      <title>ADAPTATION HOLES</title>
      <year>2006</year>
      <rating>NC-17</rating>
    </movie>
      .
      .
      .
  </movies>
```

After the data store is defined, the grid panel is created. Note the use of `autoExpandColumn` to specify which column will expand to fill the space that is not used up by the rest of the columns. The `record` configuration option, inherited from the `XmlReader` class, indicates the `DomQuery` path to the XML element that contains record information.

If you send your dataset one page at a time from the server, the store should be configured with the `totalRecords` option, inherited from the `XmlReader` class. `totalRecords` is the `DomQuery` path used to retrieve the total number of records in the dataset.

See also...

▶ The next recipe, *Displaying JSON data generated by the server*, explains how to populate a grid with JSON data created on the server

Displaying JSON data generated by the server

This recipe explains how to populate the **Movies** grid with JSON data retrieved from the server. The loaded grid will look as shown in the following screenshot:

Movies		
Title	Rating	Year
ACADEMY DINOSAUR	PG	2006
ACE GOLDFINGER	G	2006
ADAPTATION HOLES	NC-17	2006
AFFAIR PREJUDICE	G	2006
AFRICAN EGG	G	2006
AGENT TRUMAN	PG	2006
AIRPLANE SIERRA	PG-13	2006
AIRPORT POLLOCK	R	2006
ALABAMA DEVIL	PG-13	2006
ALADDIN CALENDAR	NC-17	2006
ALAMO VIDEOTAPE	G	2006

How to do it...

1. Create a data store:

```
var store = new Ext.data.JsonStore({
    url: 'grid-json-remote.php',
    root: 'movies',
    fields: ['id', 'title', 'release_year', 'rating']
});
```

2. Define the grid panel:

```
Ext.onReady(function() {
    var grid = new Ext.grid.GridPanel({
        title:'Movies',
        store: store,
        columns: [
            { header: "ID", width: 30, dataIndex: 'id',
                sortable: true, hidden:true },
            { id: 'title-col', header: "Title", width: 180,
                dataIndex: 'title', sortable: true },
            { header: "Rating", width: 75, dataIndex: 'rating',
                sortable: true },
            { header: "Year", width: 75, dataIndex: 'release_year',
                sortable: true, align: 'center' }
        ],
        autoExpandColumn: 'title-col',
        renderTo: Ext.getBody(),
        width: 600,
        height: 300,
        loadMask: true
    });
    store.load();
});
```

How it works...

As a first step, the data store is created. This is a `JsonStore` instance that will connect to the server page. The generated JSON will have a structure similar to this:

```json
{
    "count":2,
    "movies":[{
        "film_id":"1",
        "title":"ACADEMY DINOSAUR",
        "description":"An Epic Drama of a Feminist And a Mad Scientist who
        must Battle a Teacher in The Canadian Rockies",
        "release_year":"2006",
        "rating":"PG",
        "special_features":"Deleted Scenes,Behind the Scenes"
        },
        {
            "film_id":"2",
            "title":"ACE GOLDFINGER",
            "description":"An Astounding Epistle of a Database Administrator
            And an Explorer who must Find a Car in Ancient China",
            "release_year":"2006",
            "rating":"G",
            "special_features":"Trailers,Deleted Scenes"
        }
    ]
}
```

`count` is a property that indicates the number of records retrieved, and `movies` is the array of movie records. records. The `root` configuration option of the data store will point to this array (`root:'movies'`)

Next, the grid panel that will display the JSON data is defined. Notice the use of the `autoExpandColumn` config option to specify which column will expand to fill the space not used up by the rest of the columns.

See also...

►   The previous recipe, *Displaying XML data sent by the server*, explains how to populate a grid with server-generated XML data

Creating a grid that uses server-side sorting

The grid control has the ability to instruct its data store to sort the records cache, either in place, or by requesting the store's proxy to download a refreshed version of the data object in a sorted order.

In this recipe, the **Movies** grid implements server-side sorting. By default, the **Title** column is sorted:

Clicking on any column will initiate a sort operation on the server:

After the download, the sorted data is shown:

Movies		
Title	Rating ▲	Year
DRUMLINE CYCLONE	G	2006
ACE GOLDFINGER	G	2006
SCISSORHANDS SLUMS	G	2006
AFFAIR PREJUDICE	G	2006
DUDE BLINDNESS	G	2006
AFRICAN EGG	G	2006
DUFFEL APOCALYPSE	G	2006
LIBERTY MAGNIFICENT	G	2006
DWARFS ALTER	G	2006
SECRETS PARADISE	G	2006
ALAMO VIDEOTAPE	G	2006

How to do it...

1. Define the data store:

```
var store = new Ext.data.JsonStore({
    url: 'grid-sort-remote.php',
    root: 'movies',
    idProperty: 'id',
    fields: ['id', 'title', 'release_year', 'rating'],
    remoteSort: true
});
```

2. Define the default sort:

```
store.setDefaultSort('release_year', 'desc');
```

3. Create the grid panel:

```
Ext.onReady(function() {
    var grid = new Ext.grid.GridPanel({
        title: 'Movies',
        store: store,
        columns: [
            { header: "ID", width: 30, dataIndex: 'id',
              sortable: true, hidden:true },
            { id: 'title-col', header: "Title", width: 180,
              dataIndex: 'title', sortable: true },
            { header: "Rating", width: 75, dataIndex: 'rating',
              sortable: truc },
            { header: "Year", width: 75, dataIndex: 'release_year',
```

```
                sortable: true, align: 'center' }
            ],
            autoExpandColumn: 'title-col',
            renderTo: Ext.getBody(),
            width: 600,
            height: 300,
            loadMask: true,
            columnLines:true
        });
        store.load();
    });
```

How it works...

The most important detail here is the use of the `remoteSort` config option at the time the data store is defined. When `remoteSort` is set to `true`, the store requests its proxy to provide a refreshed version of the data object in a sorted order. When `remoteSort` is `false`, the sorting occurs against the store's cache. A call to `setDefaultSort()` sets the default sort column and order to be used by the next load operation:

```
store.setDefaultSort('release_year', 'desc');
```

Another way to define the sort column and order is through the `sortInfo` config object:

```
sortInfo: {
    field: "release_year",
    direction: "DESC"
}
```

Although a discussion of the server technologies is not the intent of this book, notice that the server page will use the `sort` and `dir` parameters present in the HTTP request to implement the server-side sorting. You can inspect these parameters with the Firebug console:

Headers	Post	Response
dir DESC		
sort title		

The `sort` and `dir` parameters just reflect the values of the `field` and `direction` parameters of the `sortInfo` object.

There's more...

What's better, client-side or server-side sorting?

There is no simple answer for this question. While in-place sorting drastically reduces the number of connections to the server, as well as the bandwidth used by your application, remote sorting relieves the application of the processing required to sort the data. In general, sorting small recordsets can be easily handled in place. However, careful measuring and testing will help you to take the right approach.

See also...

> ▸ The next recipe, *Implementing data paging*, explains how to use data paging to increase your application's efficiency

Implementing data paging

Paging increases your application's efficiency. As paging reduces the amount of data exchanged with the server, it decreases the time required for the browser to render records as well as the resources needed to cache them.

In this recipe, a grid component that displays information about movies will display paged data returned by the server. The grid will use a paging toolbar to provide a means for navigating the paged data, as well as the ability to count the number of records and pages.

Movies		
Title ▲	Rating	Year
AMERICAN CIRCUS	R	2006
AMISTAD MIDSUMMER	G	2006
ANACONDA CONFESSIONS	R	2006
ANALYZE HOOSIERS	R	2006
ANGELS LIFE	G	2006
ANNIE IDENTITY	G	2006
ANONYMOUS HUMAN	NC-17	2006
ANTHEM LUKE	PG-13	2006
ANTITRUST TOMATOES	NC-17	2006
ANYTHING SAVANNA	R	2006

|◀ ◀ | Page 2 of 50 | ▶ ▶| ↻   Displaying movies 21 – 40 of 1000

How to do it...

1. Create the data store:

```
var store = new Ext.data.JsonStore({
    url: 'grid-paging-remote.php',
    root: 'movies',
    idProperty: 'id',
    totalProperty: 'count',
    fields: ['id', 'title', 'release_year', 'rating'],
    remoteSort: true
});
```

2. Set the default sort:

```
store.setDefaultSort('release_year', 'desc');
```

3. Define the grid panel:

```
Ext.onReady(function() {
    var grid = new Ext.grid.GridPanel({
        title: 'Movies',
        store: store,
        columns: [
            { header: "ID", width: 30, dataIndex: 'id',
                sortable: true, hidden:true },
            { id: 'title-col', header: "Title", width: 180,
                dataIndex: 'title', sortable: true },
            { header: "Rating", width: 75, dataIndex: 'rating',
                sortable: true },
            { header: "Year", width: 75, dataIndex: 'release_year',
                sortable: true, align: 'center' }
        ],
        autoExpandColumn: 'title-col',
        renderTo: Ext.getBody(),
        width: 600,
        height: 300,
        loadMask: true,
        columnLines:true,
        bbar: new Ext.PagingToolbar({
            pageSize: 20,
            store: store,
            displayInfo: true,
            displayMsg: 'Displaying movies {0} - {1} of {2}',
            emptyMsg: "No movies found"
        })
    });
    store.load({ params: { start: 0, limit: 20} });
});
```

How it works...

When the data store is defined, the most important detail is the use of the `idProperty` and `totalProperty` config options, which originate in the `JsonReader` class and are accepted by `JsonStore`:

```
idProperty: 'id',
totalProperty: 'count',
```

The `idProperty` config option identifies the record property that uniquely identifies a record, and `totalProperty` is the property that identifies how many records were returned.

In order to perform the paging, the grid panel uses a `PagingToolbar` instance:

```
bbar: new Ext.PagingToolbar({
    pageSize: 20,
    store: store,
    displayInfo: true,
    displayMsg: 'Displaying movies {0} - {1} of {2}',
    emptyMsg: "No movies found"
})
```

Note that you can specify the page size, a message when no data is present (`emptyMsg`), and a message when data is present (`displayMsg`).

The `displayMsg` string is formatted using the braced numbers 0-2 as tokens that are replaced by the values of the `start`, `end`, and `total` properties. These tokens should be preserved when overriding this string if you want to show the values.

You can use the `displayInfo` config option of the `PagingToolbar` to hide the `displayMessage` value.

Although a discussion on the server technologies is not the intent of this book, note that the server page will use the `start` and `limit` parameters present in the HTTP request to implement the server-side paging. These parameters can be inspected with the Firebug console:

Params	Headers	Response
_dc	1241619241626	
dir	DESC	
limit	20	
sort	release_year	
start	60	
xaction	load	

The `start` parameter is a pointer to the first record in the recordset that should be retrieved, and `limit` is the number of records to retrieve.

▶ The previous recipe, *Creating a grid that uses server-side sorting*, explains how to set up a grid panel that displays data sorted by the server

Data grouping with live group summaries

Combining a grid component with a `GroupingStore` and a `GroupingView` allows you to display records grouped by one of the available fields, and also allows you to create column summaries on the fly.

The **Movies By Category** grid in this recipe implements data grouping and live group summaries. Each group shows a summary with the number of movies in the group, the average movie length, and price:

Movies By Category

Title ▼	Rating	Length	Price
⊟ **Category: Action**			
BRIDE INTRIGUE	G	56 min	$0.99
BERETS AGENT	PG-13	77 min	$2.99
BAREFOOT MANCHURIAN	G	129 min	$2.99
ARK RIDGEMONT	NC-17	68 min	$0.99
ANTITRUST TOMATOES	NC-17	168 min	$2.99
AMERICAN CIRCUS	R	129 min	$4.99
AMADEUS HOLY	PG	113 min	$0.99
7 Movies	**Averages:**	**108 min**	**$2.42**
⊟ **Category: Animation**			
BORROWERS BEDAZZLED	G	63 min	$0.99
BLACKOUT PRIVATE	PG	85 min	$2.99
BIKINI BORROWERS	NC-17	142 min	$4.99
ARGONAUTS TOWN	PG-13	127 min	$0.99
ANACONDA CONFESSIONS	R	92 min	$0.99
ALTER VICTORY	PG-13	57 min	$0.99
6 Movies	**Averages:**	**94 min**	**$1.99**
⊟ **Category: Children**			
BETRAYED REAR	NC-17	122 min	$4.99
BENEATH RUSH	NC-17	53 min	$0.99

With the **Group By This Field** menu, users can change the way data is grouped, as well as recalculate the summaries accordingly:

Movies By Category			
Title ▾	Rating	Length	Price
⊟ Category: Action			
BRIDE INTRIGUE	G		$0.99
BERETS AGENT	PG-13		$2.99
BAREFOOT MANCHURIAN	G		$2.99
ARK RIDGEMONT	NC-17		$0.99
ANTITRUST TOMATOES	NC-17	168 min	$2.99
AMERICAN CIRCUS	R	129 min	$4.99
AMADEUS HOLY	PG	113 min	$0.99
7 Movies	Averages:	106 min	$2.42

Menu items shown over the grid:
- ↓ Sort Ascending
- ↓ Sort Descending
- Columns ▸
- Group By This Field

How to do it...

1. Create the data reader:

```
var reader = new Ext.data.JsonReader({
    idProperty: 'fid',
    root: 'movies',
    fields: ['id', 'title', 'category', 'rating',
{ name: 'length', type: 'int' },
{ name: 'price', type: 'float'}]
});
```

2. Createa a grouping store:

```
var groupingStore = new Ext.data.GroupingStore({
    url: 'grid-group-summary.php',
    reader: reader,
    sortInfo: { field: 'title', direction: "desc" },
    groupField: 'category'
});
```

3. Define the group summary:

```
var summary = new Ext.grid.GroupSummary();
```

4. Define the grid panel:

```
Ext.onReady(function() {
    var grid = new Ext.grid.GridPanel({
        title: 'Movies By Category',
        store: groupingStore,
        columns: [
            { header: "ID", width: 30, dataIndex: 'fid',
```

```
        sortable: true, hidden:true },
{ id: 'title-col',
  header: "Title",
  width: 180,
  dataIndex: 'title',
  sortable: true,
  summaryType: 'count',
  hideable: false,
  summaryRenderer: function(v, params, data){
      return ((v === 0 || v > 1) ? + v +' Movies' :
        '1 Movie');
  }
},
{ header: "Category", width: 65, dataIndex: 'category',
  sortable: true, groupName:'Category' },
{ header: "Rating",
  width: 65,
  dataIndex: 'rating',
  sortable: true,
  summaryRenderer: function(v, params, data) {
      return 'Averages:';
  },
  groupName:'Rating'
},
{ header: "Length",
  width: 65,
  dataIndex: 'length',
  sortable: true,
  align: 'right',
  renderer : function(v){
      return v + ' min';
  },
  summaryType: 'average',
  summaryRenderer: function(v, params, data) {
      return Ext.util.Format.number(v,'0') + ' min';
  },
  groupName:'Length'
},
{ header: "Price",
  width: 65,
  dataIndex: 'price',
  sortable: true,
  align: 'right',
  summaryType: 'average',
  renderer: Ext.util.Format.usMoney,
  summaryRenderer: function(v, params, data) {
      return Ext.util.Format.usMoney(v);
  },
  groupName:'Price'
}
```

```
        ],
        autoExpandColumn: 'title-col',
        renderTo: Ext.getBody(),
        width: 600,
        height: 500,
        loadMask: true,
        view: new Ext.grid.GroupingView({
            forceFit:true,
            showGroupName: true,
            enableNoGroups:false, // Required
            hideGroupedColumn: true
        }),
        plugins:summary
    });
    groupingStore.load();
});
```

How it works...

A `JsonReader` is created, together with a `GroupingStore`—a specialization of `Store` that allows for grouping records by one of the available fields. Note the use of the `groupField` config option to define the field by which the data will be grouped:

```
groupField: 'category'
```

Next comes defining a group summary:

```
var summary = new Ext.grid.GroupSummary();
```

The `GroupSummary` is a plugin used by the grid to display a summary for the grouped data:

ANTITRUST TOMATOES	NC-17	168 min	$2.99
AMERICAN CIRCUS	R	129 min	$4.99
AMADEUS HOLY	PG	113 min	$0.99
7 Movies	Averages:	106 min	$2.42

Besides using the `summary` plugin, the grid uses a `GroupingView` instance to define the ability for grouping:

```
view: new Ext.grid.GroupingView({
    forceFit:true,
    showGroupName: true,
    enableNoGroups:false, // Required
    hideGroupedColumn: true
})
```

The grouping feature is rounded up with the use of the `groupName`, `summaryType`, `summaryRenderer`, and `groupRenderer` config options on each of the grid columns. The `GroupName` config option specifies the text that should prefix the group field value in the group header line. The `SummaryType` config option can be any of the functions defined in `Ext.grid.GroupSummary.Calculations`: sum, count, max, min, and average. The `groupRenderer` function formats the grouping field value for display in the group header, and the `summaryRenderer` function formats the summary for display.

See also...

▶ The next recipe, *Creating data previews*, teaches you how to enrich the grid component by adding a row body that expands beneath each data row

▶ The *Creating a grid panel with expandable rows* recipe, covered later in this chapter, explains how to add an expandable body to each data row of a grid panel

Creating data previews

A useful feature of the Ext JS `GridPanel` is the ability to add a row body that expands beneath the data row. This body can be used to display additional information for each record.

The **Movies** grid in this recipe uses a record's row body to display the actors that star in each movie. A toolbar button allows the user to toggle the visibility of the actors' row:

How to do it...

1. Define the data store:

```
var store = new Ext.data.JsonStore({
    url: 'grid-row-body.php',
    root: 'movies',
    idProperty: 'id',
    totalProperty: 'count',
    fields: ['id', 'title', 'category', 'rating', 'actors',
{ name: 'length', type: 'int' },
{ name: 'price', type: 'float' }],
    remoteSort: true
});
store.setDefaultSort('title', 'asc');
```

2. Define the data grid:

```
Ext.onReady(function() {
    var grid = new Ext.grid.GridPanel({
        title: 'Movies',
        store: store,
        columns: [
            { header: "ID", width: 30, dataIndex: 'fid',
              sortable: true, hidden:true },
            { id: 'title-col',
              header: "Title",
              width: 180,
              dataIndex: 'title',
              sortable: true
            },
            { header: "Category", width: 65, dataIndex: 'category',
              sortable: true },
            { header: "Rating",
              width: 65,
              dataIndex: 'rating',
              sortable: true
            },
            { header: "Length",
              width: 65,
              dataIndex: 'length',
              sortable: true,
              align: 'right',
              renderer : function(v){
                  return v + ' min';
              }
            },
            { header: "Price",
              width: 65,
              dataIndex: 'price',
```

```
                sortable: true,
                align: 'right',
                renderer: Ext.util.Format.usMoney
            }
        ],
        autoExpandColumn: 'title-col',
        renderTo: Ext.getBody(),
        width: 600,
        height: 400,
        loadMask: true,
        columnLines: true,
        viewConfig: {
            forceFit: true,
            enableRowBody: true,
            showPreview: true,
            getRowClass: function(record, rowIndex, p, store) {
                if (this.showPreview) {
                    p.body = '<div class="row-preview ">
                        <img src="img/star_yellow.png" align="left"
                        style="padding-right:5px;"/><p>' +
                        record.data.actors + '</p></div>';
                    return 'x-grid3-row-expanded';
                }
                return 'x-grid3-row-collapsed';
            }
        },
        bbar: new Ext.PagingToolbar({
            pageSize. 20,
            store: store,
            displayInfo: true,
            displayMsg: 'Displaying movies {0} - {1} of {2}',
            emptyMsg: "No movies found",
            items:[
                '-',
                {
                    pressed: true,
                    enableToggle:true,
                    text: 'Show Actors',
                    toggleHandler: function(btn, pressed){
                        var view = grid.getView();
                        view.showPreview = pressed;
                        view.refresh();
                    }
                }
            ]
        })
    });
    store.load({ params: { start: 0, limit: 20} });
});
```

How it works...

The data store that provides the data for the grid is created first. This is a `JsonStore` connected to the server page. As the data preview will display the actors' information, the `actors` field is included in the field's definition of the store:

```
fields: ['id', 'title', 'category', 'rating', 'actors',
    { name: 'length', type: 'int' },
    { name: 'price', type: 'float' }]
```

Next, the grid panel is defined. The data preview configuration is found within the grid's `viewConfig` object.

The `enableRowBody` option adds a second `TR` element per row. This element is used to provide a row body that spans beneath the data row.

The `getRowClass()` function is where you can customize the row. In this case, if the `showPreview` option is `true`, the body of the row is altered so that the preview is shown:

```
getRowClass: function(record, rowIndex, p, store) {
    if (this.showPreview) {
        p.body = '<div class="row-preview ">
          <img src="img/star_yellow.png" align="left"
          style="padding-right:5px;"/><p>' +
          record.data.actors + '</p></div>';
        return 'x-grid3-row-expanded';
    }
    return 'x-grid3-row-collapsed';
}
```

The last element needed for the preview feature is the button that shows or hides the preview. This button is a part of the grid's paging toolbar. Its handler toggles the `showPreview` property and refreshes the grid's view:

```
toggleHandler: function(btn, pressed){
    var view = grid.getView();
    view.showPreview = pressed;
    view.refresh();
}
```

There's more...

Commonly, using the row body is a good option when you need to display data that wouldn't normally fit in a cell of the grid. As this area can be collapsed or expanded, it's also a good place to put non-vital information that can be hidden in order to save room, or to avoid distracting the user from the most important information in the grid.

See also...

▸ The previous recipe, *Data grouping with live group summaries*, explains how the grid panel can display records grouped by one of the available fields as well as column summaries

▸ The next recipe, *Creating a grid panel with expandable rows*, explains the use of a plugin that adds an expandable body to each data row

Creating a grid panel with expandable rows

The **Movies** grid in this recipe uses a plugin that adds an expandable body to each data row. This expandable area is used to display the actors who star in each movie:

Movies					
Title ▲	Category	Rating	Length	Price	
⊞ BLINDNESS GUN	Sci-Fi	PG-13	103 min	$4.99	
⊞ BLOOD ARGONAUTS	Family	G	71 min	$0.99	
⊟ BLUES INSTINCT	Family	G	50 min	$2.99	
☆ Cameron Streep, Groucho Dunst, Salma Nolte, Matthew Carrey					
⊞ BOILED DARES	Travel	PG	102 min	$4.99	
⊞ BONNIE HOLOCAUST	Documentar	G	63 min	$0.99	
⊞ BOOGIE AMELIE	Music	R	121 min	$4.99	
⊞ BOONDOCK BALLROOM	Travel	NC-17	76 min	$0.99	
⊟ BORN SPINAL	Travel	PG	179 min	$4.99	
☆ Kirsten Paltrow, Sissy Sobieski, Nick Stallone, Dustin Tautou, Ray Johansson, Kenneth Paltrow, Dan Streep, Rita Reynolds, Meryl Allen					
⊞ BORROWERS BEDAZZLED	Animation	G	63 min	$0.99	
⊞ BOULEVARD MOB	New	R	63 min	$0.99	
⊞ BOUND CHEAPER	Classics	PG	98 min	$0.99	
⊞ BOWFINGER GABLES	Horror	NC-17	72 min	$4.99	

|◀ ◀ Page 5 of 50 ▶ ▶| ⟳ Show Actors   Displaying movies 81 - 100 of 997

How to do it...

1. Create the data store:

```
var store = new Ext.data.JsonStore({
    url: 'grid-row-expander.php',
    root: 'movies',
    idProperty: 'id',
```

```
        totalProperty: 'count',
        fields: ['id', 'title', 'category', 'rating', 'actors',
    { name: 'length', type: 'int' },
    { name: 'price', type: 'float' }],
        remoteSort: true
    });
    store.setDefaultSort('title', 'asc');
```

2. Create the row expander:

```
var rowExpander = new Ext.grid.RowExpander({
    tpl: new Ext.Template(
        '<div class="row-preview"><img src="img/star_yellow.png"
         align="left" style="padding-right:5px;"/>
         <p>{actors}</p></div>'
    )
});
```

3. Define the grid panel:

```
Ext.onReady(function() {
    var grid = new Ext.grid.GridPanel({
        title: 'Movies',
        store: store,
        columns: [
            rowExpander,
            { header: "ID", width: 30, dataIndex: 'fid',
              sortable: true, hidden:true },
            { id: 'title-col',
              header: "Title",
              width: 180,
              dataIndex: 'title',
              sortable: true
            },
            { header: "Category", width: 65, dataIndex: 'category',
              sortable: true },
            { header: "Rating",
              width: 65,
              dataIndex: 'rating',
              sortable: true
            },
            { header: "Length",
              width: 65,
              dataIndex: 'length',
              sortable: true,
              align: 'right',
              renderer : function(v){
                  return v + ' min';
              }
            },
            { header: "Price",
```

```
            width: 65,
            dataIndex: 'price',
            sortable: true,
            align: 'right',
            renderer: Ext.util.Format.usMoney
        }
    ],
    autoExpandColumn: 'title-col',
    renderTo: Ext.getBody(),
    width: 600,
    height: 400,
    loadMask: true,
    columnLines: true,
    plugins: rowExpander,
    bbar: new Ext.PagingToolbar({
        pageSize: 20,
        store: store,
        displayInfo: true,
        displayMsg: 'Displaying movies {0} - {1} of {2}',
        emptyMsg: "No movies found
    })
});
store.load({ params: { start: 0, limit: 20} });
});
```

How it works...

The data store that provides the data for the grid is a JsonStore connected to the server page. As the data preview will display the actors' information, the actors field is included in the fields definition of the store:

```
fields: ['id', 'title', 'category', 'rating', 'actors',
    { name: 'length', type: 'int' },
    { name: 'price', type: 'float' }]
```

The RowExpander plugin provides a template for showing the row's body:

```
var rowExpander = new Ext.grid.RowExpander({
    tpl: new Ext.Template(
        '<div class="row-preview">
          <img src="img/star_yellow.png" align="left"
          style="padding-right:5px;"/><p>{actors}</p></div>'
    )
});
```

When the grid panel is defined, what is needed to show the row expander is that it is added as the first column of the grid, and also defined as a plugin:

```
columns: [rowExpander,…
plugins: rowExpander,
```

There's more...

Using the expandable row is a good option when you need to display data that would not normally fit in a cell of the grid. As this row can be collapsed or expanded, the preview area is a good place to put non-vital information that can be hidden in order to save room, or to avoid distracting the user from the most important information in the grid.

See also...

▶ The previous recipe, *Creating data previews*, teaches you how to enrich the grid component by adding a row body that expands beneath each data row

Using checkboxes to select grid rows

A common pattern for row selection is the use of a checkbox column. The **Movies** grid in this recipe shows how this can be accomplished:

Movies				
☐ Title ▲	Category	Rating	Length	Price
☐ INSTINCT AIRPORT	Sports	PG	116 min	$2.99
☐ INTENTIONS EMPIRE	Animation	PG-13	107 min	$2.99
☐ INTERVIEW LIAISONS	New	R	59 min	$4.99
☐ INTOLERABLE INTENTIONS	Documentary	PG-13	63 min	$4.99
☐ INTRIGUE WORST	Foreign	G	181 min	$0.99
☐ VASION CYCLONE	Children	PG	97 min	$2.99
☑ IRON MOON	Classics	PG	46 min	$4.99
☐ ISHTAR ROCKETEER	Animation	R	79 min	$4.99
☐ ISLAND EXORCIST	Classics	NC-17	84 min	$2.99
☐ ITALIAN AFRICAN	Travel	G	174 min	$4.99
☐ JACKET FRISCO	Drama	PG-13	181 min	$2.99
☐ JADE BUNCH	Sports	NC-17	174 min	$2.99
☐ JAPANESE RUN	Horror	G	135 min	$0.99
☐ JASON TRAP	Family	NC-17	130 min	$2.99
☐ JAWBREAKER BROOKLYN	Music	PG	118 min	$0.99

◁◁ ◁ Page 24 of 50 ▷ ▷▷ ⟳   Displaying movies 461 – 480 of 997

How to do it...

1. Create the data store:

```
var store = new Ext.data.JsonStore({
    url: 'grid-checkbox-selection.php',
    root: 'movies',
    idProperty: 'id',
    totalProperty: 'count',
    fields: ['id', 'title', 'category', 'rating', 'actors',
{ name: 'length', type: 'int' },
{ name: 'price', type: 'float' }],
    remoteSort: true
});
store.setDefaultSort('title', 'asc');
```

2. Create a checkbox selection model:

```
var checkboxSel = new Ext.grid.CheckboxSelectionModel();
```

3. Define the grid panel that uses the checkbox selection model:

```
Ext.onReady(function() {
    var grid = new Ext.grid.GridPanel({
        title: 'Movies',
        store: store,
        sm:checkboxSel,
        columns: [
            checkboxSel,
            {header: "ID", width: 30, dataIndex: 'fid',
                sortable: true, hidden:true },
            { id: 'title-col',
              header: "Title",
              width: 180,
              dataIndex: 'title',
              sortable: true
            },
            { header: "Category", width: 85, dataIndex: 'category',
              sortable: true },
            { header: "Rating",
              width: 65,
              dataIndex: 'rating',
              sortable: true
            },
            { header: "Length",
```

```
                width: 65,
                dataIndex: 'length',
                sortable: true,
                align: 'right',
                renderer : function(v){
                    return v + ' min';
                }
            },
            { header: "Price",
              width: 65,
              dataIndex: 'price',
              sortable: true,
              align: 'right',
              renderer: Ext.util.Format.usMoney
            }
        ],
        autoExpandColumn: 'title-col',
        renderTo: Ext.getBody(),
        width: 600,
        height: 400,
        loadMask: true,
        columnLines: true,
        bbar: new Ext.PagingToolbar({
            pageSize: 20,
            store: store,
            displayInfo: true,
            displayMsg: 'Displaying movies {0} - {1} of {2}',
            emptyMsg: "No movies found"
        })
    });
    store.load({ params: { start: 0, limit: 20} });
});
```

How it works...

The checkbox selection feature is defined with the addition of a
CheckboxSelectionModel instance:

```
var checkboxSel = new Ext.grid.CheckboxSelectionModel();
```

When the grid panel is defined, adding the `CheckboxSelectionModel` instance to the list of columns completes the feature implementation:

```
sm:checkboxSel,
columns: [checkboxSel,...
```

There's more...

You can combine the checkbox selection with the row expander feature explained in the previous recipe:

```
var rowExpander = new Ext.grid.RowExpander({
    tpl: new Ext.Template(
        '<div class="row-preview "><img src="img/star_yellow.png"
        align="left" style="padding-right:5px;"/>
        <p>{actors}</p></div>'
    )
});
```

What is needed is to add the `rowExpander`, along with the checkbox selection, to the columns of the grid, and also specify the `rowExpander` as a plugin:

```
columns. [checkboxSel,rowExpander,...]
plugins: rowExpander,
```

This is how the grid looks:

		Title ▲	Category	Rating	Length	Price
☐	⊞	WONDERFUL DROP	Foreign	NC-17	126 min	$2.99
☐	⊞	WONDERLAND CHRISTMAS	Sci-Fi	PG	111 min	$4.99
☐	⊞	WONKA SEA	Animation	NC-17	85 min	$2.99
☑	⊟	WORDS HUNTER	Music	PG	116 min	$2.99
	☆	Gene Willis, Susan Davis, Scarlett Bening, Adam Hopper, Fay Winslet, Ian Tandy				
☐	⊞	WORKER TARZAN	Travel	R	139 min	$2.99
☑	⊟	WORKING MICROCOSMOS	Travel	R	74 min	$4.99
	☆	Val Bolger, Kenneth Torn, Lucille Dee, Geoffrey Heston, Rock Dukakis				
☐	⊞	WORLD LEATHERNECKS	Horror	PG-13	171 min	$0.99
☐	⊞	WORST BANGER	Action	PG	185 min	$2.99
☐	⊞	WRATH MILE	Documentary	NC-17	176 min	$0.99
☐	⊞	WRONG BEHAVIOR	Children	PG-13	178 min	$2.99
☐	⊞	WYOMING STORM	New	PG-13	100 min	$4.99
☐	⊞	YENTL IDAHO	Horror	R	86 min	$4.99
☐	⊞	YOUNG LANGUAGE	Documentary	G	183 min	$0.99

Page 50 of 50 Displaying movies 981 - 997 of 997

A limitation of the checkbox selection model presented in this recipe is that when you switch data pages, your row selection is lost. This can be solved by modifying the selection model so that it preserves the selection state across data pages.

Numbering rows in a grid panel

Another common pattern when working with grid components is numbered rows. The **Movies** grid in this recipe exemplifies how this can be accomplished:

	Title ▲	Category	Rating	Length	Price
1	ACADEMY DINOSAUR	Documentary	PG	86 min	$0.99
2	GOLDFINGER	Horror	G	48 min	$4.99
3	ADAPTATION HOLES	Documentary	NC-17	50 min	$2.99
4	AFFAIR PREJUDICE	Horror	G	117 min	$2.99
5	AFRICAN EGG	Family	G	130 min	$2.99
6	AGENT TRUMAN	Foreign	PG	169 min	$2.99
7	AIRPLANE SIERRA	Comedy	PG-13	62 min	$4.99
8	AIRPORT POLLOCK	Horror	R	54 min	$4.99
9	ALABAMA DEVIL	Horror	PG-13	114 min	$2.99
10	ALADDIN CALENDAR	Sports	NC-17	63 min	$4.99
11	ALAMO VIDEOTAPE	Foreign	G	126 min	$0.99
12	ALASKA PHANTOM	Music	PG	136 min	$0.99
13	ALI FOREVER	Horror	PG	150 min	$4.99
14	ALICE FANTASIA	Classics	NC-17	94 min	$0.99
15	ALIEN CENTER	Foreign	NC-17	46 min	$2.99
16	ALLEY EVOLUTION	Foreign	NC-17	180 min	$2.99

How to do it...

1. Define the data store:

```
var store = new Ext.data.JsonStore({
   url: 'grid-row-numberer.php',
   root: 'movies',
   idProperty: 'id',
   totalProperty: 'count',
   fields: ['id', 'title', 'category', 'rating', 'actors',
{ name: 'length', type: 'int' },
{ name: 'price', type: 'float' }],
   remoteSort: true
});
store.setDefaultSort('title', 'asc');
```

2. Define the grid panel. The first column of the grid is of the RowNumberer type:

```
Ext.onReady(function() {
    var grid = new Ext.grid.GridPanel({
        title: 'Movies',
        store: store,
        columns: [
            new Ext.grid.RowNumberer(),
            {header: "ID", width: 30, dataIndex: 'fid',
              sortable: true, hidden:true },
            { id: 'title-col',
              header: "Title",
              width: 180,
              dataIndex: 'title',
              sortable: true
            },
            { header: "Category", width: 85, dataIndex: 'category',
              sortable: true },
            { header: "Rating",
              width: 65,
              dataIndex: 'rating',
              sortable: true
            },
            { header: "Length",
              width: 65,
              dataIndex: 'length',
              sortable: true,
              align: 'right',
              renderer : function(v){
                  return v + ' min';
              }
            },
            { header: "Price",
              width: 65,
              dataIndex: 'price',
              sortable: true,
              align: 'right',
              renderer: Ext.util.Format.usMoney
            }
        ],
        autoExpandColumn: 'title-col',
        renderTo: Ext.getBody(),
        width: 600,
        height: 400,
        loadMask: true
    })
    store.load();
});
```

How it works...

When the grid panel is defined, the first column should be a `RowNumberer` instance:

```
columns: [new Ext.grid.RowNumberer(),…
```

`RowNumberer` accepts the `header` and `width` config options.

Changing grid panel data using cell editors

The **Customers** grid built in this recipe illustrates how different cell editors are used to allow for in-place editing of a data record.

A text field can be used as a cell editor as shown in the following screenshot:

Customers				
Name	Address	Zip Code	Phone	City
ZACHARY HITE	98 Pyongyang Boulevard	88749	191958435142	Akron
RICHARD MCCRARY	913 Coacalco de Berriozbal Loop	42141	262088367001	Arlington
DIANA ALEXANDER	1308 Arecibo Way	30695	6171054059	Augusta-Richmond
SCOTT SHELLEY	587 Benguela Manor	91590	165450987037	Aurora
CLINTON BUFORD	43 Vilnius Manor	79814	484500282381	Aurora
WILMA RICHARDS	660 Jedda Boulevard	25053	168758068397	Bellevue
VALERIE BLACK	782 Mosul Street	25545	885899703621	Brockton
KARL SEAL	1427 Tabuk Place	31342	214756839122	Cape Coral
BETTY WHITE	770 Bydgoszcz Avenue	16266	517338314235	Citrus Heights
EVA RAMOS	1666 Beni-Mellal Place	13377	9099941466	Clarksville
RENEE LANE	533 al-Ayn Boulevard	8862	662227486184	Compton
BRYAN HARDISON	530 Lausanne Lane	11067	775235029633	Dallas
SHELLY WATTS	32 Pudukkottai Lane	38834	967274728547	Dayton
JACOB LANCE	1866 al-Qatif Avenue	89420	546793516940	El Monte
ALICE STEWART	1135 Izumisano Parkway	48150	171822533480	Fontana
RENE MCALISTER	1895 Zhezqazghan Drive	36693	137809746111	Garden Grove
IAN STILL	1894 Boa Vista Way	77464	239357986667	Garland
KIM CRUZ	333 Goinia Way	78625	909029256431	Grand Prairie
VERONICA STONE	369 Papeete Way	66639	170117068815	Greensboro
NATHANIEL ADAM	786 Matsue Way	37469	111177206479	Joliet

Combo boxes can also serve as cell editors:

Customers				
Name	Address	Zip Code	Phone	City
ZACHARY HITE	98 Pyongyang Boulevard	88749	191958435142	Akron
RICHARD MCCRARY	913 Coacalco de Berriozbal Loop	42141	262088367001	Arlington
DIANA ALEXANDER	1308 Arecibo Way	30695	6171054059	Kansas City
SCOTT SHELLEY	587 Benguela Manor	91590	165450987937	Lancaster
CLINTON BUFORD	43 Vilnius Manor	79814	484596282381	Laredo
WILMA RICHARDS	660 Jedda Boulevard	25053	168758068397	Lincoln
VALERIE BLACK	782 Mosul Street	25545	885899703621	Manchester
KARL SEAL	1427 Tabuk Place	31342	214756839122	Memphis
BETTY WHITE	770 Bydgoszcz Avenue	16266	517338314235	Peoria
EVA RAMOS	1666 Beni-Mellal Place	13377	9099941466	Roanoke
RENEE LANE	533 al-Ayn Boulevard	8862	662227486184	Rockford
BRYAN HARDISON	530 Lausanne Lane	11067	775235029633	Saint Louis
SHELLY WATTS	32 Pudukkottai Lane	38834	967274728547	Salinas
JACOB LANCE	1866 al-Qatif Avenue	89420	546793516940	San Bernardinc
ALICE STEWART	1135 Izumisano Parkway	48150	171822533480	Sterling Height
RENE MCALISTER	1895 Zhezqazghan Drive	36693	137809746111	Sunnyvale
IAN STILL	1894 Boa Vista Way	77464	239357966667	Tallahassee / Warren / Garland
KIM CRUZ	333 Goinia Way	78625	909029256431	Grand Prairie
VERONICA STONE	369 Papeete Way	66639	170117068816	Greensboro
NATHANIEL ADAM	786 Matsue Way	37469	111177206479	Joliet

How to do it...

1. Define the customers' data store:

```
var customersStore = new Ext.data.JsonStore({
    url: 'grid-editor.php',
    baseParams: { xaction: 'customers' },
    root: 'customers',
    idProperty: 'ID',
    fields: ['ID', 'name', 'address', 'zip code', 'phone', 'city'],
    writer: new Ext.data.JsonWriter()
});
```

2. Define the cities data store. This store will feed the cities lookup:

```
var citiesStore = new Ext.data.JsonStore({
    url: 'grid-editor.php',
    baseParams: { xaction: 'cities' },
    root: 'cities',
    fields: ['city_id', 'city']
});
```

3. Create the grid panel:

```
Ext.onReady(function() {
    var grid = new Ext.grid.EditorGridPanel({
        title:'Customers',
        store: customersStore,
        columns: [
            { header: "ID", width: 30, dataIndex: 'ID',
              sortable: true, hidden:true },
            { id: 'name',
              header: "Name",
              width: 180,
              dataIndex: 'name',
              sortable: true,
              editor: new Ext.form.TextField({
                  allowBlank: false
              })
            },
            { id:'address',
              header: "Address",
              width: 160,
              dataIndex: 'address',
              sortable: true,
              editor: new Ext.form.TextField({
                  allowBlank: false
              })
            },
            { header: "Zip Code",
              width: 65,
              dataIndex: 'zip code',
              sortable: true, align: 'left',
              editor: new Ext.form.NumberField({
                  allowBlank: false,
                  allowNegative: false,
                  style: 'text-align:left'
              })
```

```
                },
                { header: "Phone",
                  width: 95,
                  dataIndex: 'phone',
                  sortable: true,
                  align: 'left',
                  editor: new Ext.form.NumberField({
                      allowBlank: false,
                      allowNegative: false,
                      style: 'text-align:left'
                  })
                },
                { header: "City",
                  width: 95,
                  dataIndex: 'city',
                  sortable: true,
                  align: 'left',
                  editor: new Ext.form.ComboBox({
                      store: citiesStore,
                      displayField: 'city',
                      valueField: 'city_id',
                      editable: false,
                      mode: 'remote',
                      forceSelection: true,
                      triggerAction: 'all',
                      selectOnFocus: true
                  })
                }
            ],
            autoExpandColumn: 'address',
            renderTo: Ext.getBody(),
            width: 750,
            height: 500,
            loadMask: true,
            clicksToEdit:'1'
        });
    customersStore.load();
});
```

How it works...

After defining the `customersStore` data store, the `citiesStore` is created. The `citiesStore` will feed the `ComboBox` that serves as an editor for the cities column:

```
var citiesStore = new Ext.data.JsonStore({
   url: 'grid-editor.php',
   baseParams: { xaction: 'cities' },
   root: 'cities',
   fields: ['city_id', 'city']
});
```

When defining the grid panel, each editable column specifies an editor. The `name` and `address` columns use `TextField` instances as editors:

```
editor: new Ext.form.TextField({
   allowBlank: false
})
```

The `zip code` and `phone` editors are `NumberField` instances:

```
editor: new Ext.form.NumberField({
   allowBlank: false,
   allowNegative: false,
   style: 'text-align:left'
})
```

The editor for the `city` column is a `ComboBox` instance fed by the `citiesStore`:

```
editor: new Ext.form.ComboBox({
   store: citiesStore,
   displayField: 'city',
   valueField: 'city_id',
   editable: false,
   mode: 'remote',
   forceSelection: true,
   triggerAction: 'all',
   selectOnFocus: true
})
```

Normally, a column editor activates when a column cell is double-clicked. You can change this to a single-click using the `clicksToEdit` config option:

```
clicksToEdit:'1'
```

See also...

▶ The next recipe, *Automatic uploading of data edited with a grid*, teaches you how data edits in a grid panel can be automatically propagated to the server

▶ The, *Performing batch uploads of data edited with a grid* recipe (covered later in this chapter) explains how to cache record changes and send them to the server as a batch

Automatic uploading of data edited with a grid

The **Customers** grid in this recipe illustrates how a grid component and its data store can be configured so that the data edited in the grid is automatically propagated to the server.

In case of changes to any editable cell, the updated value will be uploaded to the server:

Name	Address	Zip Code	Phone	City
ZACHARY HITE	98 Pyongyang Boulevard	88749	191958435142	Akron
RICHARD MCCRARY	913 Coacalco de Berriozbal Loop	42141	262088367001	Arlington
DIANA ALEXANDER	1309 Arecibo Way	30695	6171054059	Augusta-Richmon(
SCOTT SHELLEY	587 Benguela Manor	91590	165450987037	Aurora
CLINTON BUFORD	43 Vilnius Manor	79814	484500282381	Aurora
WILMA RICHARDS	660 Jedda Boulevard	26063	168750000307	Bellevue
VALERIE BLACK	782 Mosul Street	25545	885899703621	Brockton
KARL SEAL	1427 Tabuk Place	31342	214756839122	Cape Coral
BETTY WHITE	770 Bydgoszcz Avenue	16266	517338314235	Citrus Heights
EVA RAMOS	1666 Beni-Mellal Place	13377	9099941466	Clarksville
RENEE LANE	533 al-Ayn Boulevard	8862	662227486184	Compton
BRYAN HARDISON	530 Lausanne Lane	11067	775235029633	Dallas
SHELLY WATTS	32 Pudukkottai Lane	38834	967274728547	Dayton
JACOB LANCE	1866 al-Qatif Avenue	89420	546793516940	El Monte
ALICE STEWART	1135 Izumisano Parkway	48150	171822533480	Fontana
RENE MCALISTER	1895 Zhezqazghan Drive	36693	137809746111	Garden Grove
IAN STILL	1894 Boa Vista Way	77464	239357986667	Garland
KIM CRUZ	333 Goinia Way	78625	909029256431	Grand Prairie
VERONICA STONE	369 Papeete Way	66639	170117068815	Greensboro
NATHANIEL ADAM	786 Matsue Way	37469	111177206479	Joliet

How to do it...

1. Create a store for customers' data:

```
var customersStore = new Ext.data.JsonStore({
    url: 'grid-auto-save.php',
    root: 'customers',
    idProperty: 'ID',
    successProperty:'success',
    fields: ['ID', 'name', 'address', 'zip code', 'phone', 'city'],
    writer: new Ext.data.JsonWriter()
});
```

2. Create a store for cities' data:

```
var citiesStore = new Ext.data.JsonStore({
    url: 'grid-editor.php',
    baseParams: { xaction: 'cities' },
    root: 'cities',
    fields: ['city_id', 'city']
});
```

3. Define the grid panel:

```
Ext.onReady(function() {
    var grid = new Ext.grid.EditorGridPanel({
        title:'Customers',
        store: customersStore,
        columns: [
            { header: "ID", width: 30, dataIndex: 'ID',
              sortable: true, hidden:true },
            { id: 'name',
              header: "Name",
              width: 160,
              dataIndex: 'name',
              sortable: true,
              editor: new Ext.form.TextField({
                  allowBlank: false
              })
            },
            { id: 'address',
              header: "Address",
              width: 150,
              dataIndex: 'address',
              sortable: true,
              editor: new Ext.form.TextField({
                  allowBlank: false
              })
```

```
        },
        { header: "Zip Code",
          width: 65,
          dataIndex: 'zip code',
          sortable: true, align: 'left',
          editor: new Ext.form.NumberField({
              allowBlank: false,
              allowNegative: false,
              style: 'text-align:left'
          })
        },
        { header: "Phone",
          width: 95,
          dataIndex: 'phone',
          sortable: true,
          align: 'left',

          editor: new Ext.form.NumberField({
              allowBlank: false,
              allowNegative: false,
              style: 'text-align:left'
          })
        },
        { header: "City",
          width: 95,
          dataIndex: 'city',
          sortable: true,
          align: 'left',
          editor: new Ext.form.ComboBox({
              store: citiesStore,
              displayField: 'city',
              valueField: 'city_id',
              editable: false,
              mode: 'remote',
              forceSelection: true,
              triggerAction: 'all',
              selectOnFocus: true
          })
        }
    ],
    autoExpandColumn: 'address',
    renderTo: Ext.getBody(),
    width: 750,
    height: 500,
    loadMask: true,
    clicksToEdit: 1,
    tbar: { items: [
      { text: 'Save Changes',
        iconCls:'btn-save',
        handler: function() {
```

```
                customersStore.save();
            }
        }
    ]},
    batchSave: false
});
customersStore.load();
});
```

How it works...

The first step in implementing the save feature is defining a data writer for the grid's data store:

```
var customersStore = new Ext.data.JsonStore({
    url: 'grid-auto-save.php',
    root: 'customers',
    idProperty: 'ID',
    successProperty:'success',
    fields: ['ID', 'name', 'address', 'zip code', 'phone', 'city'],
    writer: new Ext.data.JsonWriter(),
    autoSave: true,
    batch: true
});
```

In the store's definition, the `idProperty` option is inherited from the `JsonReader` class and is used to specify which record property serves as its unique ID. This is important because the store inspects a record's ID in order to determine whether the record is new or is simply being edited. Also, `successProperty` (inherited from `JsonReader`) is used to identify the request's property that indicates whether any of the **CRUD** operations succeeded.

> The acronym CRUD refers to all of the major functions that need to be implemented in a relational database application to consider it complete. Each letter in the acronym can be mapped to a standard SQL statement:
>
> Create: INSERT
> Read (Retrieve): SELECT
> Update: UPDATE
> Delete (Destroy): DELETE

Each editable column in the grid specifies an editor. The name and address columns use the `TextField` instances as editors:

```
editor: new Ext.form.TextField({
    allowBlank: false
})
```

The zip code and phone editors are NumberField instances:

```
editor: new Ext.form.NumberField({
    allowBlank: false,
    allowNegative: false,
    style: 'text-align:left'
})
```

The editor for the city column is a ComboBox instance fed by the citiesStore:

```
editor: new Ext.form.ComboBox({
    store: citiesStore,
    displayField: 'city',
    valueField: 'city_id',
    editable: false,
    mode: 'remote',
    forceSelection: true,
    triggerAction: 'all',
    selectOnFocus: true
})
```

With every record change, the save() method of customersStore initiates a request to the server. You can inspect the parameters sent with the Firebug console:

The xaction parameter indicates an update operation. xaction is accompanied by the record ID (ID) and the changed properties of the updated record.

The server page should handle the request to save the data and return the modified information. If the operation succeeds, the server code should also include in the response a success property set to true: success = true.

There's more...

Automatically uploading any cell changes relieves the user from manually having to initiate an upload. However, depending on your bandwidth and performance constraints, this might not be the optimal approach for applications where users will perform a large number of updates in short periods of time. For such cases, it's also possible to send your updates to the server in batches. (See the *Performing batch uploads of data edited with a grid* recipe.)

See also...

▷ The previous recipe, *Changing grid panel data using cell editors*, explains how to use the different cell editors to allow for in-place editing of record data

▷ The next recipe, *Performing batch uploads of data edited with a grid*, explains how to cache record changes and send them to the server as a batch

Performing batch uploads of data edited with a grid

This recipe illustrates how a grid component and its data store can be configured so that record changes are locally cached in the store and automatically sent to the server as a batch at a later time.

Multiple edits in the **Customers** grid can be batched and sent to the server by clicking on the **Save Changes** button:

Name	Address	Zip Code	Phone	City
ZACHARY HITE	98 Pyongyang Boulevard	88749	191958435142	Akron
RICHARD MCCRARY	913 Coacalco de Berriozbal Loop	42141	262088367001	Arlington
JAMES ALEXANDER	1308 South Arecibo Way	30697	6171054059	101
DEBBY SHELLEY	5873 Benguela Manor	91593	165450987037	Aurora
CLINTON BUFORD	43 Vilnius Manor	79814	484500282381	Aurora
WILMA RICHARDS	660 Jedda Boulevard	25053	168758068397	Bellevue
VALERIE BLACK	782 Mosul Street	25545	885899703621	Brockton
KARL SEAL	1427 Tabuk Place	31342	214756839122	Cape Coral
BETTY WHITE	770 Bydgoszcz Avenue	16266	517338314235	Citrus Heights
EVA RAMOS	1666 Beni-Mellal Place	13377	9099941466	Clarksville
RENEE LANE	533 al-Ayn Boulevard	8862	662227486184	Compton
BRYAN HARDISON	530 Lausanne Lane	11067	775235029633	Dallas
SHELLY WATTS	32 Pudukkottai Lane	38834	967274728547	Dayton
JACOB LANCE	1866 al-Qatif Avenue	89420	546793516940	El Monte
ALICE STEWART	1135 Izumisano Parkway	48150	171822533480	Fontana
RENE MCALISTER	1895 Zhezqazghan Drive	36693	137809746111	Garden Grove
IAN STILL	1894 Boa Vista Way	77464	239357986667	Garland
KIM CRUZ	333 Goinia Way	78625	909029256431	Grand Prairie
VERONICA STONE	369 Papeete Way	66639	170117068815	Greensboro

How to do it...

1. Create a data store for the customers' information:

```
var customersStore = new Ext.data.JsonStore({
    url: 'grid-batch-save.php',
    root: 'customers',
    idProperty: 'ID',
    successProperty: 'success',
    fields: ['ID', 'name', 'address', 'zip code', 'phone', 'city'],
    writer: new Ext.data.JsonWriter(),
    autoSave: false,
    batch:true
});
```

2. Create a data store that will hold the cities list:

```
var citiesStore = new Ext.data.JsonStore({
    url: 'grid-editor.php',
    baseParams: { xaction: 'cities' },
    root: 'cities',
    fields: ['city id', 'city']
});
```

3. Define the grid panel:

```
Ext.onReady(function() {
    var grid = new Ext.grid.EditorGridPanel({
        title:'Customers',
        store: customersStore,
        columns: [
            { header: "ID", width: 30, dataIndex: 'ID',
              sortable: true, hidden:true },
            { id: 'name',
              header: "Name",
              width: 130,
              dataIndex: 'name',
              sortable: true,
              editor: new Ext.form.TextField({
                  allowBlank: false
              })
            },
            { id: 'address',
              header: "Address",
```

```
            width: 150,
            dataIndex: 'address',
            sortable: true,
            editor: new Ext.form.TextField({
                allowBlank: false
            })
        },
        { header: "Zip Code",
            width: 65,
            dataIndex: 'zip code',
            sortable: true, align: 'left',
            editor: new Ext.form.NumberField({
                allowBlank: false,
                allowNegative: false,
                style: 'text-align:left'
            })
        },
        { header: "Phone",
            width: 95,
            dataIndex: 'phone',
            sortable: true,
            align: 'left',
            editor: new Ext.form.NumberField({
                allowBlank: false,
                allowNegative: false,
                style: 'text-align:left'
            })
        },
        { header: "City",
            width: 95,
            dataIndex: 'city',
            sortable: true,
            align: 'left',
            editor: new Ext.form.ComboBox({
                store: citiesStore,
                displayField: 'city',
                valueField: 'city_id',
                editable: false,
                mode: 'remote',
                forceSelection: true,
                triggerAction: 'all',
```

```
                    selectOnFocus: true
                })
            }
        ],
        autoExpandColumn: 'address',
        renderTo: Ext.getBody(),
        width: 750,
        height: 500,
        loadMask: true,
        clicksToEdit: 1
    });
    customersStore.load();
});
```

How it works...

To implement the save feature you have to define a data writer for the grid's data store:

```
var customersStore = new Ext.data.JsonStore({
    url: 'grid-batch-save.php',
    root: 'customers',
    idProperty: 'ID',
    successProperty: 'success',
    fields: ['ID', 'name', 'address', 'zip code', 'phone', 'city'],
    writer: new Ext.data.JsonWriter(),
    autoSave:false,
    batch:true
});
```

To enable batch updates, you need to set the batch config option to true. This makes the store accumulate all the record changes, which will be automatically sent to the server when its save() method is called.

Notice that batch = true only applies when autoSave = false. If autoSave = true and a record is changed, the store will automatically send the record to the server.

The idProperty option, inherited from the JsonReader class, is used to specify which record property serves as the record's unique ID. This is important because the store inspects a record's ID in order to determine whether the record is new or is simply being edited. The successProperty, also inherited from JsonReader, is used to identify the request's property that indicates whether any of the CRUD operations succeeded.

Each editable column in the grid specifies an editor. The name and address columns use the TextField instances as editors:

```
editor: new Ext.form.TextField({
   allowBlank: false
})
```

The zip code and phone editors are the NumberField instances:

```
editor: new Ext.form.NumberField({
   allowBlank: false,
   allowNegative: false,
   style: 'text-align:left'
})
```

The editor for the city column is a ComboBox instance fed by the citiesStore:

```
editor: new Ext.form.ComboBox({
   store: citiesStore,
   displayField: 'city',
   valueField: 'city_id',
   editable: false,
   mode: 'remote',
   forceSelection: true,
   triggerAction: 'all',
   selectOnFocus: true
})
```

The grid's toolbar includes a **Save Changes** button that triggers the save operation:

```
tbar: { items: [
   { text: 'Save Changes',
      iconCls:'btn-save',
      handler: function() {
         customersStore.save();
      }
   }
]},
```

As the store is configured for batch saves (`batchSave - true`), all of the accumulated record changes are automatically sent to the server upon a call to `save()`. The Firebug console provides a view into the request:

Headers	Post	Response

```
       ID  ["305","96"]
customers  [{"city":"120","ID":"305"},{"address":"1322 Arecibo Way","ID":"96"}]
   xaction  update
```

The request's `xaction` parameter indicates a save operation. `xaction` is accompanied by the record ID (`ID`) and the changed properties of each of the updated records.

The server page should handle the request to save the data and return the modified information. To indicate whether the request was successful or not, a `success` property should be included in the response.

There's more...

It's possible to write a code to implement batch updates automatically. For example, the updates can be triggered after a period of inactivity in the application, or at fixed intervals.

See also...

▶ The *Changing grid panel data using cell editors* recipe (covered earlier in this chapter) explains how to use the different cell editors to allow for in-place editing of record data

▶ The previous recipe, *Automatic uploading of data edited with a grid*, teaches you how data edits in a grid panel can be automatically propagated to the server

Changing a grid's data store and columns at runtime

A sought-after ability in grid components is changing the column's definitions at runtime. With the latest version of Ext JS, accomplishing this is very simple.

In this recipe, you will learn how to have a grid component switch from displaying customers' information to displaying movies' information with the click of a button.

Initially, the grid panel is configured to display the customers' information:

After clicking on the **Movies** button, the grid displays the movies' information as shown in the next screenshot. Note how the grid's columns change to reflect the fields of the records displayed.

How to do it...

1. Create a data store to hold the customers' information:

```
var customersStore = new Ext.data.JsonStore({
    url: 'grid-reconfigure.php',
    root: 'customers',
    baseParams:{xaction:'customers'},
    fields: ['ID', 'name', 'address', 'zip code', 'phone', 'city']
});
```

2. Create another data store that will hold the movies' records:

```
var moviesStore = new Ext.data.JsonStore({
    url: 'grid-reconfigure.php',
    root: 'movies',
    baseParams:{xaction:'movies'},
    fields: ['id', 'title', 'release_year', 'rating']
});
```

3. Create a column model for displaying the customers' records:

```
var customersColumnModel = new Ext.grid.ColumnModel([
    { header: "ID", width: 30, dataIndex: 'ID', sortable: true,
      hidden: true },
    { id: 'name', header: "Name", width: 130, dataIndex: 'name',
      sortable: true },
    { id: 'autoexpand',header: "Address",width: 150,
      dataIndex: 'address',sortable: true},
    { header: "Zip Code",width: 65,dataIndex: 'zip code',
      sortable: true, align: 'left'},
    { header: "Phone", width: 95,dataIndex: 'phone',
      sortable: true,align: 'left'},
    { header: "City",width: 95,dataIndex: 'city',
      sortable: true,align: 'left'}
]);
```

4. Create the column model for the movies' records:

```
var moviesColumnModel = new Ext.grid.ColumnModel([
    { header: "ID", width: 30, dataIndex: 'ID', sortable: true,
      hidden: true },
    { id: 'autoexpand', header: "Title", width: 180,
      dataIndex: 'title', sortable: true },
    { header: "Rating", width: 75, dataIndex: 'rating',
      sortable: true },
    { header: "Year", width: 75, dataIndex: 'release_year',
      sortable: true, align: 'center' }
```

```
    ]);
```

5. Create a grid panel:

```
Ext.onReady(function() {
    var grid = new Ext.grid.GridPanel({
        title: 'Customers',
        store: customersStore,
        cm: customersColumnModel,
        autoExpandColumn: 'autoexpand',
        renderTo: Ext.getBody(),
        width: 750,
        height: 500,
        loadMask: true,
        clicksToEdit: 1,
        tbar: { items: [
            { text: 'Movies',
              handler: function() {
                  grid.setTitle('Movies');
                  grid.reconfigure(moviesStore, moviesColumnModel);
                  moviesStore.load();
              }
            },'-',
            { text: 'Customers',
              handler: function() {
                  grid.setTitle('Customers');
                  grid.reconfigure(customersStore,
                    customersColumnModel);
                  moviesStore.load();
              }
            }
        ]}
    });
    customersStore.load();
});
```

How it works...

The two data stores that will fill the grid with data are created first. They are followed by a pair of the ColumnModel instances that match each of the stores' field collections.

The magic occurs inside the handlers for the grid's toolbar's buttons. Besides changing the grid's title, they call the reconfigure() function. As the name of this function implies, it reconfigures the grid to use a different Store and ColumnModel by binding the view to new objects and refreshing it:

```
handler: function() {
    grid.setTitle('Customers');
    grid.reconfigure(customersStore, customersColumnModel);
    cutomersStore.load();
```

When using reconfigure(), you need to take into account that some settings, such as autoExpandcolumn, may become invalid. Plugins and PagingToolbar instances will remain bound to the old store and will need to be individually re-bound to the new store.

6

More Applications of Grid and List Views

This chapter covers the following recipes:

- ▶ Creating a master-details view with a grid and a panel
- ▶ Creating a master-details view with a grid and a form
- ▶ Creating a master-details view with a combo box and a grid
- ▶ Creating a master-details view with two grids
- ▶ Displaying large recordsets with a buffered grid
- ▶ Using the lightweight `ListView` class
- ▶ Editing rows with the `RowEditor` plugin
- ▶ Adding tool tips to grid cells
- ▶ Using the `PropertyGrid` class
- ▶ Using drag-and-drop between two grids

Introduction

In this chapter, we continue exploring the presentation of information using grid-like components. Besides multiple ways of displaying master-details relationships, the recipes in this chapter cover the drag-and-drop features of the grid components, data editing with the new `RowEditor` class, as well as the new lightweight `ListView` component.

Creating a master-details view with a grid and a panel

A master-detail interface can be built using a grid and a panel component. In this recipe, the movie details are displayed on the basis of the current record selection in the master object—the movies list.

Movies				
Title ▲	Category	Rating	Length	Price
ACADEMY DINOSAUR	Documentary	PG	86 min	$0.99
ACE GOLDFINGER	Horror	G	48 min	$4.99
ADAPTATION HOLES	Documentary	NC-17	50 min	$2.99
AFFAIR PREJUDICE	Horror	G	117 min	$2.99
AFRICAN EGG	Family	G	130 min	$2.99
AGENT TRUMAN	Foreign	PG	169 min	$2.99
AIRPLANE SIERRA	Comedy	PG-13	62 min	$4.99
AIRPORT POLLOCK	Horror	R	54 min	$4.99
ALABAMA DEVIL	Horror	PG-13	114 min	$2.99
ALADDIN CALENDAR	Sports	NC-17	63 min	$4.99
ALAMO VIDEOTAPE	Foreign	G	126 min	$0.99

|◄ Page 1 of 67 ► ►| ⟳   Displaying movies 1 - 15 of 997

ALABAMA DEVIL

Category: Horror

Length: 114 min.

Rating: PG-13

Price: $2.99

A Thoughtful Panorama of a Database Administrator And a Mad Scientist who must Outgun a Mad Scientist in A Jet Boat

Getting ready...

The sample data used in this chapter's recipes comes from the Sakila sample database.

> You can obtain the Sakila database, as well as the installation instructions, at `http://dev.mysql.com/doc`.

How to do it...

1. Create the data store:

```
var store = new Ext.data.JsonStore({
    url: 'grid-data-binding.php',
    root: 'movies',
    idProperty: 'id',
    totalProperty: 'count',
    fields: ['id', 'title', 'category', 'rating', 'actors',
             { name: 'length', type: 'int' },
             { name: 'price', type: 'float' },
             'description'],
    remoteSort: true
});
store.setDefaultSort('title', 'asc');
```

2. Define the data grid:

```
var grid = new Ext.grid.GridPanel({
    store: store,
    height: 300,
    split: true,
    region: 'north',
    columns: [{ header: "ID", width: 30, dataIndex: 'fid',
                sortable: true, hidden: true },
       { id: 'title-col',
         header: "Title",
         width: 180,
         dataIndex: 'title',
         sortable: true
       },
       { header: "Category", width: 65, dataIndex: 'category',
         sortable: true },
       { header: "Rating",
         width: 65,
         dataIndex: 'rating',
         sortable: true
       },
       { header: "Length",
         width: 65,
         dataIndex: 'length',
         sortable: true,
         align: 'right',
```

```
            renderer: function(v) {
               return v + ' min';
            }
         },
         { header: "Price",
           width: 65,
           dataIndex: 'price',
           sortable: true,
           align: 'right',
           renderer: Ext.util.Format.usMoney
         }
      ],
      sm: new Ext.grid.RowSelectionModel({ singleSelect: true }),
      viewConfig: {
         forceFit: true
      },
      bbar: new Ext.PagingToolbar({
         pageSize: 15,
         store: store,
         displayInfo: true,
         displayMsg: 'Displaying movies {0} - {1} of {2}',
         emptyMsg: "No movies found"
      })
   });
```

3. Create a template for displaying the movie details:

```
var movieTpl = new Ext.XTemplate('<div class="movie-details">',
   '<a href="#" target="_blank">{title}</a><br/>',
   'Category: {category}<br/>',
   'Length: {length} min.<br/>',
   'Rating: {rating}<br/>',
   'Price: {[fm.usMoney(values.price)]}<br/>',
   '{description}<br/></div>'
);
```

4. Define a container for the grid and the movie details panel:

```
Ext.onReady(function() {
   var moviesPanel = new Ext.Panel({
      renderTo: Ext.getBody(),
      frame: true,
      title: 'Movies',
      width: 600,
      height: 500,
      layout: 'border',
      items: [grid,
         {
            id: 'detailPanel',
            region: 'center',
            bodyStyle: {
```

```
                background: '#ffffff',
                padding: '10px'
            },
            html:'Please select a movie'
        }
    ]
});
```

5. Add a handler for the `rowselect` event of the grid. This will update the details panel information:

```
grid.getSelectionModel().on('rowselect',
    function(sm, rowIdx, r) {
        var detailPanel = Ext.getCmp('detailPanel');
        movieTpl.overwrite(detailPanel.body, r.data);
    });
```

6. Load the movies list from the server:

```
    store.load({ params: { start: 0, limit: 15} });
}); // onReady
```

How it works...

The trick to this recipe resides in the handler for the `rowselect` event. This function uses the XTemplate instance, `movieTpl`, to write the movie details to the panel's body:

```
grid.getSelectionModel().on('rowselect', function(sm, rowIdx, r) {
    var detailPanel = Ext.getCmp('detailPanel');
    movieTpl.overwrite(detailPanel.body, r.data);
});
```

Note how `XTemplate` also allows formatting of the movie properties:

```
var movieTpl = new Ext.XTemplate('<div class="movie-details">',
    '<a href="#" target="_blank">{title}</a><br/>',
    'Category: {category}<br/>',
    'Length: {length} min.<br/>',
    'Rating: {rating}<br/>',
    'Price: {[fm.usMoney(values.price)]}<br/>',
    '{description}<br/></div>'
);
```

There's more...

As you can see, this approach is used when the details will be displayed in a read-only view, for example, previewing an email message or an RSS feed item.

See also...

▶ The next recipe, *Creating a master-details view with a grid and a form*, explains how to display the properties of a data record using a form

▶ In the *Creating a master-details view with a combo box and a grid* recipe (covered later in this chapter), you will learn how to use a combo box to filter the records shown in a grid

▶ The *Creating a master-details view with two grids* recipe (covered later in this chapter) shows how to use two grids for displaying the master-details data relationships

Creating a master-details view with a grid and a form

Another common master-detail UI uses a grid to present a master list and form elements to present the details of the selected record on the grid.

In this recipe, a `FormPanel` displays the details of movies as they are selected on the grid:

How to do it...

1. Define the data store for the movies list:

```
var moviesStore = new Ext.data.JsonStore({
    url: 'grid-form-master-details.php',
    root: 'movies',
    totalProperty: 'count',
```

```
    baseParams: { action: 'movies' },
    fields: [{ name: 'film_id' },
  { name: 'title' },
  { name: 'rating' },
  { name: 'length', type: 'int' },
  { name: 'price', type: 'float'}]
});
```

2. Create the movies grid panel:

```
var moviesGrid = new Ext.grid.GridPanel({
    store: moviesStore,
    columns: [
        { header: "ID", width: 30, dataIndex: 'film_id',
          sortable: true, hidden: true },
        { id: 'title-col',
          header: "Title",
          width: 180,
          dataIndex: 'title',
          sortable: true
        },
        { header: "Rating",
          dataIndex: 'rating',
          sortable: true
        },
        { header: "Length",
          dataIndex: 'length',
          sortable: true,
          align: 'right',
          renderer: function(v) {
             return v + ' min';
          }
        },
        { header: "Price",
          dataIndex: 'price',
          sortable: true,
          align: 'right',
          renderer: Ext.util.Format.usMoney
        }
    ],
    autoExpandColumn: 'title-col',
    width: 330,
```

```
        height: 300,
        loadMask: true,
        columnLines: true,
        viewConfig: {
            forceFit: true
        }
    });
```

3. Define a fieldset for displaying the movie details:

```
var fieldset = {
    columnWidth: 0.5,
    xtype: 'fieldset',
    labelWidth: 90,
    title: 'Movie details',
    defaults: { width: 230 },
    defaultType: 'textfield',
    autoHeight: true,
    bodyStyle: Ext.isIE ? 'padding:0 0 5px 15px;' :
        'padding:10px 15px;',
    items: [{
        id: 'title',
        fieldLabel: 'Title',
        name: 'title'
    }, {
        id: 'rating',
        fieldLabel: 'Rating',
        name: 'rating',
        width: 55,
        style: 'text-align:right;'
    }, {
        id:'length',
        xtype:'numberfield',
        fieldLabel: 'Length (min)',
        name: 'length',
        width: 55,
        style: 'text-align:right;'
    }, {
        id: 'price',
        xtype: 'numberfield',
        fieldLabel: 'Price (USD)',
        name: 'price',
```

```
                width: 55,
                style:'text-align:right;'
        }]
    }
```

4. Now, define the form that contains the grid and the fieldset:

```
Ext.onReady(function() {
    var moviesForm = new Ext.FormPanel({
        id: 'movies-form',
        renderTo: Ext.getBody() ,
        frame: true,
        labelAlign: 'left',
        title: 'Movies List',
        bodyStyle: 'padding:5px',
        width: 750,
        layout: 'column',
        items: [{ columnWidth: 0.5,
            items: [moviesGrid]
          }, fieldset]
    });
```

5. Add a handler for the grid's `rowselect` event. This function will update the movie details in the fieldset:

```
moviesGrid.getSelectionModel().on('rowselect', function(sm,
  rowIndex, record) {
    moviesForm.getForm().loadRecord(record);
});
```

6. Add a handler for the store's `load` event in order to select the first record after data is retrieved from the server:

```
    moviesStore.on('load', function(store, records, options) {
        if (records && records.length > 0) {
            moviesGrid.getSelectionModel().selectFirstRow();
        }
    });
    moviesStore.load();
}); // onReady
```

How it works...

The form's fields are updated with the movie's details when a grid row is selected:

```
moviesGrid.getSelectionModel().on('rowselect',
    function(sm, rowIndex, record) {
        moviesForm.getForm().loadRecord(record);
});
```

You can use the form's `loadRecord(record)` function to load the record into the form. This function works by calling `setValues(...)` with the record data. You can also try to load data into an individual field using the `setValue(...)` function. For example, the `title` field can be changed like this:

```
Ext.getCmp('title').setValue(record.data.title);
```

There's more...

This approach is commonly used in scenarios where the details view must provide facilities for editing the viewed data. If you need a read-only details view, you might choose the grid and panel approach described in the *Creating a master-details view with a grid and a panel* recipe.

See also...

> ▶ The previous recipe, *Creating a master-details view with a grid and a panel*, teaches you how to use a panel to display details about a grid's selected record

> ▶ In the next recipe, *Creating a master-details view with a combo box and a grid*, you will learn how to use a combo box to filter the records shown in a grid

> ▶ The *Creating a master-details view with two grids* recipe (covered later in this chapter) shows how to use two grids for displaying the master-details data relationships

Creating a master-details view with a combo box and a grid

Here's another way of displaying related information in a master-details type of view. In this example, a `ComboBox` component displays a list of movie categories that control the movies list displayed on the `GridPanel` component.

Movies					
Category:	Family				
Title	Category	Rating	Length	Price	
AFRICAN EGG	Family	G	130 min	$2.99	
APACHE DIVINE	Family	NC-17	92 min	$4.99	
ATLANTIS CAUSE	Family	G	170 min	$2.99	
BAKED CLEOPATRA	Family	G	182 min	$2.99	
BANG KWAI	Family	NC-17	87 min	$2.99	
BEDAZZLED MARRIED	Family	PG	73 min	$0.99	
BILKO ANONYMOUS	Family	PG-13	100 min	$4.99	
BLANKET BEVERLY	Family	G	148 min	$2.99	
BLOOD ARGONAUTS	Family	G	71 min	$0.99	
BLUES INSTINCT	Family	G	50 min	$2.99	
BRAVEHEART HUMAN	Family	PG-13	176 min	$2.99	
CHASING FIGHT	Family	PG	114 min	$4.99	
CHISUM BEHAVIOR	Family	G	124 min	$4.99	
CHOCOLAT HARRY	Family	NC-17	101 min	$0.99	
CONFUSED CANDLES	Family	PG-13	122 min	$2.99	

How to do it...

1. Create the data store for the combo box:

```
var categoriesStore = new Ext.data.JsonStore({
    url: 'grid-combo-cascading.php',
    root: 'categories',
    baseParams: { action: 'categories' },
    fields: ['category_id', 'name']
});
```

2. Create the data store for the grid:

```
var moviesStore = new Ext.data.JsonStore({
    url: 'grid-combo-cascading.php',
    root: 'movies',
    totalProperty: 'count',
    baseParams: { action: 'movies' },
    fields: ['id', 'title', 'category', 'rating',
            { name: 'length', type: 'int' },
            { name: 'price', type: 'float'}]
});
```

3. Define the categories combo box:

```
var categoriesCombo = {
   xtype: 'combo',
   store: categoriesStore,
   displayField: 'name',
   valueField: 'category_id',
   editable: false,
   mode: 'remote',
   forceSelection: true,
   triggerAction: 'all',
   emptyText: 'Select a category...',
   selectOnFocus: true,
   listeners: {
      'select': function(cmb, rec, idx) {
         moviesStore.load({
                 params: { 'category': this.getValue() }
         });
      }
   }
}
```

4. Define the movies grid and place the categories combo box in the grid's toolbar:

```
Ext.onReady(function() {
   var moviesGrid = new Ext.grid.GridPanel({
       title: 'Movies',
       renderTo: Ext.getBody(),
       store: moviesStore,
       columns: [{ header: "ID", width: 30, dataIndex: 'fid',
                   sortable: true, hidden: true },
          { id: 'title-col',
            header: "Title",
            width: 180,
            dataIndex: 'title',
            sortable: true
          },
          { header: "Category", width: 65, dataIndex: 'category',
            sortable: true },
          { header: "Rating",
            width: 65,
            dataIndex: 'rating',
            sortable: true
```

```
        },
        { header: "Length",
          width: 65,
          dataIndex: 'length',
          sortable: true,
          align: 'right',
          renderer: function(v) {
             return v + ' min';
          }
        },
        { header: "Price",
          width: 65,
          dataIndex: 'price',
          sortable: true,
          align: 'right',
          renderer: Ext.util.Format.usMoney
        }
      ],
      autoExpandColumn: 'title-col',
      width: 570,
      height: 400,
      loadMask: true,
      columnLines: true,
      viewConfig: {
         forceFit: true
      },
      tbar: new Ext.Toolbar({
         items: [{ xtype: 'tbtext', text: 'Category:' }, ' ',
            categoriesCombo]
      })
   });
}); // onReady
```

How it works...

The categories combo box is easily placed in the grid panel's toolbar:

```
tbar: new Ext.Toolbar({
    items: [{ xtype: 'tbtext', text: 'Category:' }, ' ',
      categoriesCombo]
})
```

The handler for the `select` event of the combo box calls the `load()` method of the `moviesStore`, submitting the selected category to the server:

```
listeners: {
    'select': function(cmb, rec, idx) {
        moviesStore.load({
            params: { 'category': this.getValue() }
        });
    }
}
```

There's more...

This is a convenient approach when the amount of data displayed on the details grid is too large. By using a combo box to filter the details information, you reduce the data being moved and focus the user's attention on the information that's relevant in a given context.

You're not restricted to using a ComboBox component as the master data filter. You can also use components such as checkboxes, or devise a more complex filtering UI built with multiple input elements.

See also...

- ▶ The *Creating a master-details view with a grid and a panel* recipe (covered earlier in this chapter) teaches you how to use a panel to display details about a grid's selected record

- ▶ The previous recipe, *Creating a master-details view with a grid and a form*, explains how to display the properties of a data record using a form

- ▶ The next recipe, *Creating a master-details view with two grids*, shows how to use two grids for displaying the master-details data relationships

Creating a master-details view with two grids

A pair of grids is a very typical combination for displaying master-detail relationships. Here's an example using actors' and movies' information. When an actress is selected in the **Actors** grid, her movies will be shown by the **Movies** grid like this:

Actors	
First Name	Last Name
PENELOPE	GUINESS
NICK	WAHLBERG
ED	CHASE
JENNIFER	DAVIS
JOHNNY	LOLLOBRIGIDA
BETTE	NICHOLSON
GRACE	MOSTEL

Movies staring BETTE NICHOLSON

Title	Rating	Length	Price
ANTITRUST TOMATOES	NC-17	168 min	$2.99
BANG KWAI	NC-17	87 min	$2.99
BEAST HUNCHBACK	R	89 min	$4.99
BIKINI BORROWERS	NC 17	142 min	$4.99
CALENDAR GUNFIGHT	NC-17	120 min	$4.99
COAST RAINBOW	PG	55 min	$0.99
COLDBLOODED DARLING	G	70 min	$4.99
CROSSROADS CASUALTIES	G	153 min	$2.99
DROP WATERFRONT	R	178 min	$4.99
IGBY MAKER	NC-17	160 min	$4.99
KRAMER CHOCOLATE	R	171 min	$2.99

How to do it...

1. Create a data store for the actors grid:

```
var actorsStore = new Ext.data.JsonStore({
    url: 'grid-master-details.php',
    root: 'actors',
    baseParams: { action: 'actors' },
    fields: ['actor_id', 'first_name', 'last_name']
});
```

2. Create a data store for the movies grid:

```
var moviesStore = new Ext.data.JsonStore({
    url: 'grid-master-details.php',
    root: 'movies',
    totalProperty: 'count',
    baseParams: { action: 'movies' },
    fields: ['film_id', 'title', 'rating',
            { name: 'length', type: 'int' },
            { name: 'price', type: 'float'}]
});
```

3. Define the actors grid:

```
Ext.onReady(function() {
    var actorsGrid = new Ext.grid.GridPanel({
        title: 'Actors',
        renderTo: 'actors-div',
        store: actorsStore,
        sm: new Ext.grid.RowSelectionModel({ singleSelect: true }),
        columns: [{ header: "actor_id", width: 30, dataIndex: 'fid',
                sortable: true, hidden: true },
            { id: 'first-name',
                header: "First Name",
                width: 150,
                dataIndex: 'first_name',
                sortable: true
            },
            { id: 'last-name',
                header: "Last Name",
                width: 150,
                dataIndex: 'last_name',
                sortable: true
            }
        ],
        autoExpandColumn: 'last-name',
        width: 570,
        height: 200,
        loadMask: true,
        viewConfig: {
            forceFit: true
        }
    });
```

4. Define the movies grid:

```
var moviesGrid = new Ext.grid.GridPanel({
    title: 'Movies',
    renderTo: 'movies-div',
    store: moviesStore,
    columns: [{ header: "ID", width: 30, dataIndex: 'film_id',
                sortable: true, hidden: true },
        { id: 'title-col',
            header: "Title",
            width: 180,
            dataIndex: 'title',
            sortable: true
        },
        { header: "Rating",
            width: 65,
            dataIndex: 'rating',
            sortable: true
        },
        { header: "Length",
            width: 65,
            dataIndex: 'length',
            sortable: true,
            align: 'right',
            renderer: function(v) {
                return v + ' min';
            }
        },
        { header: "Price",
            width: 65,
            dataIndex: 'price',
            sortable: true,
            align: 'right',
            renderer: Ext.util.Format.usMoney
        }
    ],
    autoExpandColumn: 'title-col',
    width: 570,
    height: 300,
    loadMask: true,
    columnLines: true,
```

```
            viewConfig: {
                forceFit: true
            }
        });
```

5. Add a handler for the `rowselect` event of the actors grid:

```
actorsGrid.getSelectionModel().on('rowselect',
    function(sm, rowIndex, record) {
        moviesGrid.setTitle('Movies starring ' +
            record.data.first_name + ' ' + record.data.last_name);
        moviesStore.load({ params: { 'actor':
            record.data.actor_id} });
    });
actorsStore.load();
}); // onReady
```

How it works...

The `rowselect` event's handler in the actors grid updates the movies grid panel's title and calls the `load()` method on the movies store, which submits the selected actor's id to the server and retrieves the filtered movies list:

```
actorsGrid.getSelectionModel().on('rowselect',
    function(sm, rowIndex, record) {
        moviesGrid.setTitle('Movies starring ' +
            record.data.first_name + ' ' + record.data.last_name);
        moviesStore.load({
            params: { 'actor': record.data.actor_id}
        });
    });
```

Note how the actors grid allows for selecting one actor at a time using the `singleSelect` config option on its selection model:

```
sm: new Ext.grid.RowSelectionModel({ singleSelect: true }),
```

There's more...

Use this approach when you need to display one-to-many relationships. One-to-one relationships are better shown with the grid and panel, or grid and form fields approaches described in the *Creating a master-details view with a grid and a panel* and *Creating a master-details view with a grid and a form* recipes.

- ▶ The *Creating a master-details view with a grid and a panel* recipe (covered earlier in this chapter) teaches you how to use a panel to display details about a grid's selected record

- ▶ The *Creating a master-details view with a grid and a form* recipe (covered earlier in this chapter) explains how to display the properties of a data record using a form

- ▶ In the previous recipe, *Creating a master-details view with a combo box and a grid*, you learned how to use a combo box to filter the records shown in a grid

Displaying large recordsets with a buffered grid

Sometimes, it is convenient to render grid rows as they are needed, in order to improve performance in the presence of large recordsets. The movies grid in this recipe uses the new `BufferView` class, which provides the grid with the ability to render rows as they scroll into view. The end result will look like this:

Movies					
	Title ▲	Category	Rating	Length	Price
872	TALENTED HOMICIDE	Sports	PG	173 min	$0.99
873	TARZAN VIDEOTAPE	Horror	PG-13	91 min	$2.99
874	TAXI KICK	Music	PG-13	64 min	$0.99
875	TEEN APOLLO	Travel	G	74 min	$4.99
876	TELEGRAPH VOYAGE	Music	PG	148 min	$4.99
877	TELEMARK HEARTBREAKERS	Animation	PG-13	152 min	$2.99
878	TEMPLE ATTRACTION	Horror	PG	71 min	$4.99
879	TENENBAUMS COMMAND	Drama	PG-13	99 min	$0.99
880	TEQUILA PAST	Children	PG	53 min	$4.99
881	TERMINATOR CLUB	Music	R	88 min	$4.99
882	TEXAS WATCH	Horror	NC-17	179 min	$0.99
883	THEORY MERMAID	Animation	PG-13	184 min	$0.99

How to do it...

1. Include the `BufferView.js` file:

```
<script type="text/javascript" src="BufferView.js"></script>
```

> The `BufferView.js` file can be obtained from the Ext JS 3.0 samples at
> `http://extjs.com/deploy/dev/examples/grid/buffer.html`.

2. Define the movies data store:

```
var store = new Ext.data.JsonStore({
    url: 'grid-buffer-view.php',
    root: 'movies',
    idProperty: 'id',
    totalProperty: 'count',
    fields: ['id', 'title', 'category', 'rating', 'actors',
             { name: 'length', type: 'int' },
             { name: 'price', type: 'float' },
             'description'],
    remoteSort: true
});
store.setDefaultSort('title', 'asc');
```

3. Create a grid that will display the movies list and use a `BufferView` instance as its view:

```
Ext.onReady(function() {
    var grid = new Ext.grid.GridPanel({
        title: 'Movies',
        store: store,
        width:600,
        height: 300,
        loadMask: true,
        renderTo: Ext.getBody(),
        view: new Ext.ux.BufferView({
            // Render rows as they come into viewable area.
            scrollDelay: false
        }),
        autoExpandColumn: 'title-col',
        columns: [
            new Ext.grid.RowNumberer(),
            { header: "ID", width: 30, dataIndex: 'fid',
              sortable: true, hidden: true },
            { id: 'title-col',
                header: "Title",
                width: 180,
                dataIndex: 'title',
                sortable: true
            },
            { header: "Category", width: 65,
              dataIndex: 'category', sortable: true },
            { header: "Rating",
                width: 65,
```

```
                      dataIndex: 'rating',
                      sortable: true
                  },
                  { header: "Length",
                      width: 65,
                      dataIndex: 'length',
                      sortable: true,
                      align: 'right',
                      renderer: function(v) {
                          return v + ' min';
                      }
                  },
                  { header: "Price",
                      width: 65,
                      dataIndex: 'price',
                      sortable: true,
                      align: 'right',
                      renderer: Ext.util.Format.usMoney
                  }
              ],
              viewConfig: {
                  forceFit: true
              }
          });
          store.load();
      }); // onReady
```

How it works...

Rows can be rendered as they come into view with the use of the `BufferView` instance as the grid panel's view:

```
view: new Ext.ux.BufferView({
    // Render rows as they come into viewable area.
    scrollDelay: false
}),
```

The `BufferView` class is a custom `GridView` that caches a number of the rows that have already been rendered. This cache can be changed with the `cacheSize` config option.

See also...

▶ The next recipe, *Using the lightweight ListView class*, explains how to display the read-only tabular data with a little overhead

Using the lightweight ListView class

The new `ListView` class is a high-performance, lightweight implementation of a grid-like display. In this recipe, we use it to display a read-only list of movies as shown in the following screenshot:

Movies List				
Title ▲	**Category**	**Rating**	**Length**	**Price**
EGG IGBY	Documentary	PG	67 min	$2.99
EGYPT TENENBAUMS	Horror	PG	85 min	$0.99
ELEMENT FREDDY	Comedy	NC-17	115 min	$4.99
ELEPHANT TROJAN	Horror	PG-13	126 min	$4.99
ELF MURDER	Music	NC-17	155 min	$4.99
ELIZABETH SHANE	Sports	NC-17	152 min	$4.99
EMPIRE MALKOVICH	Children	G	177 min	$0.99
ENCINO ELF	Games	G	143 min	$0.99
ENCOUNTERS CURTAIN	Drama	NC-17	92 min	$0.99
ENDING CROWDS	New	NC-17	85 min	$0.99
ENEMY ODDS	Music	NC-17	77 min	$4.99
ENGLISH BULWORTH	Sci-Fi	PG-13	51 min	$0.99
ENOUGH RAGING	Travel	NC-17	158 min	$2.99

How to do it...

1. Create a data store for the movies list view:

```
var store = new Ext.data.JsonStore({
    url: 'grid-listview.php',
    root: 'movies',
    idProperty: 'id',
    totalProperty: 'count',
    fields: ['id', 'title', 'category', 'rating',
            { name: 'length', type: 'int' },
            { name: 'price', type: 'float' },
            'description']
});
store.setDefaultSort('title', 'asc');
```

2. Define the movies list view:

```
Ext.onReady(function() {
    var moviesListView = new Ext.ListView({
        store: store,
        multiSelect: false,
        emptyText: 'No images to display',
```

```
          reserveScrollOffset: true,
          loadingText: 'Loading movies...',
          columns: [{
             header: 'Title',
             width: .4,
             dataIndex: 'title'
          }, {
                header: 'Category',
                width: .15,
                dataIndex: 'category'
          }, {
                header: 'Rating',
                dataIndex: 'rating',
                width: .15,
                align: 'right'
          }, {
                header: 'Length',
                dataIndex: 'length',
                width: .15,
                align: 'right',
                tpl: '{length} min'
          }, {
                header: 'Price',
                dataIndex: 'price',
                width: .15,
                align: 'right',
                tpl: '{price:usMoney}'
          }]
       });
```

3. Build a container for the list view:

```
       var moviesPanel = new Ext.Panel({
          id: 'movies-panel',
          renderTo: Ext.getBody(),
          width: 525,
          height: 300,
          layout: 'fit',
          title: 'Movies List',
          items: moviesListView
       });
       store.load();
    }); // onReady
```

How it works...

The `ListView` class uses templates to render the data in any required format, such as in the `Length` and `Price` columns:

```
{
    header: 'Length',
    dataIndex: 'length',
    width: .15,
    align: 'right',
    tpl: '{length} min'
}, {
    header: 'Price',
    dataIndex: 'price',
    width: .15,
    align: 'right',
    tpl: '{price:usMoney}'
}
```

Although `ListView` has no horizontal scrolling, it provides selection, column resizing, sorting, and other features inherited from the `DataView` class. Column widths are specified by percentage, based on the container width and the number of columns.

There's more...

With the addition of the `ListView` class to Ext JS, you have another option for displaying tabular information—especially if you're implementing a read-only UI that does not require all of the features of the `GridPanel` component.

See also...

> ▶ The previous recipe, *Displaying large recordsets with a buffered grid*, explains how to improve your UI's performance in the presence of large recordsets

Editing rows with the RowEditor plugin

The `RowEditor` plugin is another great addition to Ext, which allows you to rapidly edit full rows in a grid. The **Customers** grid in this recipe shows you how to use `RowEditor`.

Customers			
➕ New ✖ Delete			
First Name	**Last Name**	**Phone**	**Email**
MARY	SMITH	28303384290	MARY.SMITH@sakilacustomer.org
PATRICIA	JOHNSON	838635286649	PATRICIA.JOHNSON@sakilacustomer.org
LINDA	WILLIAMS	448477190408	LINDA.WILLIAMS@sakilacustomer.org
BARBARA	JONES	705814003527	BARBARA.JONES@sakilacustomer.org
ELIZABETH	BROWN	10655648674	ELIZABETH.BROWN@sakilacustomer.org
JENNIFER	DAVIS	[Update] [Cancel]	JENNIFER.DAVIS@sakilacustomer.org
MARIA	MILLER		MARIA.MILLER@sakilacustomer.org
SUSAN	WILSON	657282285970	SUSAN.WILSON@sakilacustomer.org
MARGARET	MOORE	380657522649	MARGARET.MOORE@sakilacustomer.org
DOROTHY	TAYLOR	648856936185	DOROTHY.TAYLOR@sakilacustomer.org
LISA	ANDERSON	635297277345	LISA.ANDERSON@sakilacustomer.org
NANCY	THOMAS	465887807014	NANCY.THOMAS@sakilacustomer.org
KAREN	JACKSON	695479687538	KAREN.JACKSON@sakilacustomer.org
BETTY	WHITE	517338314235	BETTY.WHITE@sakilacustomer.org
HELEN	HARRIS	990911107354	HELEN.HARRIS@sakilacustomer.org
SANDRA	MARTIN	949312333307	SANDRA.MARTIN@sakilacustomer.org
DONNA	THOMPSON	407752414682	DONNA.THOMPSON@sakilacustomer.org
CAROL	GARCIA	747791594069	CAROL.GARCIA@sakilacustomer.org
RUTH	MARTINEZ	272572357893	RUTH.MARTINEZ@sakilacustomer.org

How to do It...

1. Include the `RowEditor.js` file in your project:

    ```
    <script type="text/javascript" src="RowEditor.js"></script>
    ```

    The `RowEditor.js` file can be obtained from the Ext JS 3.0 samples at `http://extjs.com/deploy/dev/examples/grid/row-editor.html`.

2. Define the fields for the customers data store:

    ```
    var custFields = [{
        name:'ID',
        type: 'int'
    },{
        name: 'first_name',
        type: 'string'
    }, {
        name: 'last_name',
        type: 'string'
    }, {
    ```

```
            name:'phone',
            type:'string'
    }, {
            name: 'email',
            type: 'string'
}]
        var Customer = Ext.data.Record.create(custFields);
```

3. Create a data store for the customers grid:

```
var customersStore = new Ext.data.JsonStore({
    url: 'grid-row-editor.php',
    root: 'customers',
    fields: custFields
});
```

4. Create a data store for the cities combo box:

```
var citiesStore = new Ext.data.JsonStore({
    url: 'grid-row-editor.php',
    baseParams: { xaction: 'cities' },
    root: 'cities',
    fields: ['city_id', 'city']
});
```

5. Define the RowEditor instance:

```
var editor = new Ext.ux.RowEditor({
    saveText: 'Update'
});
```

6. Build an EditorGridPanel with a toolbar containing the **New** and **Delete** customer buttons:

```
Ext.onReady(function() {
    var grid = new Ext.grid.EditorGridPanel({
        title: 'Customers',
        store: customersStore,
        plugins: [editor],
        sm: new Ext.grid.RowSelectionModel({ singleSelect: true }),
        tbar: [{
            iconCls: 'icon-add',
            text: 'New',
            handler: function() {
                var cust = new Customer({
                    Id:'0',
                    first_name: '[First name]',
```

```
                last_name: '[Last Name]',
                phone:'[Phone Number]',
                email: 'user@domain.com'
            });
            editor.stopEditing();
            customersStore.insert(0, cust);
            grid.getView().refresh();
            grid.getSelectionModel().selectRow(0);
            editor.startEditing(0);
        }
    },'-', {
        ref: '../removeBtn',
        iconCls: 'icon-del',
        text: 'Delete',
        disabled: true,
        handler: function() {
            editor.stopEditing();
            var s = grid.getSelectionModel().getSelections();
            for (var i = 0, r; r = s[i]; i++) {
                customersStore.remove(r);
            }
        }
    }],
    columns: [
    { header: "ID", width: 30, dataIndex: 'ID',
      sortable: true, hidden: true },
    { id: 'fname',
        header: "First Name",
        width: 180,
        dataIndex: 'first_name',
        sortable: true,
        editor: new Ext.form.TextField({
            allowBlank: false
        })
    },
    { id: 'lname',
        header: "Last Name",
        width: 160,
        dataIndex: 'last_name',
        sortable: true,
        editor: new Ext.form.TextField({
```

```
                        allowBlank: false
                    })
                },
                { header: "Phone",
                    width: 135,
                    dataIndex: 'phone',
                    sortable: true,
                    align: 'left',
                    editor: new Ext.form.TextField({
                        allowBlank: false
                    })
                },
                { id:'email',
                    header: "Email",
                    width: 95,
                    dataIndex: 'email',
                    sortable: true,
                    align: 'left',
                    editor: new Ext.form.TextField({
                        allowBlank: false,
                        vtype: 'email'
                    })
                }
            ],
            autoExpandColumn:'email',
            renderTo: Ext.getBody(),
            width: 750,
            height: 500,
            loadMask: true
        });
        grid.getSelectionModel().on('selectionchange', function(sm) {
            grid.removeBtn.setDisabled(sm.getCount() < 1);
        });
        customersStore.load();
    }); // onReady
```

How it works...

New records are created in the handler for the **New** button:

```
tbar: [{
    iconCls: 'icon-add',
    text: 'New',
    handler: function() {
        var cust = new Customer({
            Id:'0',
            first_name: '[First name]',
            last_name: '[Last Name]',
```

```
        phone:'[Phone Number]',
          email: 'user@domain.com'
      });
      editor.stopEditing();
      customersStore.insert(0, cust);
      grid.getView().refresh();
      grid.getSelectionModel().selectRow(0);
      editor.startEditing(0);
    }
  }
```

After a new `Customer` instance is added to the customers store, the grid's view is refreshed and the `RowEditor` component is put in edit mode so that the user can enter values for the newly created record.

Deletions are implemented in the handler for the **Delete** button. Changes through the `RowEditor` components are interrupted with a call to `stopEditing()`, and any selected records in the grid are removed from the store:

```
  {
      ref: '../removeBtn',
      iconCls: 'icon-del',
      text: 'Delete',
      disabled: true,
      handler: function() {
      editor.stopEditing();
      var s = grid.getSelectionModel().getSelections();
      for (var i - 0, r; r - s[i]; i++) {
          customersStore.remove(r);
      }
  }
```

Double-clicking on any row activates the `RowEditor` component for editing the selected record.

See also...

> ▶ The *Changing grid panel data using cell editors* recipe from Chapter 5 explains how to use the different cell editors to allow for in-place editing of the record data

Adding tool tips to grid cells

This recipe teaches you how to add tool tips to the columns of the grid component. The grid created using this recipe will look like this:

How to do it...

1. Start the QuickTips singleton:

   ```
   Ext.QuickTips.init();
   ```

2. Create the fields for the customers grid:

   ```
   var custFields = [{
           name:'ID',
           type: 'int'
   },{
           name: 'first_name',
           type: 'string'
   }, {
           name: 'last_name',
           type: 'string'
   }, {
           name:'phone',
           type:'string'
   }, {
   ```

```
        name: 'email',
        type: 'string'
}]
```

3. Create a `Customer` record based on the already defined customer fields:

```
var Customer = Ext.data.Record.create(custFields);
```

4. Create the data store for the customers grid:

```
var customersStore = new Ext.data.JsonStore({
    url: 'grid-cell-qtip.php',
    root: 'customers',
    fields: custFields
});
```

5. An `XTemplate` instance defines the format of the tool tips:

```
var tpl = new
  Ext.XTemplate('<div><b>Phone:</b> {phone}</div>',
     '<div><b>Email</b>: {email}</div>');
```

6. Define a custom rendering function for the grid's cells. This renderer uses the above `XTemplate` to provide a cell tool tip:

```
var renderCell = function(val, cell, record) {
    var qtip = this.tpl.apply(record.data);
    return '<div qtip="' + qtip + '">' + val + '</div>';
}
```

7. Build the customers grid and use the already defined renderer function on the `First Name` and `Last Name` columns:

```
Ext.onReady(function() {
    var grid = new Ext.grid.GridPanel({
        title: 'Customers',
        store: customersStore,
        sm: new Ext.grid.RowSelectionModel({ singleSelect: true }),
          columns: [
          { header: "ID", width: 30, dataIndex: 'ID',
            sortable: true, hidden: true },
          { id: 'fname',
              header: "First Name",
              width: 180,
              dataIndex: 'first_name',
              sortable: true,
              renderer: this.renderCell.createDelegate(this)
          },
```

```
                        { id: 'lname',k
                            header: "Last Name",
                            width: 160,
                            dataIndex: 'last_name',
                            sortable: true,
                            renderer: this.renderCell.createDelegate(this)
                        }],
                        autoExpandColumn:'lname',
                        renderTo: Ext.getBody(),
                        width: 400,
                        height: 350,
                        loadMask: true
                    });
                    customersStore.load();
                }); // onReady
```

How it works...

The tooltips are drawn through the use of a custom renderer function for the First Name and Last Name columns:

```
{ id: 'fname',
    header: "First Name",
    width: 180,
    dataIndex: 'first_name',
    sortable: true,
    renderer: this.renderCell.createDelegate(this)
},
{ id: 'lname',
    header: "Last Name",
    width: 160,
    dataIndex: 'last_name',
    sortable: true,
    renderer: this.renderCell.createDelegate(this)
}
```

In the renderer function, an XTemplate instance is used to format the contents of the tooltip. There is also a div with the qtip attribute that allows displaying the tooltip information together with the cell's value:

```
var renderCell = function(val, cell, record) {
    var qtip = this.tpl.apply(record.data);
    return '<div qtip="' + qtip + '">' + val + '</div>';
}
```

Using the PropertyGrid class

The `PropertyGrid` class is a grid implementation similar to the property grids so commonly used in different IDEs. Each row in the property grid represents a property of some object. In this example, each row represents a property of a movie from a movies list:

How to do it...

1. Create a data store for the property grid:

```
var moviesStore = new Ext.data.JsonStore({
    url: 'grid-property-grid.php',
    root: 'movies',
    totalProperty: 'count',
    baseParams: { action: 'movies' },
    fields: [{ name: 'film_id' },
        { name: 'title' },
        { name: 'rating' },
        { name: 'length', type: 'int' },
        { name: 'price', type: 'float' },
        { name: 'last_rented', type:'date'}]
});
```

2. Define the property grid:

```
Ext.onReady(function() {
    var movieGrid = new Ext.grid.PropertyGrid({
        title: 'Properties Grid',
        autoHeight: true,
        width: 300,
        renderTo: Ext.getBody()
    });
```

3. A handler for the store's `load` event will set the first record as the source for the property grid:

```
moviesStore.on('load', function(store, records, options) {
    if (records && records.length > 0) {
        movieGrid.setSource(moviesStore.getAt(0).data);
    }
});
moviesStore.load();
}); // onReady
```

How it works...

A call to `setSource()` specifies the record containing the data for the property grid. In this example, the first record retrieved from the server is used:

```
moviesStore.on('load', function(store, records, options) {
    if (records && records.length > 0) {
        movieGrid.setSource(moviesStore.getAt(0).data);
    }
});
```

Through its column model (`PropertyColumnModel` class), `PropertyGrid` has the ability to display editors for the date, string, number and boolean data types.

Using drag-and-drop between two grids

If you have worked with data mining and analysis interfaces, you have probably seen the application of drag-and-drop feature between two grids. This recipe explains how you can enable drag-and-drop between two grids in Ext JS.

The example uses a **Movies** grid and a **Selected Movies** grid, as shown in the next screenshot:

Movies			
Title	**Rating**	**Length**	**Price**
ALASKA PHANTOM	PG	136 min	$0.99
ALI FOREVER	PG	150 min	$4.99
ALICE FANTASIA	NC-17	94 min	$0.99
ALIEN CENTER	NC-17	46 min	$2.99
ALLEY EVOLUTION	NC-17	180 min	$2.99
ALONE TRIP	R	82 min	$0.99
ALTER VICTORY	PG-13	57 min	$0.99
AMADEUS HOLY	PG	113 min	$0.99
AMELIE HELLFIGHTERS	R	79 min	$4.99
AMERICAN CIRCUS	R	129 min	$4.99
AMISTAD MIDSUMMER	G	85 min	$2.99

Selected Movies			
Title	**Rating**	**Length**	**Price**

3 selected rows

If you drag the selected rows in the **Movies** grid and drop them in the **Selected Movies** grid, the grids' data stores will be updated to reflect the changes:

Movies			
Title	**Rating**	**Length**	**Price**
ALASKA PHANTOM	PG	136 min	$0.99
ALI FOREVER	PG	150 min	$4.99
ALONE TRIP	R	82 min	$0.99
ALTER VICTORY	PG-13	57 min	$0.99
AMADEUS HOLY	PG	113 min	$0.99
AMELIE HELLFIGHTERS	R	79 min	$4.99
AMERICAN CIRCUS	R	129 min	$4.99
AMISTAD MIDSUMMER	G	85 min	$2.99
ANACONDA CONFESSIONS	R	92 min	$0.99
ANALYZE HOOSIERS	R	181 min	$2.99
ANGELS LIFE	G	74 min	$2.99

Selected Movies			
Title ▲	**Rating**	**Length**	**Price**
ALICE FANTASIA	NC-17	94 min	$0.99
ALIEN CENTER	NC-17	46 min	$2.99
ALLEY EVOLUTION	NC-17	180 min	$2.99

How to do it...

1. Create fields for the two data stores used:

```
var sharedFields = ['film_id', 'title', 'rating',
    { name: 'length', type: 'int' },
    { name: 'price', type: 'float' }
]
```

2. Create a data store for the available movies grid:

```
var moviesStore = new Ext.data.JsonStore({
    url: 'grid-to-grid-drag-drop.php',
    root: 'movies',
    totalProperty: 'count',
    baseParams: { action: 'movies' },
    fields: sharedFields
});
```

3. Create a data store for the selected movies grid:

```
var selectedMoviesStore = new Ext.data.JsonStore({
    root: 'movies',
    fields: sharedFields
});
```

4. Define the colums that both grids will display:

```
var sharedColumns = { header: "ID",
        width: 30,
        dataIndex: 'film_id',
        sortable: true,
        hidden: true
    },
    { id: 'title-col',
      header: "Title",
      width: 180,
      dataIndex: 'title',
      sortable: true
    },
    { header: "Rating",
        width: 45,
        dataIndex: 'rating',
        sortable: true
    },
    { header: "Length",
        width: 45,
        dataIndex: 'length',
```

```
            sortable: true,
            align: 'right',
            renderer: function(v) {
                return v + ' min';
            }
        },
        { header: "Price",
            width: 45,
            dataIndex: 'price',
            sortable: true,
            align: 'right',
            renderer: Ext.util.Format.usMoney
        }
    ]
```

5. Create the available movies grid. Make sure drag-and-drop is enabled and a ddGroup is defined:

```
Ext.onReady(function() {
    var moviesGrid = new Ext.grid.GridPanel({
        title: 'Movies',
        enableDragDrop: true,
        ddGroup: 'selectedMoviesDDGroup',
        renderTo: 'movies-div',
        store: moviesStore,
        columns: sharedColumns,
        autoExpandColumn: 'title-col',
        width: 370,
        height: 300,
        loadMask: true,
        columnLines: true,
        viewConfig: {
            forceFit: true
        }
    });
```

6. Create the selected movies grid. As with the first grid, make sure drag-and-drop is enabled and a ddGroup is defined:

```
    var selectedMoviesGrid = new Ext.grid.GridPanel({
        title: 'Selected Movies',
        enableDragDrop: true,
        ddGroup: 'availableMoviesDDGroup',
        renderTo: 'selected-movies-div',
        store: selectedMoviesStore,
        columns: sharedColumns,
```

```
        autoExpandColumn: 'title-col',
        width: 370,
        height: 300,
        loadMask: true,
        columnLines: true,
        viewConfig: {
            forceFit: true
        }
    });
```

7. Define a drop target for the available movies grid:

```
var moviesGridDropTargetEl =
    moviesGrid.getView().el.dom.childNodes[0].childNodes[1];
var moviesGridDropTarget = new
    Ext.dd.DropTarget(moviesGridDropTargetEl, {
    ddGroup: 'availableMoviesDDGroup',
    copy: true,
    notifyDrop: function(ddSource, e, data) {
        function addRow(record, index, allItems) {
            var foundItem = moviesStore.find('title',
                record.data.name);
            if (foundItem == -1) {
                moviesStore.add(record);
                moviesStore.sort('title', 'ASC');
                ddSource.grid.store.remove(record);
            }
        }
        Ext.each(ddSource.dragData.selections, addRow);
        return (true);
    }
});
// This will make sure we only drop to the view container
var selectedMoviesGridDropTargetEl =
selectedMoviesGrid.getView().el.dom.childNodes[0].childNodes[1]
```

8. Define a drop target for the selected movies grid:

```
var selectedMoviesGridDropTarget = new
Ext.dd.DropTarget(selectedMoviesGridDropTargetEl, {
    ddGroup: 'selectedMoviesDDGroup',
    copy: false,
    notifyDrop: function(ddSource, e, data) {
        function addRow(record, index, allItems) {
```

```
        var foundItem = selectedMoviesStore.find('title',
          record.data.name);
        if (foundItem == -1) {
          selectedMoviesStore.add(record);
          selectedMoviesStore.sort('title', 'ASC');
          ddSource.grid.store.remove(record);
        }
      }
      Ext.each(ddSource.dragData.selections, addRow);
      return (true);
    }
  });
  moviesStore.load();
}); // onReady
```

How it works...

Although the figures portray dragging rows from the available movies grid to the selected movies grid, it is also possible to move rows back to the available movies grid. The explanation for this is that both grids have drag-and-drop enabled.

Each grid contains a drop target that allows for dropping rows coming from the other grid. Visually, it appears that the rows are moving from one grid to the other. In reality, records are being removed from the source store and added to the target store. These changes in the stores cause the grids to refresh.

The notifyDrop() functions in each drop target call the addRow() function for each of the selected records on the source store:

```
Ext.each(ddSource.dragData.selections, addRow);
```

AddRow() adds the record to the target store and removes it from the source store:

```
function addRow(record, index, allItems) {
    var foundItem = selectedMoviesStore.find('title',
      record.data.name);
    if (foundItem == -1) {
      selectedMoviesStore.add(record);
      selectedMoviesStore.sort('title', 'ASC');
      ddSource.grid.store.remove(record);
    }
}
```

7

Keeping Tabs on Your Trees

In this chapter, you will learn the following recipes:

- ▸ Handling tab activation
- ▸ Loading tab data with Ajax
- ▸ Adding tabs dynamically
- ▸ Enhancing a `TabPanel` with plugins: The `Close` menu
- ▸ Enhancing a `TabPanel` with plugins: The `TabScroller` menu
- ▸ Populating nodes with server-side data, reordering nodes
- ▸ Tree and panel in a master-details relationship
- ▸ Multi-column TreePanel
- ▸ Drag-and-drop between tree panels
- ▸ Drag-and-drop from a tree to a panel

Introduction

This chapter explores how `TabPanel` widgets can be used to group components or information under the same container. It also explains how hierarchical views of information can be built using the Ext JS tree view widget.

Handling tab activation

This recipe explains how you can execute code when a `TabPanel`'s tab is activated. In this recipe's sample tab panel, activating the second tab initiates a request, which will populate the tab with server-side data. You can see this in the following screenshot:

How to do it...

1. Define the `TabPanel` and add a listener for the `activate` event:

```
Ext.onReady(function() {
    var tabs = new Ext.TabPanel({
        renderTo: document.body,
        activeTab: 0,
        width: 500,
        height: 250,
        plain: true,
        defaults: { autoScroll: true },
        items: [{
            title: 'First Tab',
            HTML: ""
        },{
            title: 'Load on tab activation',
            bodyStyle: 'padding:5px;',
            listeners: { activate: activationHandler }
        }]
    });
```

2. Create the handler function for the `activate` event:

```
    function activationHandler(tab) {
        tab.load({ url: 'tabs-ajax-load.php', params:
        'xaction=load' });
        }
});
```

How it works...

The `activate` event indicates that a panel has been visually activated. The handler for this event is passed a reference to the activated panel.

Panels do not directly support being activated, unless they are children of a `TabPanel`. However, there are some panel subclasses (such as the `Window` class) that support activation.

See also...

▶ The next recipe, *Loading tab data with Ajax*, explains how to load content into a tab when the tab is first activated

▶ The *Adding tabs dynamically* recipe (covered later in this chapter) illustrates how the dynamic addition of tabs to a tab panel can be implemented

Loading tab data with Ajax

In this recipe, you will learn how to load static and dynamic content into a `TabPanel`'s tab when the tab is first activated.

A sample `TabPanel`'s tabs will load data from an HTML file, as seen below:

Another tab will receive its contents from a server page that makes a database call, as shown in the following screenshot:

Getting ready...

The sample data used in this recipe comes from the Sakila sample database.

 You can obtain the Sakila database, as well as the installation instructions, at `http://dev.mysql.com/doc`.

How to do it...

1. Define the `Tabpanel`:

```
Ext.onReady(function() {
    var tabs = new Ext.TabPanel({
        renderTo: document.body,
        activeTab: 0,
        width: 500,
        height: 250,
        plain: true,
        defaults: { autoScroll: true },
```

2. On the tabs, use the `autoLoad` config option to specify the page that will provide the tab's contents:

```
items: [{
        title: 'First Tab',
        HTML: ""
    }, {
        title: 'Ajax load from HTML file',
        bodyStyle: 'padding:5px;',
        autoLoad: { url: 'tabs-ajax-load-data.HTML' }
    }, {
    title: 'Ajax load from DB',
        bodyStyle:'padding:5px;',
        autoLoad: { url: 'tabs-ajax-load.php' }
    }
    ]
});
});
```

How it works...

When the `autoLoad` option is present, the panel will try to load its contents immediately upon rendering. The URL specified in `autoLoad` becomes the default URL for the panel's body element, and it may be refreshed at any time.

See also...

- ▶ The *Handling tab activation* recipe (seen previously in this chapter) shows how you can execute code when a `TabPanel`'s tab is activated
- ▶ The next recipe, *Adding tabs dynamically*, teaches you how the dynamic addition of tabs to a `TabPanel` can be implemented

Adding tabs dynamically

A scenario found in many web applications is the dynamic addition of tabs to a `TabPanel`. This recipe teaches you a simple way of using a button that, when it is clicked on, executes code that creates a tab, as shown in the following screenshot:

How to do it...

1. Define the `TabPanel`:

```
Ext.onReady(function() {
    var tabs=new Ext.TabPanel({
        renderTo: 'tabs',
        resizeTabs: true,
        minTabWidth: 115,
        tabWidth: 135,
        enableTabScroll: true,
        width: 500,
        height: 250,
        defaults: { autoScroll: true }
    });
```

2. Add a few tabs to start up with:

```
// Create some tabs.
    var index=0;
    while (index < 3) {
        addTab(index);
        index++;
    }
```

3. Create a function that adds tabs dynamically:

```
function addTab(index) {
    var tab=tabs.add({
        title: 'New Tab ' + (index),
        iconCls: 'icon-tab',
        bodyStyle:'padding: 5px',
        HTML: 'Tab Body ' + (index) + '<br/><br/>',
        closable: true
    });
    tab.show();
}
```

4. Define a button that will call the newly created function:

```
var btn=new Ext.Button({
        text: 'Add a tab',
        handler: addTab,
        iconCls: 'icon-new-tab'
    })
    btn.render('button');
});
```

How it works...

You can dynamically add tabs (panels) to a `TabPanel` by calling the `TabPanel`'s `add()` method and passing the desired configuration for the tab. This is possible because the `TabPanel` uses a `Ext.layout.CardLayout` layout manager, which handles the sizing and positioning of child components.

Other layout managers that support the dynamic addition of child components are `Ext.layout.AnchorLayout`, `Ext.layout.FormLayout`, and `Ext.layout.TableLayout`.

See also...

▸ The previous recipe, *Loading tab data with Ajax*, explains how to load content into a tab when the tab is first activated

> ► The *Handling tab activation* recipe (seen earlier in this chapter) explains how you can execute code when a `TabPanel`'s tab is activated

Enhancing a TabPanel with plugins: The Close menu

This is another example of extending a component's features. Here, you'll use the `TabCloseMenu` plugin to add a **Close** menu to the tabs in a `TabPanel`. This menu allows the user to close either the selected tab, or all the tabs but the selected one, as seen in the following screenshot:

Getting ready...

In order to use the `TabCloseMenu` plugin, you need to locate and include the `TabCloseMenu.js` file. The `TabCloseMenu.js` file can be obtained from this book's sample code.

How to do it...

1. Create the styles for the button and the tabs:

```css
<style type="text/css">
        .icon-new-tab
        {
        background:url(img/add2.png) 0 no-repeat !important;
        }
        .icon-tab
        {
        background:url(img/star-yellow.png) 0 no-repeat
!important;
        }
</style>
```

2. Include the `TabCloseMenu.js` plugin file:

```html
<script src="TabCloseMenu.js" type="text/javascript"></script>
```

3. Define the `TabPanel` and assign an instance of the `TabCloseMenu` class to the plugin's `config` object:

```
Ext.onReady(function() {
    var tabs = new Ext.TabPanel({
        renderTo: 'tabs',
        resizeTabs: true,
        minTabWidth: 115,
        tabWidth: 135,
        enableTabScroll: true,
        width: 500,
        height: 250,
        defaults: { autoScroll: true },
        plugins: new Ext.ux.TabCloseMenu()
    });
    // Create some tabs.
    var index = 0;
    while (index < 3) {
        addTab();
    }
```

4. Create a function that adds tabs on the fly:

```
function addTab() {
        var tab=tabs.add({
            title: 'New Tab '+(++index),
            iconCls: 'icon-tab',
            bodyStyle:'padding: 5px',
            HTML: 'Tab Body '+(index)+'<br/><br/>',
            closable: true
        });
        tab.show();
}
```

5. Define a button that will call the newly created function:

```
var btn=new Ext.Button({
        text: 'Add a tab',
        handler: addTab,
        iconCls: 'icon-new-tab'
    })
    btn.render('button');
});
```

How it works...

The `TabCloseMenu` plugin adds a `Close` menu to the tabs with two actions. One action is to close the active panel and the other one is to close all the panels, except the active panel. The menu's code looks like this:

```
menu=new Ext.menu.Menu({
    items: [{
        id: tabs.id+'-close',
        text: 'Close',
        handler: function() {
            tabs.remove(ctxItem);
        }
    }, {
        id: tabs.id+'-close-others',
        text: 'Close All But This',
        handler: function() {
            tabs.items.each(function(item) {
                if (item.closable && item!=ctxItem) {
                    tabs.remove(item);
                }
            });
        }
    }]
});
```

Observe how the act of closing a tab consists of instructing the container panel to remove the tab component from its items collection.

You can customize this menu (text, icons, for example) by modifying the code in the TabCloseMenu.js file and also the styles defined for the plugin.

See also...

▸ The next recipe, *Enhancing a TabPanel with plugins: The TabScroller menu*, explains how to create a menu that provides easy access to any of the tabs of a TabPanel

Enhancing a TabPanel with plugins: The TabScroller menu

The TabScrollerMenu plugin is another example of how to extend a component's features. Used on a TabPanel, this plugin builds a menu that provides easy access to any of the tabs without having to resort to the panel's default tab-scrolling behavior, as seen below:

Getting ready...

Obtain the `TabScrollerMenu.js`, `tab-scroller-menu.gif`, and `tab-scroller-menu.css` files from the Ext JS samples page at `http://extjs.com/deploy/dev/examples/tabs/tab-scroller-menu.html`.

How to do it...

1. Create the styles for the button and tabs:

```
icon-new-tab
{
    background:url(img/add2.png) 0 no-repeat !important;
}
icon-tab
{
    background:url(img/star-yellow.png) 0 no-repeat !important;
}
```

2. Include the styles used in the `TabScrollerMenu` plugin:

```
<link href="tab-scroller-menu.css" rel="stylesheet" type="text/css" />
```

3. Include the `TabScrollerMenu` plugin file:

```
<script src="TabScrollerMenu.js" type="text/javascript"></script>
```

4. Create an instance of the `TabScrollerMenu` class that will be used by the `TabPanel`:

```
Ext.onReady(function() {
    Ext.QuickTips.init();
    var scrollerMenu = new Ext.ux.TabScrollerMenu({
        maxText: 15,
        pageSize: 5,
        menuPrefixText:'Tabs'
    });
```

5. Define the `TabPanel` and use the `scrollerMenu` plugin:

```
var tabs = new Ext.TabPanel({
        renderTo: 'tabs',
        resizeTabs: true,
        enableTabScroll: true,
        minTabWidth: 100,
        width: 500,
```

```
        height: 250,
        defaults: { autoScroll: true },
        plugins: [scrollerMenu]
    });
```

6. Add enough tabs so that the `TabScrollerMenu` can be shown:

```
// Create some tabs.
    var index = 0;
    while (index < 15) {
        var tab = tabs.add({
            title: 'New Tab ' + (++index),
            iconCls: 'icon-tab',
            bodyStyle: 'padding: 5px',
            HTML: 'Tab Body ' + (index) + '<br/><br/>',
            closable: true
        });
        tab.show();
    }
});
```

How it works...

The `TabScrollerMenu` class is a plugin that inserts a context menu in the header area of the `TabPanel` instance. This menu contains an item for each tab of the `TabPanel`. Clicking on any of these items activates the corresponding tab.

There's more...

A disadvantage of tabbed interfaces presents itself when dealing with many tabs at once, particularly when the number of tabs exceeds the available area of the container. Using this plugin helps to deal with tab clutter by giving the user fast access to any tab, without having to resort to the default scrolling behavior of the `TabPanel`.

See also...

▶ The *Enhancing a TabPanel with plugins: The Close menu,* explains how to enhance a `TabPanel` with a menu that allows the user to close either the selected tab, or all the tabs but the selected one

Populating tree nodes with server-side data

This recipe explains how you can use dynamic content to populate the nodes of a TreePanel. The TreePanel in this recipe belongs to a fictitious report development tool and it will display various properties of a reporting project, as shown in the following screenshot:

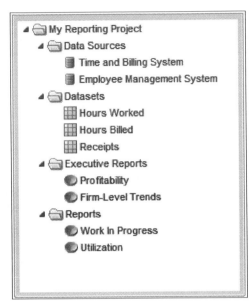

How to do it...

1. Create styles for the tree-node icons:

```
report
{
    background:url(img/pie-chart.png) 0 no-repeat !important;
}
dataset
{
    background:url(img/table.png) 0 no-repeat !important;
}
datasource
{
    background:url(img/data.png) 0 no-repeat !important;
}
```

2. Define the `TreePanel`:

```
Ext.onReady(function() {
    var tree = new Ext.tree.TreePanel({
        el: 'tree-reorder',
        frame:true,
        width: 250,
        height:400,
        useArrows: true,
        autoScroll: true,
        animate: true,
        enableDD: true,
        containerScroll: true,
        border: false,
        dataUrl: 'tree-ajax-load.php',
```

3. In the `TreePanel`, create the `root` node and finish the tree's definition:

```
root: {
        nodeType: 'async',
        text: 'My Reporting Project',
        draggable: false,
        id: 'project'
    }
});
```

4. Render the tree:

```
tree.render();
```

5. Expand the root node and its child nodes. This causes the data to be retrieved from the server:

```
tree.getRootNode().expand(true);
});
```

How it works...

The `dataUrl` config option is the URL from which a JSON string representing an array of node definition objects is requested. These node definition objects will become the child nodes of the tree. To simplify the example, `dataUrl` is specified directly on the `TreePanel` instead of explicitly creating a `TreeLoader` instance.

Expanding the `root` node with a call to `expand(true)` causes the root's children nodes to expand as well.

Tree and panel in a master-details relationship

A master-details page interface can be built using a tree and a panel component.
In this recipe, you'll use a panel to display additional details about the selected node on
a `TreePanel`, as seen in the following screenshot:

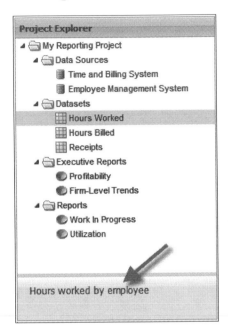

How to do it...

1. Create the styles for the tree node icons:

```
report
{
    background:url(img/pie-chart.png) 0 no-repeat !important;
}
dataset
{
    background:url(img/table.png) 0 no-repeat !important;
}
datasource
{
    background:url(img/data.png) 0 no-repeat !important;
}
```

2. Create the initial text for the panel body:

```
var pnlBody = 'Select an item to see its information';
```

3. Create and compile a template to be used on the panel body:

```
var tpl = new Ext.Template('<p>{description}</p>');
tpl.compile();
```

4. Define the `TreePanel`:

```
Ext.onReady(function() {
    var tree = new Ext.tree.TreePanel({
        height: 350,
        region:'center',
        useArrows: true,
        autoScroll: true,
        animate: true,
        enableDD: true,
        containerScroll: true,
        border: false,
        dataUrl: 'tree-panel-master-details.php',
        root: {
            nodeType: 'async',
            text: 'My Reporting Project',
            draggable: false,
            id: 'project'
        }
    });
```

5. Define the container for the `TreePanel` and details panel, and define the details panel in line:

```
    new Ext.Panel({
        title: 'Project Explorer',
        renderTo: document.body,
        layout: 'border',
        width: 250,
        height: 500,
        items: [tree, {
            region: 'south',
            id: 'details-panel',
            autoScroll: true,
            split: true,
            height: 150,
            baseCls: 'x-box-mc',
```

```
                HTML: pnlBody,
                bodyStyle:'padding:5px'
        }]
    });
```

6. Attach a handler to the tree's selection model so that you can update the details panel when the selected node changes:

```
    tree.getSelectionModel().on('selectionchange', function(tree,
    node) {
            var el = Ext.getCmp('details-panel').body;
            tpl.overwrite(el, node.attributes);
    })
```

7. Expand the tree's root node and its children:

```
    tree.getRootNode().expand(true);
    });
```

How it works...

All the action occurs when a tree node is selected, so a handler for the `selectionchange` event is used. Inside the handler, a call to the `overwrite(...)` method of the `Ext.Template` instance makes it possible to write the selected node's `description` to the body of the panel.

Since all the selected node's attributes are passed in the call to `Ext.Template` `overwrite(...)`, you can easily add more details to the panel's body by altering the declaration of the template. For example, you could add the node's `name` using the following code:

```
    var tpl=new Ext.Template('<p>Name: {name}<br/>{description}</
    p>');
```

There's more...

This solution can be used when the node's underlying data object has numerous properties that need to be clearly displayed. When the amount of detail is minimal, using a tool tip on the node might suffice.

See also...

▸   The *Drag-and-drop from a tree to a panel* recipe (seen later in this chapter) teaches you how to drop tree nodes onto a panel and have the panel display details about the dropped node

The multi-column TreePanel

This recipe describes how to add grid view-like features to a `TreePanel` using a plugin, as seen in the following screenshot:

Getting ready...

The `column-tree.css`, `column-tree.js`, and `ColumnNodeUI.js` files used in this recipe can be obtained from the Ext JS 3.0 samples page at `http://extjs.com/deploy/dev/examples/tree/column-tree.html`.

How to do it...

1. Add the styles needed for the multi-column tree:

   ```
   <link href="column-tree.css" rel="stylesheet" type="text/css" />
   ```

2. Add the `ColumnNodeUI` class and `ColumTree` class definitions, contained in the `ColumnNodeUI.js` and `column-tree.js` files:

   ```
   <script type="text/javascript" src="../ux/ColumnNodeUI.js"></script>
   <script src="column-tree.js" type="text/javascript"></script>
   ```

3. Create an instance of the `ColumnTree` class:

   ```
   Ext.onReady(function() {
       var tree = new Ext.tree.ColumnTree({
           width: 620,
           height: 300,
           rootVisible: false,
           autoScroll: true,
           title: 'Product Backlog',
   ```

```
                    renderTo: Ext.getBody(),
```

4. In the `ColumnTree` instance declaration, define the multiple columns of the tree:

```
columns: [{
            header: 'Item',
            width: 400,
            dataIndex: 'task'
       }, {
            header: 'Planned',
            width: 60,
            dataIndex: 'planned'
       }, {
            header: 'Actual',
            width: 60,
            dataIndex: 'actual'
       }, {
            header: 'Status',
            width: 80,
            dataIndex: 'status'
   }],
```

5. Define the loader for the multi-column tree and use an instance of the `ColumnNodeUI` class as the UI provider:

```
loader: new Ext.tree.TreeLoader({
            dataUrl: 'column-tree-data.txt',
            requestMethod:'GET',
            uiProviders: {
                'col': Ext.tree.ColumnNodeUI
            }
       }),
       root: new Ext.tree.AsyncTreeNode({
            text: 'Tasks'
       })
   });
});
```

How it works...

The `ColumnTree` class is a `TreePanel` extension that displays nodes in a multi-column fashion. The multi-column display is achieved by using the `ColumnNodeUI` class, an extension of `TreeNodeUI`, as the node's UI implementation.

`ColumnTree` requires a definition of the tree columns through the `columns` config option. Observe how each column in the tree is tied to a property of the node's underlying data object by means of the `dataIndex` config option:

```
columns: [{
        header: 'Item',
        width: 400,
        dataIndex: 'task'
    }, {
        header: 'Planned',
        width: 60,
        dataIndex: 'planned'
    }, {
        header: 'Actual',
        width: 60,
        dataIndex: 'actual'
    }, {
        header: 'Status',
        width: 80,
        dataIndex: 'status'
    }]
```

There's more...

This recipe can be used when the node's underlying data object has numerous properties that need to be clearly displayed. Be mindful that you need to allocate sufficient screen real estate for the additional tree columns.

Drag-and-drop between tree panels

Dragging and dropping nodes between two trees is an easy-to-accomplish task due to the native drag-and-drop support in the `TreePanel`. This recipe explains how it's done, as shown in the following screenshot:

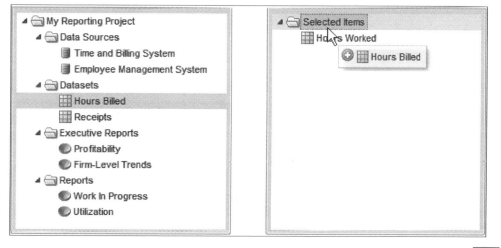

How to do it...

1. Create the styles for the tree-node icons:

```
report
{
    background:url(img/pie-chart.png) 0 no-repeat !important;
}
dataset
{
    background:url(img/table.png) 0 no-repeat !important;
}
datasource
{
    background:url(img/data.png) 0 no-repeat !important;
}
```

2. Define the source tree. Be sure to enable the drag-and-drop feature:

```
Ext.onReady(function() {
    var leftTree = new Ext.tree.TreePanel({
        el: 'leftTree',
        frame:true,
        width: 250,
        height:400,
        useArrows: true,
        autoScroll: true,
        animate: true,
        enableDD: true,
        dropConfig: {appendOnly:true},
        containerScroll: true,
        border: false,
        loader: {
            dataUrl: 'tree-drag-drop-trees.php',
            baseParams: { tree: 'leftTree' }
        },
        root: {
            nodeType: 'async',
            text: 'My Reporting Project',
            draggable: false,
            id: 'project'
        }
    });
```

3. Define the destination tree. Enable drag-and-drop on this one, too:

```
var rightTree = new Ext.tree.TreePanel({
        el: 'rightTree',
        frame: true,
        width: 250,
        height: 400,
        useArrows: true,
        autoScroll: true,
        animate: true,
        enableDD: true,
        dropConfig: {appendOnly:true},
        containerScroll: true,
        border: false,
        loader:{
            dataUrl: 'tree-drag-drop-trees.php',
            baseParams:{tree:'rightTree'}
        },
        root: {
            text: 'Selected Items',
            draggable: false,
            id: 'selected-items'
        }
    });
```

4. Render both trees and expand their root nodes:

```
    leftTree.render();
    rightTree.render();
    leftTree.getRootNode().expand(true);
    rightTree.getRootNode().expand(false);
    });
```

How it works...

The `TreePanel` class has a native support for the drag-and-drop feature. Setting the `enableDD` config option to `true` is all that is needed to obtain the desired results.

See also...

> ▸ The next recipe, *Drag-and-drop from a tree to a panel*, teaches you how to drop tree nodes onto a panel and program the panel to display details about the dropped node

Drag-and-drop from a tree to a panel

This is another take on the master-details interfaces with a tree and a panel component, but this time it has the ability to drop tree nodes onto the details panel, as shown below:

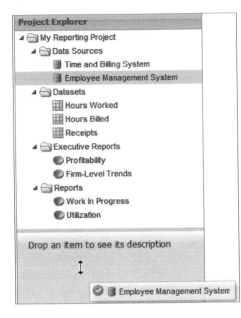

After a node is dropped on the panel, the panel will display the underlying data object's description, as seen in the following screenshot:

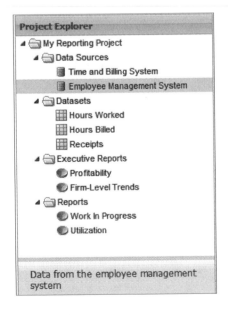

How to do it...

1. Create the styles for the tree-node icons:

```
report
{
    background:url(img/pie-chart.png) 0 no-repeat !important;
}
dataset
{
    background:url(img/table.png) 0 no-repeat !important;
}
datasource
{
    background:url(img/data.png) 0 no-repeat !important;
}
```

2. Create the initial text to show on the details panel:

```
var pnlBody='Drop an item to see its description';
```

3. Create and compile a template to be used on the panel body:

```
var tpl=new Ext.Template('<p class="">{description}</p>');
tpl.compile();
```

4. Define the TreePanel:

```
Ext.onReady(function() {
    var tree = new Ext.tree.TreePanel({
        height: 350,
        region:'center',
        useArrows: true,
        autoScroll: true,
        animate: true,
        enableDD: true,
        ddGroup: 'treeDDGroup',
        containerScroll: true,
        border: false,
        dataUrl: 'tree-panel-drag-drop.php',
        root: {
            nodeType: 'async',
            text: 'My Reporting Project',
            draggable: false,
            id: 'project'
        }
    });
```

5. Define a container for the `TreePanel` and the details panel:

```
new Ext.Panel({
    title: 'Project Explorer',
    renderTo: document.body,
    layout: 'border',
    width: 250,
    height: 500,
```

6. Define the details panel inline:

```
items: [tree, new Ext.Panel({
            region: 'south',
            id: 'details-panel',
            autoScroll: true,
            split: true,
            height: 150,
            baseCls:'x-box-mc',
            HTML: pnlBody,
            bodyStyle:'padding:5px'
        })]
});
```

7. Define the details panel's body as a drop target for items dragged from the tree:

```
var detailsPanel = Ext.getCmp('details-panel');
var pnlDropTargetEl = detailsPanel.body;
var pnlDropTarget = new Ext.dd.DropTarget(pnlDropTargetEl, {
            ddGroup: 'treeDDGroup',
            copy: false,
            notifyDrop: function(ddSource, e, data) {
                var el = detailsPanel.body;
                tpl.overwrite(el, data.node.attributes);
                return true;
            }
});
```

8. Retrieve the tree's nodes:

```
    tree.getRootNode().expand(true);
});
```

How it works...

As the `TreePanel` natively supports the drag-and-drop operations, all you need is to give the details panel the ability to catch the nodes that will be dropped onto its body. This is accomplished by creating an `Ext.dd.DropTarget` instance and adding it to the body of the details panel.

You'll need to specify that the `DropTarget` will interact only with objects originating from the tree by configuring it with the tree's `ddGroup`:

```
ddGroup: 'treeDDGroup'
```

The `notifyDrop` function is called when a node has been dropped. This is where you call the `overwrite(...)` method of the `Ext.Template` instance, which makes it possible to write the selected node's `description` to the body of the panel.

Observe how `notifyDrop` returns `true` to signal to the drag source that the drop was successful.

See also...

▶ The *Drag-and-drop between tree panels* recipe (seen earlier in this chapter) explains how nodes could be dragged and dropped between two tree panels

▶ The *Tree and panel in a master-details relationship* recipe (seen earlier in this chapter) illustrates how a `Panel` could be set up to display details about the selected node on a `TreePanel`

8

Making Progress with Menus and Toolbars

This chapter will teach you the following recipes:

- ▸ Placing buttons in a toolbar
- ▸ Working with the new ButtonGroup component
- ▸ Placing menus in a toolbar
- ▸ Commonly used menu items
- ▸ Embedding a progress bar in a status bar
- ▸ Creating a custom look for the status bar items
- ▸ Using a progress bar to indicate that your application is busy
- ▸ Using a progress bar to report progress updates
- ▸ Changing the look of a progress bar

Introduction

In this chapter, you will learn how to use menus, toolbars, and progress bars. Along with an examination of the commonly used menu items, the recipes in this chapter will teach you how to work with the new ButtonGroup component as well as the different ways to set up toolbars and progress bars in your applications.

Placing buttons in a toolbar

You can embed different types of components in a toolbar. This recipe teaches you how to build a toolbar that contains image-only, text-only and image/text buttons, a toggle button, and a combo box.

How to do it...

1. Create the styles for the toolbar items:

```
#tbar
{
    width:600px;
}
.icon-data
{
    background:url(img/data.png) 0 no-repeat !important;
}
.icon-chart
{
    background:url(img/pie-chart.png) 0 no-repeat !important;
}
.icon-table
{
    background:url(img/table.png) 0 no-repeat !important;
}
```

2. Define a data store for the combo box:

```
Ext.onReady(function() {
    Ext.QuickTips.init();
    var makesStore = new Ext.data.ArrayStore({
        fields: ['make'],
        data: makes // from cars.js
    });
```

3. Create a toolbar and define the buttons and combo box inline:

```
var tb = new Ext.Toolbar({
    renderTo: 'tbar',
    items: [{
        iconCls: 'icon-data',
```

```
            tooltip: 'Icon only button',
            handler:clickHandler
        }, '-',
        {
            text: 'Text Button'
        }, '-',
        {
            text: 'Image/Text Button',
            iconCls: 'icon-chart'
        }, '-',
        {
            text: 'Toggle Button',
            iconCls: 'icon-table',
            enableToggle: true,
            toggleHandler: toggleHandler,
            pressed: true
        }, '->', 'Make: ',
        {
            xtype: 'combo',
            store: makesStore,
            displayField: 'make',
            typeAhead: true,
            mode: 'local',
            triggerAction: 'all',
            emptyText: 'Select a make...',
            selectOnFocus: true,
            width: 135
        }]
    });
```

4. Finally, create handlers for the push button and the toggle button:

```
function clickHandler(btn) {
    Ext.Msg.alert('clickHandler', 'button pressed');
}
function toggleHandler(item, pressed) {
    Ext.Msg.alert('toggleHandler', 'toggle pressed');
}
```

How it works...

The buttons and the combo box are declared inline. While the standard button uses a click handler through the `handler` config option, the toggle button requires the `toggleHandler` config option.

The button icons are set with the `iconCls` option, using the classes declared in the first step of the recipe.

As an example, note the use of the `Toolbar.Separator` instances in this fragment:

```
}, '-', {
  text: 'Text Button'
}, '-', {
    text: 'Image/Text Button',
    iconCls: 'icon-chart'
}, '-', {
```

Using `'-'` to declare a `Toolbar.Separator` is equivalent to using `xtype: 'tbseparator'`. Similarly, using `'->'` to declare `Toolbar.Fill` is equivalent to using `xtype:'tbfill'`.

See also...

> ▶ The next recipe, *Working with the new ButtonGroup component*, explains how to use the `ButtonGroup` class to organize a series of related buttons

Working with the new ButtonGroup component

A welcome addition to Ext JS is the ability to organize buttons in groups. Here's how to create a panel with a toolbar that contains two button groups:

How to do it...

1. Create the styles for the buttons:

```css
#tbar
{
    width:600px;
}
.icon-data
{
    background:url(img/data.png) 0 no-repeat !important;
}
.icon-chart
{
    background:url(img/pie-chart.png) 0 no-repeat !important;
}
.icon-table
{
    background:url(img/table.png) 0 no-repeat !important;
}
.icon-sort-asc
{
    background:url(img/sort-asc.png) 0 no-repeat !important;
}
.icon-sort-desc
{
    background:url(img/sort-desc.png) 0 no-repeat !important;
}
.icon-filter
{
    background:url(img/funnel.png) 0 no-repeat !important;
}
```

2. Define a panel that will host the toolbar:

```javascript
Ext.onReady(function() {
    var pnl = new Ext.Panel({
        title: 'My Application',
        renderTo:'pnl-div',
        height: 300,
        width: 500,
        bodyStyle: 'padding:10px',
        autoScroll: true,
```

3. Define a toolbar inline and create two button groups:

```javascript
tbar: [{
    xtype: 'buttongroup',
    title: 'Data Connections',
    columns: 1,
    defaults: {
        scale: 'small'
```

```
                },
                items: [{
                    xtype:'button',
                    text: 'Data Sources',
                    iconCls:'icon-data'
                }, {
                    xtype: 'button',
                    text: 'Tables',
                    iconCls: 'icon-table'
                }, {
                    xtype: 'button',
                    text: 'Reports',
                    iconCls: 'icon-chart'
                }]
            }, {
                xtype: 'buttongroup',
                title: 'Sort & Filter',
                columns: 1,
                defaults: {
                    scale: 'small'
                },
                items: [{
                    xtype: 'button',
                    text: 'Sort Ascending',
                    iconCls: 'icon-sort-asc'
                }, {
                    xtype: 'button',
                    text: 'Sort Descending',
                    iconCls: 'icon-sort-desc'
                }, {
                    xtype: 'button',
                    text: 'Filter',
                    iconCls: 'icon-filter'
                }]
            }]
```

How it works...

Using a button group consists of adding a step to the process of adding buttons, or other items, to a toolbar. Instead of adding the items directly to the toolbar, you need to firstly define the group and then add the items to the group:

```
tbar: [{
    xtype: 'buttongroup',
    title: 'Data Connections',
    columns: 1,
    defaults: {
        scale: 'small'
    },
```

```
items: [{
    xtype:'button',
    text: 'Data Sources',
    iconCls:'icon-data'
}, {
    xtype: 'button',
    text: 'Tables',
    iconCls: 'icon-table'
}, {
    xtype: 'button',
    text: 'Reports',
    iconCls: 'icon-chart'
}]
}
```

See also...

▸ The next recipe, *Placing buttons in a toolbar*, illustrates how you can embed different types of components in a toolbar

Placing menus in a toolbar

In this recipe, you will see how simple it is to use menus inside a toolbar. The panel's toolbar that we will build, contains a standard button and a split button, both with menus.

How to do it...

1. Create the styles for the buttons:

```
#tbar
{
    width:600px;
}
.icon-data
{
    background:url(img/data.png) 0 no-repeat !important;
}
```

```
.icon-chart
{
    background:url(img/pie-chart.png) 0 no-repeat !important;
}
.icon-table
{
    background:url(img/table.png) 0 no-repeat !important;
}
```

2. Create a click handler for the menus:

```
Ext.onReady(function() {
    Ext.QuickTips.init();
    var clickHandler = function(action) {
        alert('Menu clicked: "' + action + '"');
    };
```

3. Create a window to host the toolbar:

```
var wnd = new Ext.Window({
    title: 'Toolbar with menus',
    closable: false,
    height: 300,
    width: 500,
    bodyStyle: 'padding:10px',
    autoScroll: true,
```

4. Define the window's toolbar inline, and add the buttons and their respective menus:

```
tbar: [{
    text: 'Button with menu',
    iconCls: 'icon-table',
    menu: [
        { text: 'Menu 1',
          handler:clickHandler.createCallback('Menu 1'),
          iconCls: 'icon-data' },
        { text: 'Menu 1',
          handler: clickHandler.createCallback('Menu 2'),
          iconCls: 'icon-data'}]
}, '-',
{
    xtype: 'splitbutton',
    text: 'Split button with menu',
    iconCls: 'icon-chart',
    handler: clickHandler.createCallback('Split button with
      menu'),
    menu: [
        { text: 'Menu 3',
          handler: clickHandler.createCallback('Menu 3'),
          iconCls: 'icon-data' },
```

```
            { text: 'Menu 4',
              handler: clickHandler.createCallback('Menu 4'),
              iconCls: 'icon-data'}]
       }]
   });
```

5. Finally, show the window:

```
wnd.show();
```

How it works...

This is a simple procedure. Note how the split button is declared with the `xtype:`
`'splitbutton'` config option. Also, observe how the `createCallback()` function is used
to invoke the `clickHandler()` function with the correct arguments for each button.

See also...

▸ The next recipe, *Commonly used menu items*, shows the different items that can be
used in a menu

Commonly used menu items

To show you the different items that can be used in a menu, we will build a menu that
contains radio items, a checkbox menu, a date menu, and a color menu.

This is how the radio options and checkbox menu will look:

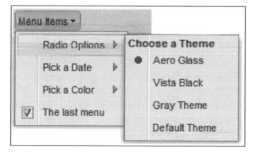

The **Pick a Date** menu item will display a date picker, as shown in the next screenshot:

The **Pick a Color** menu item displays a color picker, as seen here:

How to do it...

1. Create a handler for the checkbox menu:

```
Ext.onReady(function() {
    Ext.QuickTips.init();
    var onCheckHandler = function(item, checked) {
        Ext.Msg.alert('Menu checked', item.text + ', checked: ' +
        (checked ? 'checked' : 'unchecked'));
    };
```

2. Define a date menu:

```
var dateMenu = new Ext.menu.DateMenu({
    handler: function(dp, date) {
        Ext.Msg.alert('Date picker', date);
    }
});
```

3. Define a color menu:

```
var colorMenu = new Ext.menu.ColorMenu({
    handler: function(cm, color) {
        Ext.Msg.alert('Color picker', String.format('You picked
        {0}.', color));
    }
});
```

4. Create a main menu. Now add the date and color menus, as well as a few inline menus:

```
var menu = new Ext.menu.Menu({
    id: 'mainMenu',
    items: [{
        text: 'Radio Options',
        menu: {
            items: [
                '<b>Choose a Theme</b>',
                {
                    text: 'Aero Glass',
                    checked: true,
                    group: 'theme',
                    checkHandler: onCheckHandler
                }, {
                    text: 'Vista Black',
                    checked: false,
                    group: 'theme',
                    checkHandler: onCheckHandler
                }, {
                    text: 'Gray Theme',
                    checked: false,
                    group: 'theme',
                    checkHandler: onCheckHandler
                }, {
                    text: 'Default Theme',
                    checked: false,
                    group: 'theme',
                    checkHandler: onCheckHandler
                }
            ]
        }
    },
    {
        text: 'Pick a Date',
        iconCls: 'calendar',
        menu: dateMenu
    },
    {
```

```
            text: 'Pick a Color',
            menu: colorMenu
        },
        {
            text: 'The last menu',
            checked: true,
            checkHandler: onCheckHandler
        }]
    });
```

5. Create a toolbar and add the main menu:

```
var tb = new Ext.Toolbar({
    renderTo: 'tbar',
    items: [{
        text: 'Menu Items',
        menu: menu
    }]
});
```

How it works...

After defining the date and color pickers, the main menu is built. This menu contains the pickers, as well as a few more items that are defined inline.

To display checked items (see the `checked: true` config option) with a radio button instead of a checkbox, the menu items need to be defined using the `group` config option. This is how the theme selector menu is built:

```
menu: {
    items: [
        '<b>Choose a Theme</b>',
        {
            text: 'Aero Glass',
            checked: true,
            group: 'theme',
            checkHandler: onCheckHandler
        },
        {
            text: 'Vista Black',
            checked: false,
            group: 'theme',
            checkHandler: onCheckHandler
```

See also...

▶ The *Placing buttons in a toolbar* recipe (covered earlier in this chapter) illustrates how you can embed different types of components in a toolbar

Embedding a progress bar in a status bar

This recipe explains how to embed a progress bar in a panel's status bar, a scenario found in countless user interfaces:

How to do it...

1. Create a click handler that will simulate a long-running activity and update the progress bar:

```
Ext.onReady(function() {
    var loadFn = function(btn, statusBar) {
        btn = Ext.getCmp(btn);
        btn.disable();
        Ext.fly('statusTxt').update('Saving...');
        pBar.wait({
            interval: 200,
            duration: 5000,
            increment: 15,
            fn: function() {
                btn.enable();
                Ext.fly('statusTxt').update('Done');
            }
        });
    };
```

2. Create an instance of the progress bar:

```
var pBar = new Ext.ProgressBar({
    id: 'pBar',
    width: 100
});
```

3. Create a host panel and embed the progress bar in the `bbar` of the panel. Also, add a button that will start the progress bar updates:

```
var pnl = new Ext.Panel({
    title: 'Status bar with progress bar',
    renderTo: 'pnl1',
    width: 400,
    height: 200,
    bodyStyle: 'padding:10px;',
    items: [{
        xtype: 'button',
        id: 'btn',
        text: 'Save',
        width:'75',
        handler: loadFn.createCallback('btn', 'sBar')
    }],
    bbar: {
        id: 'sBar',
        items: [{ xtype: 'tbtext', text: '',id:'statusTxt' },'->',
            pBar]
    }
});
```

How it works...

The first step consists of creating `loadFn`, a function that simulates a long-running operation, so that we can see the progress bar animation when the button is clicked. The heart of `loadFn` is a call to `ProgressBar.wait(...)`, which initiates the progress bar in an auto-update mode.

And this is how the status bar is embedded in the `bbar` of the panel:

```
bbar: {
    id: 'sBar',
    items: [{ xtype: 'tbtext', text: '',id:'statusTxt' },'->', pBar]
```

Observe how the progress bar is sent to the rightmost location in the status bar with the help of a `Toolbar.Fill` instance, declared with `'->'`.

See also...

  ▶ The next recipe, *Creating a custom look for the status bar items*, shows how you can easily change the look of a status bar's items using custom styles

Creating a custom look for the status bar items

Customizing the look of toolbar items is relatively simple. In this recipe, you will learn how to create toolbar items with a sunken look that can be found in many desktop applications:

Status bar sunken text items
Cached: 15   Uploaded: 7   Invalid: 2

How to do it...

1. Create the styles that will provide the custom look of the status bar text items:

```
.custom-status-text-panel
{
    border-top:1px solid #99BBE8;
    border-right:1px solid #fff;
    border-bottom:1px solid #fff;
    border-left:1px solid #99BBE8;
    padding:1px 2px 2px 1px;
}
```

2. Create a host panel:

```
Ext.onReady(function() {
    var pnl = new Ext.Panel({
        title: 'Status bar with sunken text items',
        renderTo: 'pnl1',
        width: 400,
        height: 200,
        bodyStyle: 'padding:10px;',
```

3. Define the panel's bbar with the text items:

```
bbar: {
    id: 'sBar',
    items: [
        { id: 'cachedCount', xtype:'tbtext',
          text: 'Cached: 15' }, ' ',
```

```
                { id: 'uploadedCount', xtype: 'tbtext',
                  text: 'Uploaded: 7' }, ' ',
                { id: 'invalidCount', xtype: 'tbtext',
                  text: 'Invalid: 2' }
            ]
        },
```

4. Now, add a handler for the `afterrender` event and use it to modify the styles of the text items:

```
listeners: {
    'afterrender': {
        fn: function() {
            Ext.fly(Ext.getCmp('cachedCount').getEl()).parent().
                addClass('custom-status-text-panel');
            Ext.fly(Ext.getCmp('uploadedCount').getEl()).parent().
                addClass('custom-status-text-panel');
            Ext.fly(Ext.getCmp('invalidCount').getEl()).parent().
                addClass('custom-status-text-panel');
        },
        delay:500
    }
}
```

How it works...

The actual look of the items is defined by the style in the `custom-status-text-panel` CSS class.

After the host panel and toolbar are created and rendered, the look of the items is changed by applying the style to each of the TD elements that contain the items. For example:

```
Ext.fly(Ext.getCmp('uploadedCount').getEl()).parent().
    addClass('custom-status-text-panel');
```

See also...

▶ The previous recipe, *Embedding a progress bar in a status bar*, explains how a progress bar can be embedded in a panel's status bar

Using a progress bar to indicate that your application is busy

This recipe teaches you how to use a progress bar to indicate that your application is busy performing an operation. The next screenshot shows a progress bar built using this recipe:

How to do it...

1. Define the progress bar:

```
Ext.onReady(function() {
    Ext.QuickTips.init();
    var pBar = new Ext.ProgressBar({
        id: 'pBar',
        width: 300,
        renderTo: 'pBarDiv'
    });
```

2. Add a handler for the update event and use it to update the **wait** message:

```
pBar.on('update', function(val) {
    //Handle this event if you need to
    // execute code at each progress interval.
    Ext.fly('pBarText').dom.innerHTML += '.';
});
```

3. Create a click handler for the button that will simulate a long-running activity:

```
var btn = Ext.get('btn');
btn.on('click', function() {
    Ext.fly('pBarText').update('Please wait');
    btn.dom.disabled = true;
    pBar.wait({
        interval: 200,
        duration: 5000,
        increment: 15,
        fn: function() {
            btn.dom.disabled = false;
```

```
              Ext.fly('pBarText').update('Done');
          }
      });
  });
```

4. Add the button to the page:

    ```
    <button id="btn">Start long-running operation</button>
    ```

How it works...

After creating the progress bar, the handler for its `update` event is created. While I use this handler simply to update the text message, you can use it to execute some other code every time that a progress interval occurs.

The click handler for the button calls the progress bar's `wait (...)` function, which causes the progress bar to auto-update at the configured `interval` and reset itself after the configured `duration`:

```
pBar.wait({
    interval: 200,
    duration: 5000,
    increment: 15,
    fn: function() {
        btn.dom.disabled = false;
        Ext.fly('pBarText').update('Done');
    }
});
```

There's more...

The progress bar can also be configured to run indefinitely by not passing the `duration` config option. Clearing the progress bar in this scenario requires a call to the `reset()` function.

See also...

▶ The next recipe, *Using a progress bar to report progress updates*, illustrates how a progress bar can be set up to notify the user that progress is being made in the execution of an operation

▶ The *Changing the look of a progress bar* recipe (covered later in this chapter) shows you how easy it is to change the look of the progress bar using custom styles

Using a progress bar to report progress updates

As its name indicates, a progress bar can be used to notify the user that progress is being made at each step of a long-running operation.

This recipe explains how it is accomplished by using a progress bar to indicate when each of the 10 steps of a fictitious long-running operation are executed:

How to do it...

1. Create an object that will encapsulate the simulation of a long-running operation:

```
var Loader = function() {
}
```

2. Inside the Loader class, create a function that will update the progress bar status:

```
var f = function(v, pbar, btn, count, cb) {
    return function() {
        if (v > count) {
            btn.dom.disabled = false;
            cb();
        }
        else {
            pbar.updateProgress(v / count, 'Loading item ' + v +
                ' of ' + count + '...');
        }
    };
};
```

3. The start() method of the Loader class will trigger the simulation of a long-running operation:

```
return {
    start: function(pbar, btn, count, cb) {
        btn.dom.disabled = true;
        var ms = 5000 / count;
        for (var i = 1; i < (count + 2); i++) {
            setTimeout(f(i, pbar, btn, count, cb), i * ms);
```

```
                  }
              }
          }
      } ();
```

4. Now, it's time to define the progress bar:

```
Ext.onReady(function() {
    var pBar = new Ext.ProgressBar({
        id: 'pBar',
        width: 300,
        renderTo: 'pBarDiv',
        text: 'Loading...'
    });
```

5. After the progress bar, a `click` handler for the button triggers the simulation:

```
        var btn = Ext.get('btn');
        btn.on('click', function() {
            Loader.start(pBar, Ext.get('btn'), 10, function() {
                Ext.getCmp('pBar').reset(true);
                Ext.fly('pBarText').update('Finished').show();
            });
        });
    });
```

6. Add the button to the page:

```
        <button id="btn">Start long-running operation</button>
```

How it works...

The `Loader` class simulates a long-running operation. Its `start(...)` function sets up a timer that periodically invokes the function `f()`, which, in turn, updates the progress bar via `ProgressBar.updateProgress(...)`.

In a real-world scenario, `updateProgress(...)` will be called upon the completion of each of the steps of a long-running operation.

See also...

▶ The previous recipe, *Using a progress bar to indicate that your application is busy*, shows how the progress bar can help to inform users that the UI is busy performing an operation

▶ The next recipe, *Changing the look of a progress bar*, shows you how easy it is to change the look of the progress bar using custom styles

Changing the look of a progress bar

In this recipe, you will learn how easy it is to change the look of the progress bar.

Let's see how it is done.

How to do it...

1. Create the styles for the custom look of the progress bar:

```
.x-progress-wrap.custom {
    height:17px;
    border:1px solid #cccccc;
    overflow:hidden;
    padding:0 2px;
}
.ext-ie .x-progress-wrap.custom {
    height:19px;
}
.custom .x-progress-inner {
    height:17px;
    background: #fff;
}
.custom .x-progress-bar {
    height:15px;
    background:transparent url(img/pbar.gif) repeat-x 0 0;
    border-top:1px solid #BEBEBE;
    border-bottom:1px solid #EFEFEF;
    border-right:0;
}
```

2. Define the progress bar and specify that it will use the `custom` CSS class:

```
Ext.onReady(function() {
    var pBar = new Ext.ProgressBar({
        id: 'pBar',
```

```
        width: 300,
        renderTo: 'pBarDiv',
        cls:'custom'
    });
```

3. Now, create a handler for the progress bar's `update` event that will change the status message shown on the page:

```
pBar.on('update', function(val) {
    //Handle this event if you need to
    // execute code at each progress interval.
    Ext.fly('pBarText').dom.innerHTML += '.';
});
```

4. Create a `click` handler for the button, which simulates a long-running operation:

```
    var btn = Ext.get('btn');
    btn.on('click', function() {
        Ext.fly('pBarText').update('Please wait');
        btn.dom.disabled = true;
        pBar.wait({
            interval: 200,
            duration: 5000,
            increment: 15,
            fn: function() {
                btn.dom.disabled = false;
                Ext.fly('pBarText').update('Done');
            }
        });
    });
});
```

5. Finally, add the button to the page:

```
<button id="btn">Start long-running operation</button>
```

How it works...

Needless to say, the look of the progress bar component is defined by a number of styles. After defining the custom styles in the first step, you just need to make the progress bar aware of these styles by using the `cls` config option:

```
var pBar = new Ext.ProgressBar({
    id: 'pBar',
    width: 300,
    renderTo: 'pBarDiv',
    cls:'custom'
});
```

See also...

▶ The *Using a progress bar to indicate that your application is busy* recipe (covered earlier in this chapter) shows how the progress bar can help to inform users that the user interface is busy performing an operation

▶ The previous recipe, *Using a progress bar to report progress updates*, illustrates how a progress bar can be set up to notify the user at each step of a long-running operation

9
Well-charted Territory

These are the recipes that you will learn in this chapter:

- ▸ Setting up a line chart to display local data
- ▸ Setting up a line chart to display data retrieved from the server
- ▸ Setting up a column chart to display local data
- ▸ Setting up a column chart to display data retrieved from the server
- ▸ Displaying local data with a pie chart
- ▸ Displaying remote data with a pie chart
- ▸ Using a chart component to display multiple data series
- ▸ Creating an auto-refreshing chart
- ▸ Configuring the Slider component to display a custom tip
- ▸ Enhancing the Slider component with custom tick marks

Introduction

This chapter covers the Chart and Slider components. It explores the different chart types, typical usage scenarios of charts when working with visual presentation of data, and the approaches to configuring and customizing the look of the slider widget.

Setting up a line chart to display local data

This recipe explains how to create a line chart that displays data stored in a local array. The array will contain income by month data for a fictitious movie rental company. The chart's X-axis will represent the time-scale (months), whereas the income information will be reflected on the Y-axis. This can be seen in the following screenshot:

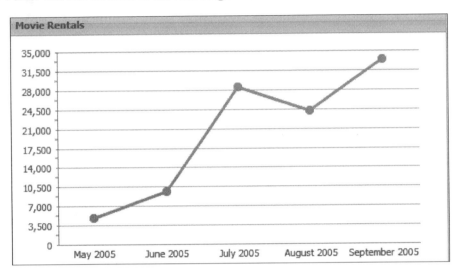

How to do it...

1. Set the URL to load the chart from:

    ```
    Ext.chart.Chart.CHART_URL = '../ext3/charts.swf';
    ```

2. Define the data store:

    ```
    Ext.onReady(function() {
        var rentalsStore = new Ext.data.JsonStore({
            fields: ['month', 'payments'],
            data: [
            { month: 'May 2005', payments: 4824.43 },
            { month: 'June 2005', payments: 9631.88 },
            { month: 'July 2005', payments: 28373.89 },
            { month: 'August 2005', payments: 24072.13 },
            { month: 'September 2005', payments: 33475.55 }
            ]
        });
    ```

3. Create a panel that will contain your chart and define the chart within the panel:

```
var pnl = new Ext.Panel({
    title: 'Movie Rentals',
    renderTo: Ext.getBody(),
    width: 500,
    height: 300,
    layout: 'fit',
    items: {
        xtype: 'linechart',
        store: rentalsStore,
        xField: 'month',
        yField: 'payments',
        yAxis: new Ext.chart.NumericAxis({
            displayName: 'Rentals',
            labelRenderer : Ext.util.Format.
numberRenderer('0,0')
        })
    }
});
});
```

How it works...

To specify a line chart, use `xtype = 'linechart'`; or use `Ext.chart.LineChart` if you want to create the chart explicitly.

To display local data, simply use a local array as the data for the grid's data store.

Notice the presence of an `Ext.util.Format.numberRenderer` instance to format the labels of the Y-axis.

See also...

▶ The next recipe, _Setting up a line chart to display data retrieved from the server_, explains how to create and configure a line chart so that it displays the data that has been downloaded from the server

Setting up a line chart to display data retrieved from the server

This recipe explains how to set up a line chart to display remote data. As with the previous recipe, the information displayed will be income-by-month figures for a fictitious movie rental company. In this case, a server page will retrieve this information from a database and make it available to the chart, as seen in the following screenshot:

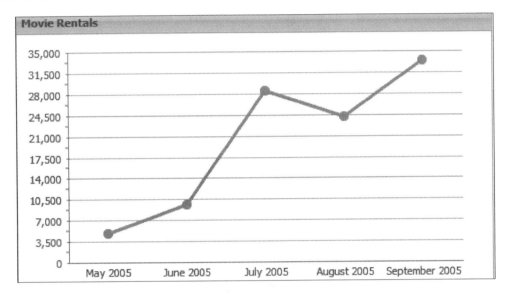

How to do it...

1. Set the URL to load the chart from:

    ```
    Ext.chart.Chart.CHART_URL = '../ext3/charts.swf';
    ```

2. Define the data store:

    ```
    Ext.onReady(function() {
        var rentalsStore = new Ext.data.JsonStore({
            url: 'chart-line-remote.php',
            root: 'rentals',
            fields: ['month', 'payments'],
            autoLoad: true
        });
    ```

3. Create a panel that will contain your chart and define it within the panel:

```
var pnl = new Ext.Panel({
    title: 'Movie Rentals',
    renderTo: Ext.getBody(),
    width: 500,
    height: 300,
    layout: 'fit',
    items: {
        xtype: 'linechart',
        store: rentalsStore,
        xField: 'month',
        yField: 'payments',
        yAxis: new Ext.chart.NumericAxis({
            displayName: 'Rentals',
            labelRenderer : Ext.util.Format.
numberRenderer('0,0')
        })
    }
});
});
```

How it works...

To specify a line chart, use `xtype - 'linechart'`; or use `Ext.chart.LineChart` if you want to create the chart explicitly.

As with other Ext JS data-consuming widgets; to display remote data, simply use a store that acquires the data from a URL:

```
url: 'chart-line-remote.php'
```

Notice the presence of an `Ext.util.Format.numberRenderer` instance to format the labels of the Y-axis.

See also...

▶   The previous recipe, *Setting up a line chart to display local data*, explains how to create a line chart and configure it to display data stored in a local array

Setting up a column chart to display local data

Using a column chart to display local data is very simple. As seen previously in the *How to set up a line chart to display local data* recipe, the data source used in this recipe is an array that contains income-by-month information for a fictitious movie rental company. Similarly, the chart's X-axis will represent the time-scale (months); whereas income information will be reflected on the Y-axis, as shown in the following screenshot:

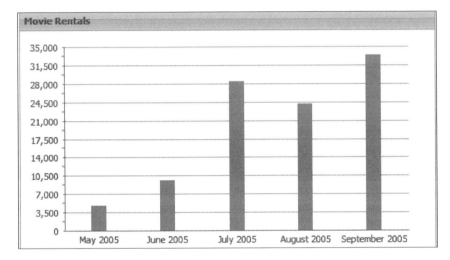

How to do it...

1. Set the URL to load the chart from:

```
Ext.chart.Chart.CHART_URL = '../ext3/charts.swf';
```

2. Define the data store:

```
Ext.onReady(function() {
    var rentalsStore = new Ext.data.JsonStore({
        fields: ['month', 'payments'],
        data: [
        { month: 'May 2005', payments: 4824.43 },
        { month: 'June 2005', payments: 9631.88 },
        { month: 'July 2005', payments: 28373.89 },
        { month: 'August 2005', payments: 24072.13 },
        { month: 'September 2005', payments: 33475.55 }
        ]
    });
```

3. Create a panel that will contain your chart and define it within the panel:

```
var pnl = new Ext.Panel({
    title: 'Movie Rentals',
    renderTo: Ext.getBody(),
    width: 500,
    height: 300,
    layout: 'fit',
    items: {
        xtype: 'columnchart',
        store: rentalsStore,
        xField: 'month',
        yField: 'payments',
        yAxis: new Ext.chart.NumericAxis({
        displayName: 'Rentals',
        labelRenderer : Ext.util.Format.numberRenderer('0,0')
        })
    }
});
});
```

How it works...

The grid is connected to the data in the local array through its data store.

To specify a column chart type, use `xtype = 'columnchart'`; or use `Ext.chart.ColumnChart` if you want to create the chart explicitly.

Notice the presence of an `Ext.util.Format.numberRenderer` instance to format the labels of the Y-axis.

See also...

▶ The next recipe, *Setting up a column chart to display data retrieved from the server*, explains what is needed to configure a column chart, so that it displays data that has been downloaded from the server

Setting up a column chart to display data retrieved from the server

In this recipe, you'll see how a column chart is set up to display data that has been downloaded from the server. As seen in previous chart recipes, the chart will display income-by-month figures for a fictitious movie rental company. A server page will retrieve this information from a database and make it available to the chart, as seen in the following screenshot:

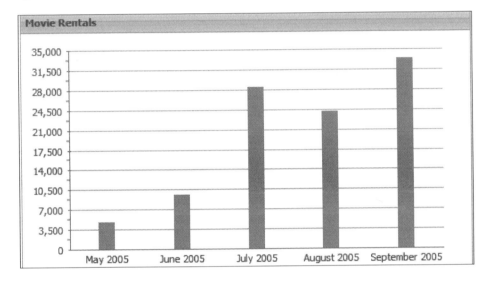

How to do it...

1. Set the URL to load the chart from:

    ```
    Ext.chart.Chart.CHART_URL = '../ext3/charts.swf';
    ```

2. Define the data store:

    ```
    Ext.onReady(function() {
        var rentalsStore = new Ext.data.JsonStore({
            url: 'chart-line-remote.php',
            root: 'rentals',
            fields: ['month', 'payments'],
            autoLoad: true
        });
    ```

3. Create a panel that will contain your chart and define it within the panel:

```
var pnl = new Ext.Panel({
    title: 'Movie Rentals',
    renderTo: Ext.getBody(),
    width: 500,
    height: 300,
    layout: 'fit',
    items: {
        xtype: 'columnchart',
        store: rentalsStore,
        xField: 'month',
        yField: 'payments',
        yAxis: new Ext.chart.NumericAxis({
            displayName: 'Rentals',
            labelRenderer : Ext.util.Format.numberRenderer('0,0')
        })
    }
});
});
```

How it works...

When it comes to data store configuration, the chart is no different than other Ext JS data-consuming widgets. To display remote data, simply use a store that acquires the data from a URL:

```
url: 'chart-line-remote.php'
```

Use `xtype = 'columnchart'` to specify a column chart type. You can also use `Ext.chart.ColumnChart` if you need to create the chart explicitly.

Notice the `Ext.util.Format.numberRenderer` instance of the format for the labels of the Y-axis.

See also...

► The previous recipe, *Setting up a column chart to display local data*, explains how to create a column chart and configure it, so that it displays data stored in a local array

Displaying local data with a pie chart

This recipe teaches you to create a pie chart that displays data stored in a local array. The data source used in this recipe is an array that contains movie sales information for a fictitious movie rental company. Each slice of the pie represents the amount of sales for a given movie category, as seen in the following screenshot:

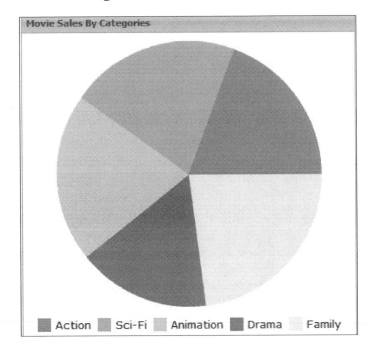

How to do it...

1. Set the URL to load the chart from:

   ```
   Ext.chart.Chart.CHART_URL = '../ext3/charts.swf';
   ```

2. Define the data store:

   ```
   Ext.onReady(function() {
       var salesStore = new Ext.data.JsonStore({
           fields: ['category', 'total_sales'],
           data: [
           { category: 'Action', total_sales: 4375.85 },
           { category: 'Sci-Fi', total_sales: 4756.98 },
           { category: 'Animation', total_sales: 4656.30 },
           { category: 'Drama', total_sales: 3722.54 },
           { category: 'Family', total_sales: 5226.07 }
           ]
       });
   ```

3. Create a panel that will contain your chart and define the chart within the panel:

```
var pnl = new Ext.Panel({
    title: 'Movie Sales By Categories',
    renderTo: Ext.getBody(),
    width: 400,
    height: 400,
    items: {
        xtype: 'piechart',
        store: salesStore,
        categoryField: 'category',
        dataField: 'total_sales',
        extraStyle:
        {
            legend:
            {
                display: 'bottom',
                padding: 5,
                font:
                {
                    family: 'Tahoma',
                    size: 13
                }
            }
        }
    }
});
```

How it works...

The grid is connected to the data in the local array through its data store.

To specify a pie chart, use `xtype = 'piechart'`; or use `Ext.chart.PieChart` If you want to create the chart explicitly.

While the `categoryField` configuration option specifies what data store field will define the chart's slices, the `dataField` option defines what field will define the dimensions of each slice.

The `extraStyle` config option is used to add styles, or override the styles defined by the `chartStyle` config option. In this case, we use it to define the position of the chart's legend. You can also use it to override the default `font`, `dataTip`, `padding`, and `animationEnabled` options.

There's more...

In general, the use of pie charts is controvertial due to the difficulty in comparing different slices of the same chart or data across different charts. However, these charts can be an effective way of displaying information in some cases—in particular if the purpose is to compare the size of a slice with the whole pie, rather than comparing the slices among themselves.

See also...

> ▶ The next recipe, *Displaying remote data with a pie chart*, illustrates how to configure a pie chart, so that it displays data that has been downloaded from the server

Displaying remote data with a pie chart

This recipe teaches you how to create a pie chart that displays remote data. Movie sales information for a fictitious movie rental company will be retrieved from a database and made available to the chart by a server page. Each slice of the pie represents the sales amount for a given movie category, as seen in the following screenshot:

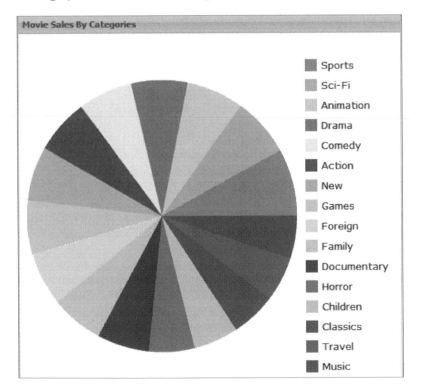

How to do it...

1. Set the URL to load the chart from:

```
Ext.chart.Chart.CHART_URL = '../ext3/charts.swf';
```

2. Define the data store:

```
Ext.onReady(function() {
    var salesStore = new Ext.data.JsonStore({
        url: 'chart-pie-remote.php',
        root: 'sales',
        fields: ['category', 'total_sales'],
        autoLoad: true
    });
```

3. Create a panel that will contain your chart and define the chart within the panel:

```
var pnl = new Ext.Panel({
    title: 'Movie Sales By Categories',
    renderTo: Ext.gctBody(),
    width: 500,
    height: 500,
    layout: 'fit',
    items: {
        xtype: 'piechart',
        store: salesStore,
        categoryField: 'category',
        dataField: 'total_sales',
        extraStyle:
        {
            legend:
            {
                display: 'right',
                padding: 5,
                font:
                {
                    family: 'Tahoma',
                    size: 13
                }
            }
        }
    });
}),
```

How it works...

To display remote data, simply use a store that acquires the data from a URL:

```
url: 'chart-pie-remote.php'
```

To specify a pie chart, use `xtype = 'piechart'`; or use `Ext.chart.PieChart` if you need to create the chart explicitly.

While the `categoryField` configuration option specifies what data store field will define the chart's slices, the `dataField` option establishes what field will define the dimensions of each slice.

The `extraStyle` config option is used to add styles, or override the styles defined by the `chartStyle` config option. In this case, use it to define the position of the chart's legend. You can also use it to override the default `font`, `dataTip`, `padding`, and `animationEnabled` options.

There's more...

In general, the use of pie charts is controvertial due to the difficulty in comparing different slices of the same chart, or data across different charts. The chart built in this recipe, with more than a dozen slices, is a good example. However, pie charts can be an effective way of displaying information in some cases, in particular if the purpose is to compare the size of a slice with the whole pie, rather than comparing the slices among themselves.

See also...

▶ The previous recipe, *Displaying local data with a pie chart*, explains how to create a pie chart and configure it to display data stored in a local array

Using a chart component to display multiple data series

The chart component supports the display of data series with different chart types. In this recipe, rental and payment information for a fictitious movie rental company will be retrieved from a database and will be made available to the chart component by a server page.

Rental data will be presented using a line chart, whereas payment data will be presented using a column chart as shown in the following screenshot:

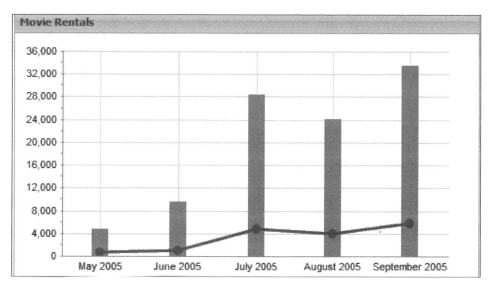

How to do it...

1. Set the URL to load the chart from:

    ```
    Ext.chart.Chart.CHART_URL = '../ext3/charts.swf';
    ```

2. Define the data store:

    ```
    Ext.onReady(function() {
        var rentalsStore = new Ext.data.JsonStore({
            url: 'chart-line-remote.php',
            root: 'rentals',
            fields: ['month', 'payments', 'filmsrented'],
            autoLoad: true
        });
    ```

3. Create a panel that will contain our chart and define the chart within the panel:

    ```
    var pnl = new Ext.Panel({
        title: 'Movie Rentals',
        renderTo: Ext.getBody(),
        width: 500,
        height: 300,
        layout: 'fit',
        items: {
            xtype: 'columnchart',
            store: rentalsStore,
            xField: 'month',
    ```

```
                    yAxis: new Ext.chart.NumericAxis({
                            displayName: 'Rentals',
                            labelRenderer : Ext.util.Format.
    numberRenderer('0,0')
                    }),
```

4. Define a `column` series:

```
                    series: [{
                        type: 'column',
                        displayName: 'Payments',
                        yField: 'payments',
                        style: { color: '#55bbcc' }
                    },
```

5. Define a `line` series:

```
                    {
                        type: 'line',
                        displayName: 'Films rented',
                        yField: 'filmsrented',
                        style:{color:'#AA3366'}
                    }],
```

6. Customize the look of the chart:

```
                    chartStyle: {
                        xAxis: {
                            color: 0x69aBc8,
                            majorTicks: {color: 0x69aBc8, length: 4},
                            minorTicks: {color: 0x69aBc8, length: 2},
                            majorGridLines: {size: 1, color: 0xeeeeee}
                        },
                        yAxis: {
                            color: 0x69aBc8,
                            majorTicks: {color: 0x69aBc8, length: 4},
                            minorTicks: {color: 0x69aBc8, length: 2},
                            majorGridLines: {size: 1, color: 0xdfe8f6}
                        }
                    }
                }
            });
        });
```

How it works...

The `type` config option defines a different type for different series; `type: 'column'` for the payment series and `type'line'` for the rental series. The `xField` config option is used once to define the X-axis as common to both the series. The `yField` option is different for each series. It maps to the `payments` and `filmsrented` fields of the data store.

The visual style of the chart can be changed using `chartStyle`. In this case, the `color`, `majorTicks`, `minorTicks`, and `majorGridlines` options are altered.

See also...

▸ The *Setting up a line chart to display data retrieved from the server* recipe (seen earlier in this chapter) explains how to create and configure a line chart to display data that has been downloaded from the server

▸ The *Setting up a column chart to display data retrieved from the server* recipe (seen previously in this chapter) explains what is needed to configure a column chart, so that it displays data that has been downloaded from the server

Creating an auto-refreshing chart

Sometimes, it is desirable to have a chart that automatically refreshes its information. This recipe shows you how to implement periodic updates of a chart's data. The **Crazy Stock Prices** chart will display fictitious stock prices, as seen in the following screenshot:

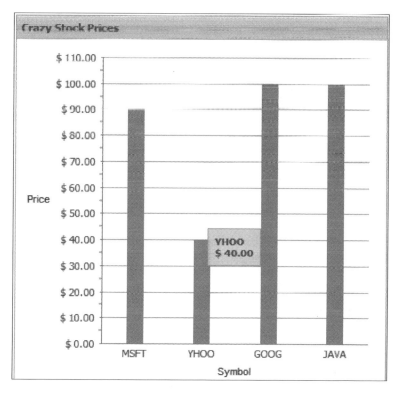

The chart's data will refresh periodically without user intervention, as seen in the following screenshot:

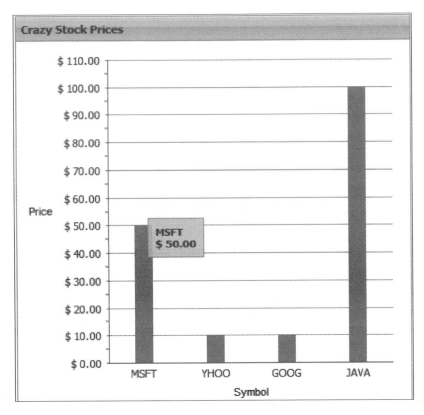

How to do it...

1. Set the URL to load the chart from:

```
Ext.chart.Chart.CHART_URL = '../ext3/charts.swf';
```

2. Create a function to generate dummy data:

```
function generateData() {
    var data = [];
    var companies = ['MSFT','YHOO','GOOG','JAVA'];
    for (var i = 0; i < 4; ++i) {
        data.push([companies[i], (Math.floor(Math.random() * 11) +
        1) * 10]);
    }
    return data;
}
```

3. Define a data store to feed the chart:

```
var store = new Ext.data.ArrayStore({
    fields: ['stock', 'price'],
    data: generateData()
});
```

4. Create a function that will be called periodically to refresh the data:

```
function refreshData() {
    store.loadData(generateData());
}
```

5. Create a panel that will contain your chart and define the chart within the panel:

```
Ext.onReady(function() {
    var pnl = new Ext.Panel({
        width: 400,
        height: 400,
        renderTo: document.body,
        title: 'Crazy Stock Prices',
        items: {
            xtype: 'columnchart',
            store: store,
            yField: 'price',
            xField: 'stock',
            xAxis: new Ext.chart.CategoryAxis({
                title: 'Symbol'
            }),
            yAxis: new Ext.chart.NumericAxis({
                title: 'Price',
                labelRenderer: Ext.util.Format.numberRenderer('$
                0,000.00')
            })
        }
    });
```

6. Set up a task to update the data at intervals:

```
    Ext.TaskMgr.start({
        run: refreshData,
        interval: 5000
    });
});
```

How it works...

What is needed in this scenario is a way to refresh the information that is saved in the chart's data store. This is accomplished with the use of the `Ext.TaskMgr` class.

`TaskMgr` is a static `Ext.util.TaskRunner` instance that can be used to run arbitrary tasks. Here, it is set up to execute the `refreshData()` function after every five seconds:

```
Ext.TaskMgr.start({
    run: refreshData,
    interval: 5000
});
```

`refreshData()`, in turn, loads a new batch of dummy data into the data store. By way of the data-binding mechanism built into the chart, an update of the data store contents will cause the chart to render the updated information.

Note that in a more robust implementation, the refresh interval would probably be a configurable option.

Configuring the Slider component to display a custom tip

The `Slider` component is a welcome addition to the Ext JS arsenal. One of the enhancements that you can make to this widget consists of adding a tool tip that displays the `Slider` component's current value as seen here:

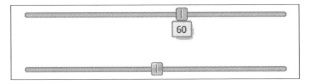

With little work, the tool tip can be made to display a friendlier message, as shown in the following screenshot:

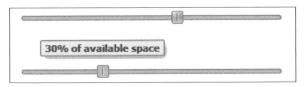

How to do it...

1. Define the `SliderTip` custom component:

> The `SliderTip` component used in this recipe is provided with the Ext JS documentation and samples at `http://www.extjs.com/deploy/dev/examples/`.

```
Ext.ux.SliderTip = Ext.extend(Ext.Tip, {
    minWidth: 10,
    offsets: [0, -10],
    init: function(slider) {
        slider.on('dragstart', this.onSlide, this);
        slider.on('drag', this.onSlide, this);
        slider.on('dragend', this.hide, this);
        slider.on('destroy', this.destroy, this);
    },
    onSlide: function(slider) {
        this.show();
        this.body.update(this.getText(slider));
        this.doAutoWidth();
        this.el.alignTo(slider.thumb, 'b-t?', this.offsets);
    },
    getText: function(slider) {
        return String(slider.getValue());
    }
});
```

2. Create the first `Slider` and set an instance of the `SliderTip` component as a plugin:

```
Ext.onReady(function() {
    var slider1 = new Ext.Slider({
        renderTo:'slider1',
        minValue: 0,
        maxValue: 100,
        width:300,
        increment: 10,
        plugins: new Ext.ux.SliderTip()
    });
```

3. Create a second `Slider` and set an instance of the `SliderTip` component as a plugin. Provide a custom message by overriding the `getText()` function of the `SliderTip` component:

```
    var slider2 = new Ext.Slider({
        renderTo: 'slider2',
        minValue: 0,
        maxValue: 100,
        width: 300,
        increment: 10,
```

```
      plugins: new Ext.ux.SliderTip({
          getText: function(slider) {
              return String.format('<b>{0}% of available space</
b>', slider.getValue());
          }
      })
   });
});
```

How it works...

The custom tip functionality comes as a courtesy of the `SliderTip` plugin. For the second `Slider`, the plugin is passed a `getText()` function that provides the custom format.

See also...

> ► The next recipe, *Enhancing the Slider component with custom tick marks*, explains another modification that you can make to the `Slider` component

Enhancing the Slider component with custom tick marks

Another enhancement you can make to the `Slider` component is adding custom tick marks. This recipe teaches you how this can be accomplished using a background image and cascading stylesheets, as seen in the following screenshot:

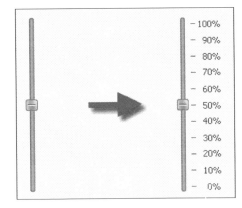

How to do it...

1. Create an image with tick marks, as seen below:

```
─ 100%
─  90%
─  80%
─  70%
─  60%
─  50%
─  40%
─  30%
─  20%
─  10%
─   0%
```

2. Create a CSS class that will be used to position the tick mark image behind the Slider:

```css
<style type="text/css">
    .vertical-slider
        {
        background: url(img/ticks-vert.gif) no-repeat 20px 20px;
        }
</style>
```

3. Define the Slider:

```javascript
Ext.onReady(function() {
    var slider = new Ext.Slider({
        renderTo:Ext.getBody(),
        vertical: true,
        minValue: 0,
        maxValue: 100,
        height: 214,
        increment: 10,
        plugins: new Ext.ux.SliderTip({
            getText: function(slider) {
                return String.format('<b>{0}% of available space
                </b>', slider.getValue());
            }
        })
    });
});
```

4. Add the `vertical-slider` CSS class to the document's body:

```html
<body class="vertical-slider" style="padding: 20px">
</body>
```

How it works...

The trick here is to position the tick marks image behind the `Slider`. This is accomplished by changing the background of the `Slider`'s container. In the above example, the `Slider`'s container is the body of the HTML document. Adding the `vertical-slider` CSS class to the document's body does the job.

When creating the tick marks image, pay attention to the height of the `Slider` and the distance between the steps (the `increment` config option). You want the image to correctly align with the `Slider`, and the tick marks to match the distance between the steps.

See also...

▶ The previous recipe, *Configuring the slider component to display a custom tip*, explains how the `Slider` component can be configured to display a custom tip

10
Patterns in Ext JS

In this chapter, you will learn the following recipes:

- ► Sharing functionality with the `Action` class
- ► Autosaving form values
- ► Saving resources with lazy component instantiation
- ► Extending a class
- ► Using code modules to achieve encapsulation
- ► Implementing a publish/subscribe mechanism with `relayEvents()`
- ► Augmenting a class with a plugin
- ► Building preconfigured classes
- ► Implementing state preservation with cookies

Introduction

In this chapter, you will explore some additional design patterns used to build robust and flexible applications with Ext JS. Besides autosaving form elements and component state management, you will be able to take a look at the patterns for building your own custom components on top of the Ext framework, along with ways for modularizing your code.

Sharing functionality with the Action class

Components such as buttons, menus, and toolbars frequently perform similar functionalities. This recipe shows you how you can use the `Action` interface to abstract a hypothetical `Import` function out of a menu, a toolbar item, and a button's handlers, effectively implementing a variant of the command design pattern. You will also learn how to use `Action` to change different configuration options of the components that use it.

In the following screenshot; a toolbar item, a menu item, and a button are all wired to perform the `Import` functionality by using the `Ext.Action` interface:

Clicking on any of the components that use the `Action` interface will execute the `Import` functionality, as seen in the following screenshot:

The `Action` interface allows you to change the text of the components that use it. In this recipe, you'll use an `Ext.Msg.prompt` to change the `Action`'s text, as seen in the following screenshot:

After entering the new text, all of the components that implement the `Action` will reflect the change, as seen in the following screenshot:

How to do it...

1. Create an `Action` instance:

```
Ext.onReady(function() {
    var action = new Ext.Action({
        iconCls: 'icon-data',
        text: 'Import',
        handler: function() {
        Ext.Msg.alert('Action executed', 'This is the Import
action executing...');
        }
    });
```

2. Now, create a panel with the different components that will use the `Action` instance:

```
var panel = new Ext.Panel({
    title: 'What you can do with Actions',
    width: 450,
    height: 200,
    bodyStyle: 'padding:10px;',
    tbar: [
        action, {
            text: 'Action Menu',
            menu: [action]
        }
    ],
    items: [
        new Ext.Button(action)
    ],
    renderTo: Ext.getBody()
});
var tb = panel.getTopToolbar();
// Buttons added to the toolbar of the Panel above    // to
test/demo doing group operations with an action
tb.add('-', {
    text: 'Disable action',
    handler: function() {
        action.setDisabled(!action.isDisabled());
        this.setText(action.isDisabled() ? 'Enable action' :
        'Disable action');
    }
}, {
    text: 'Change action text',
    handler: function() {
        Ext.Msg.prompt('Enter Text', 'Enter new text for the
        action:', function(btn, text) {
            if (btn == 'ok' && text) {
```

```
                               action.setText(text);
                               action.setHandler(function() {
                               Ext.Msg.alert('Click', 'This is the "' + text
                               + '" action executing...');
                               });
                    }
               });
          }
     }, {
          text: 'Switch action icon',
          handler: function() {
               action.setIconClass(action.getIconClass()='icon-data'
               ? 'icon-filter' : 'icon-data');
          }
     });
     tb.doLayout();
});
```

How it works...

The `Action` class allows you to share handlers, configuration options, and UI updates across any components that support the `Action` interface.

Start by creating an `Action` instance. The configuration options `iconCls`, `text`, and `handler` will be applied to the components that use it.

Next, create the different components that will use the `Action` such as a toolbar item and menu:

```
tbar: [
          action, {
               text: 'Action Menu',
               menu: [action]
          }
     ],
```

Next, create a button:

```
items: [
          new Ext.Button(action)
          ]
```

Notice how the `Action` instance functions as an item for the toolbar items. For buttons, the action instance is passed as the `config` object in the button definition.

Finally, some more components will help you to exercise the `Action` features:

A toolbar item allows you to toggle the enabled state of the `Action`:

```
{
    text: 'Disable action',
    handler: function() {
        action.setDisabled(!action.isDisabled());
        this.setText(action.isDisabled() ? 'Enable action' : 'Disable
action');
    }
}
```

A second toolbar item allows you to change the `Action`'s `text` and `handler`:

```
{
        text: 'Change action text',
        handler: function() {
            Ext.Msg.prompt('Enter Text', 'Enter new text for the
            action:', function(btn, text) {
                if (btn == 'ok' && text) {
                    action.setText(text);
                    action.setHandler(function() {
                    Ext.Msg.alert('Click', 'This is the "' + text + '"
                    action executing...');
                    });
                }
            });
        }
    }
```

There's more...

Any component that needs to use actions must support the `config` object interface, as well as the following method list: `setText(string)`, `setIconCls(string)`, `setDisabled(boolean)`, `setVisible(boolean)`, and `setHandler(function)`.

Autosaving form values

Autosave is a useful feature found in many applications. This recipe teaches you how to execute code that simulates the saving of a `TextArea`'s contents without requiring any user intervention.

Your `TextArea` will be accompanied by a couple of toolbar items that will show the character count and the last time the `TextArea` contents were saved, as seen in the following screenshot:

How to do it...

1. Create the components that will show the character count and status message:

```
Ext.onReady(function() {
    var statusMsg = new Ext.Toolbar.TextItem('');
    var charCount = new Ext.Toolbar.TextItem('Chars: 0');
```

2. Now, create a panel that will contain the the autosaving `TextArea`:

```
new Ext.Panel({
    title: 'Autosave of a form element',
    renderTo: 'autosave-form',
    width: 450,
    autoHeight: true,
    bodyStyle: 'padding:5px;',
    layout: 'fit',
    bbar: new Ext.Toolbar({
        id: 'statusBar',
        items: [charCount, '->', statusMsg]
    }),
```

3. Define the autosaving `TextArea` inside the panel. A handler for the `keypress` event will update the character count in the status bar:

```
items: {
    xtype: 'textarea',
    id: 'autosaveTextArea',
    enableKeyEvents: true,
    grow: true,
    growMin: 100,
    growMax: 200,
    listeners: {
        // Update the character count.
        'keypress': {
```

```
                          fn: function(t) {
                              var v = t.getValue();
                              var cc = v.length ? v.length : 0;
                              Ext.fly(charCount.getEl()).update('Chars:
                              ' + cc);
                          },
                          buffer: 1 // buffer to allow the value to
                          update first
                      }
                  }
              }
          });
```

4.   Another handler for the text area's `keypress` event will initiate a delayed task that, in turn, will execute the autosave routine:

```
    Ext.fly('autosaveTextArea').on('keypress', function() {
          statusMsg.setText('Last saved at ' + new Date().
format('g:i:s A'));
          // Put your save code here.
    }, this, { buffer: 1500 });
    });
```

How it works...

Your simple text editor consists of a panel with a TextArea and a toolbar, which will show the character count and the time that the TextArea value was last saved.

Use the text area's keypress event to keep track of the character count. This keypress handler displays the length of the TextArea's value in the toolbar.

```
listeners: {
              // Update the character count.
              'keypress': {
                  fn: function(t) {
                      var v = t.getValue();
                      var cc = v.length ? v.length : 0;
          Ext.fly(charCount.getEl()).update('Chars: ' + cc);
                  },
                  buffer: 1 // buffer to allow the value to update
    first
              }
          }
      }
```

The autosaving logic is also triggered by the `keypress` event in the `TextArea`. The global `flyweight` object allows you to acquire a reference to the `TextArea` and wire the event handler:

```
Ext.fly('autosaveTextArea').on('keypress', function() ....
```

You can use this event handler to call your implementation of the save feature right after updating the status bar message:

```
statusMsg.setText('Last saved at ' + new Date().format('g:i:s A'));
// Put your save code here.
```

There's more...

Use this recipe in scenarios where it's important to preserve the integrity of the information being worked on without requiring user intervention. This need is typically found when handling large documents or forms, or in environments with unreliable connectivity between your client application and the server.

Saving resources with lazy component instantiation

In large applications, instantiating all application objects when the page loads—those that are initially needed and those that might or might not be needed later—will cause a number of unused objects to be sitting in the memory.

Lazy instantiation reduces the amount of consumed resources by initially committing to memory only the configuration of the objects (and not the actual object instances) and deferring instance creation until render time. This recipe explains how lazy instantiation is done.

You will build two panels that look identical. The items of the first panel are explicitly instantiated, and this is how the panel will look:

Panel with items explicitly created
Save

The second panel's items are instantiated at render time. This is a screenshot of the second panel:

How to do it...

1. Create a function that animates the progress bars used in the panels:

```
Ext.onReady(function() {
    var loadFn = function(btn, textItem, statusBar, pBar) {
        btn = Ext.getCmp(btn);
        btn.disable();
        Ext.fly(textItem).update('Saving...');
        Ext.getCmp(pBar).wait({
            interval: 200,
            duration: 5000,
            increment: 15,
            fn: function() {
                btn.enable();
                Ext.fly(textItem).update('Done');
            }
        });
    };
```

2. Explicitly instantiate a progress bar, a button, and some toolbar items. These will be placed on the first panel:

```
var pBar = new Ext.ProgressBar({
    id: 'pBar1',
    width: 100
});
var button = new Ext.Button({
    xtype: 'button',
    id: 'btn1',
    text: 'Save',
    width: '75',
    handler: loadFn.createCallback('btn1',
    'statusTxt1','sBar1', 'pBar1')
});
```

```
var textItem = new Ext.Toolbar.TextItem({ text: '', id:
'statusTxt1' });
var fill = new Ext.Toolbar.Fill();
```

3. Create the first panel. This panel contains the items that were explicitly instantiated:

```
var pnl1 = new Ext.Panel({
    title: 'Panel with items explicitly created',
    renderTo: 'pnl1',
    width: 400,
    height: 200,
    bodyStyle: 'padding:10px;',
    items: [button],
    bbar: {
        id: 'sBar1',
        items: [textItem, fill, pBar]
    }
});
```

4. Create the second panel. In contrast with the first panel, this panel's items are defined inline:

```
var pnl2 = new Ext.Panel({
    title: 'Panel with items whose creation is deferred',
    renderTo: 'pnl2',
    width: 400,
    height: 200,
    bodyStyle: 'padding:10px;',
    items: [{xtype: 'button',
        id: 'btn2',
        text: 'Save',
        width: '75',
        handler: loadFn.createCallback('btn2',
        'statusTxt2','sBar2', 'pBar2')}],
    bbar: {
        id: 'sBar2',
        items: [{ xtype: 'tbtext', text: '', id: 'statusTxt2'
        },
            '->',
            { xtype: 'progress', id:'pBar2',width: 100 }
        ]
    }
});
});
```

How it works...

As opposed to the first panel, the second panel's components are defined inline as a set of configuration options that include the xtype property. The xtype is a symbolic name given to a class, so that it can be instantiated by the framework's component manager. For example, if you look at the second progress bar, what is committed to memory is a small configuration object:

```
{ xtype: 'progress', id:'pBar2',width: 100 }
```

When the progress bar needs to be rendered, the ComponentMgr class will execute the create(...) function:

```
create: function(config, defaultType) {
    return new types[config.xtype || defaultType](config);
}
```

As you can probably tell, the code in create(...) is equivalent to:

```
return new Ext.ProgressBar(config);
```

And this effectively produces the progress bar. But notice that the process occurs when the progress bar is about to be rendered, and not at the page-load time.

In short, lazy instantiation is achieved by using the component manager's ability to produce an instance of a class just when it is needed, based on a config object that includes the xtype, or type identifier, of the class.

Extending a class

This recipe explains how to use a class extension to create a custom field. As an example, you will build a custom TextField component that provides visual feedback indicating that it is a required field. The feedback will consist of a small glyph on the upper-left corner of the field's input elements, as seen in the following screenshot:

How to do it...

1. Define the namespace that you will use:

   ```
   Ext.ns('Ext.ux.form');
   ```

2. Define the custom field as an extension of `ext.form.TextField` and override the `onRender()` method:

```
Ext.ux.form.RequiredTextField = Ext.extend(Ext.form.TextField, {
    allowBlank: false,
    onRender: function(ct, position) {
```

3. Within `onRender()` Call the `onRender()` method of the base class:

```
Ext.ux.form.RequiredTextField.superclass.onRender.call(this, ct,
position);
```

4. Moving on to the custom behavior, calculate the glyph's location:

```
        glyphX = this.el.dom.clientLeft + this.el.dom.offsetLeft + 1;
        glyphY = this.el.dom.clientTop + this.el.dom.offsetTop + 1;
        }
});
```

5. Create the glyph's element and insert it in the DOM tree:

```
theGlyph = '<img style="position: absolute; width: 5px; height:
5px; left:'
    + glyphX + 'px; top:' + glyphY + 'px;" src="img/text-bg-reqd.
png"/>';
Ext.DomHelper.insertAfter(this.el, theGlyph);
```

6. Register the custom field with the framework:

```
Ext.reg('ux.requiredtextfield', Ext.ux.form.RequiredTextField);
```

7. Now create a panel that uses the custom field:

```
Ext.onReady(function() {
    var commentForm = new Ext.FormPanel({
        frame: true,
        renderTo:document.body,
        title: 'What is your name',
        bodyStyle: 'padding:5px',
        width: 450,
        layout: 'form',
        items: [
                {   xtype: 'ux.requiredtextfield',
                    fieldLabel: 'Name',
                    name: 'name',
                    anchor: '98%',
                    allowBlank:false
                }, {
                    xtype: 'textfield',
```

```
                              fieldLabel: 'Email',
                              name: 'email',
                              anchor: '98%',
                              vtype:'email'
                      }
                      ],
                      buttons: [{
                              text: 'Send'
                              }, {
                              text: 'Cancel'
                      }]
              });
        });
```

How it works...

To indicate that `RequiredTextField` modifies the behavior of the `TextField` class, you'll have to call `Ext.extend()`.

The first modification consists of setting the `allowBlank` property to `false` in order to signal that the field is required.

The second and most important change is overriding the `onRender()` function. Within `onRender()`, invoking the parent class's `onRender()` function guarantees that the field is rendered to the screen before the glyph is added:

```
Ext.ux.form.RequiredTextField.superclass.onRender.call(this, ct,
position);
```

Up to this point, the rendered field would look just like the native `TextField`, as seen in the following screenshot:

With the field rendered, you can use its location to determine the coordinates where the glyph will be inserted:

```
glyphX = this.el.dom.clientLeft + this.el.dom.offsetLeft + 1;
glyphY = this.el.dom.clientTop + this.el.dom.offsetTop + 1;
```

The glyph is an image inserted after the text box element of the field. It is absolute-positioned in such a way that it appears near the upper-left corner of the text box.

```
theGlyph = '<img style="position: absolute; width: 5px; height: 5px;
left:' + glyphX + 'px; top:' + glyphY + 'px;" src="img/text-bg-reqd.
png"/>';
Ext.DomHelper.insertAfter(this.el, theGlyph);
```

There's more...

The best practice for extension consists of calling Ext.extend(), and passing the original class and configuration object as arguments.

This is a simple template that you can use in your applications:

```
MyGridPanel = Ext.extend(Ext.grid.GridPanel, {
    initComponent: function() {
        // Your preprocessing here.
        // Call the parent class' initComponent.
        MyGridPanel.superclass.initComponent.call(this);
        // Your postprocessing here.  Event handling and other
        // things that require the object to exist.
    },
    yourMethod: function() {
        // Your method's body
    }
});
```

 A more detailed extension template is available in the *Extending a Ext2 Class* tutorial at http://extjs.com/learn/Tutorial:Extending_Ext2_Class.

See also...

▸ The *Augmenting a class with a plugin* recipe (to be seen later in this chapter), explains how to change the behavior of the Ext JS components by using plugins

▸ The *Building preconfigured classes* recipe (to be seen later in this chapter) illustrates a useful pattern that consists of creating classes with built-in configuration options

Using code modules to achieve encapsulation

This recipe demonstrates how to achieve encapsulation by organizing your code into modules where you can have private, privileged, and public members.

You will be building two modules, each with a private `Action` instance and a public `run()` method.

Calling a module's public `run()` method will cause the module to build and render a panel:

The first module's private `Action`, which is accessible only by the code within the module, will be assigned to the panel's **Import** toolbar button:

The second module's private `Action` will be assigned to the panel's **Filter** button:

How to do it...

1. Create a namespace for your example and define the first module:

```
Ext.namespace('BigSystem');
BigSystem.module1 = function() {
    // "action" is a private member of "module1".
    var action = new Ext.Action({
        iconCls: 'icon-data',
        text: 'Import',
        handler: function() {
            Ext.Msg.alert('Action executed', 'This is an action
form inside module1');
        }
    });
    return {
        // "run" is a public member of "module1".
        run: function() {
            var panel = new Ext.Panel({
                title: 'Module 1',
                width: 450,
                height: 200,
                bodyStyle: 'padding:10px;',
                tbar: [
                    action
                ],
```

```
                   renderTo:'mod1'
              });
         }
    }
}
```

2. Define the second module:

```
BigSystem.module2 = function() {
    // "action" is a private member of "module2".
    var action = new Ext.Action({
        iconCls: 'icon-filter',
        text: 'Filter',
        handler: function() {
            Ext.Msg.alert('Action executed', 'This is an action
form inside module2');
        }
    });
    return {
        // "run" is a public member of "module2".
        run: function() {
            var panel = new Ext.Panel({
                title: 'Module 2',
                width: 450,
                height: 200,
                bodyStyle: 'padding:10px;',
                items: [
                    new Ext.Button(action)
                ],
                renderTo:'mod2'
            });
        }
    }
}
```

3. Build an instance of each module and call each module's public member `run()`:

```
Ext.onReady(function() {
    var m1 = new BigSystem.module1();
    m1.run();
    var m2 = new BigSystem.module2();
    m2.run();
});
```

How it works...

A module is simply a function that returns an object. The returned object's properties (that is; functions or variables) become the public members of the module, and members that do not appear inside the return statement are private to the module. For example, the following module defines a `count` private variable, an `increaseCount()` private function, and the public functions `init()`, `getCount()`, and `checkCount()`:

```
module = function() {
    var count = 0; // Private Variable for the module. Not accessible
from outside
    var increaseCount = function() { // Private function. Not
accessible from outside
        count++;
    }
    return {
        init: function() { // Privileged method. Can be called from
        outside
            // Here comes the initialisation code
        },
        getCount: function() { // Privileged method. Can be called
        from outside
            return count;
        },
        checkCount: function() {
            increaseCount();
            if (this.getCount() > 10)
                alert("count is greater than 10");
        }
    }
}
```

In this recipe, you have taken advantage of the mechanism explained above to make the `run()` function of each module accessible to any calling code, whereas the `Action` instances can only be called by code within the module that defines each of them.

There's more...

Use the module pattern to expose services that can be consumed by other modules and to keep the inner workings of your modules hidden and free from coupling with external code.

See also...

▶   The *Building preconfigured classes* recipe (to be seen later in this chapter) illustrates a useful pattern that consists of creating classes with built-in configuration options

Implementing a publish/subscribe mechanism with relayEvents()

In this recipe, you'll learn how to implement a publish/subscribe mechanism, where a component listens to events generated from within other components. A very simple console listens to events that occur inside two panels, as seen in the following screenshot:

How to do it...

1. Create a namespace for your code and define a utility function that will be used by your event-handling routines:

```
Ext.ns('Dashboard');
function WriteToConsole(console, msg) {
    var prevValue = console.getValue();
    if (null == prevValue) prevValue = '';
    console.setValue(prevValue + msg);
}
```

2. Create a `Portlet` class as an extension of `Ext.Panel`:

```
Dashboard.Portlet = Ext.extend(Ext.Panel, {
    anchor: '100%',
    frame: true,
    collapsible: true,
    draggable: true,
```

3. Add some tools to the `Portlet` class and attach the `click` handlers to each tool. The `click` handlers will fire the custom events defined in the next step:

```
tools: [{
    id: 'gear',
```

```
        handler: function(e, toolEl, panel) {
            panel.fireEvent('gearClick', panel);
        }
    }, {
        id: 'help',
        handler: function(e, toolEl, panel) {
            panel.fireEvent('helpClick', panel);
        }
    }],
```

4. Define the custom events of this portlet. These are the events invoked by the `click` handlers above:

```
        this.addEvents('gearClick', 'helpClick');
    }
});
```

5. Now, it's time to use the `Portlet` class. Create a couple of portlets:

```
Ext.onReady(function() {
    var portlet1 = new Dashboard.Portlet({
        title: 'Portlet 1',
        renderTo: 'p1',
        id: 'portlet1'
    })
    var portlet2 = new Dashboard.Portlet({
        title: 'Portlet 2',
        renderTo: 'p2',
        id: 'portlet2'
    })
```

6. A `TextArea` will serve as a logging console:

```
    var console = new Ext.form.TextArea({
        renderTo: 'console',
        width: 350,
        grow: true,
        growMin: 200,
        growMax: 300
    })
```

7. Use `relayEvents()` to make the console listen to the portlet's custom events. The console is the subscriber in your publisher/subscriber model:

```
    console.relayEvents(portlet1, ['gearClick', 'helpClick']);
    console.relayEvents(portlet2, ['gearClick', 'helpClick']);
```

8. In the console, define the handlers for the portlet's `gearClick` and `helpClick` custom events:

```
console.on('gearClick', function(panel) {
    var msg = 'Gear clicked. Portlet Id = ' + panel.id + '\n';
    WriteToConsole(console,msg);
});
console.on('helpClick', function(panel) {
    var msg = 'Help clicked. Portlet Id = ' + panel.id + '\n';
    WriteToConsole(console,msg);
});
});
```

How it works...

After defining the portlets and the console, use the `relayEvents(...)` function to ensure that the console will subscribe to the `gearClick` and `helpClick` events of the portlets:

```
console.relayEvents(portlet1, ['gearClick', 'helpClick']);
console.relayEvents(portlet2, ['gearClick', 'helpClick']);
```

The `relayEvents()` function relays selected events from a specified `Observable` instance—in your case, the two portlets—as if the events were fired by its caller; in this case, the `TextArea` that serves as login console.

With the subscription created, you just need to add the code to handle the events that interest us:

```
console.on('gearClick', function(panel) {
        var msg = 'Gear clicked. Portlet Id = ' + panel.id + '\n';
        WriteToConsole(console,msg);
});
    console.on('helpClick', function(panel) {
        var msg = 'Help clicked. Portlet Id = ' + panel.id + '\n';
        WriteToConsole(console,msg);
    });
});
```

There's more...

Use this approach to achieve a loosely coupled architecture where components subscribe only to the events that are of interest to them, without requiring the event generators to have any knowledge about who the subscribers are.

This decoupling of publishers and subscribers allows for greater scalability, since publishers and subscribers can be added, changed, or removed with minimal impact on the rest of the system.

Augmenting a class with a plugin

A way to change the behavior of a class is by using plugins. This recipe explains the mechanics of a plugin through an example plugin that provides visual feedback that indicates when a `TextField` or `TextArea` is a required field. The feedback will consist of a small glyph on the upper-left corner of the field's input elements, as seen in the following screenshot:

How to do it...

1. Define a couple of namespaces to encapsulate your `plugin` class:

   ```
   Ext.ns('Ext.ux', 'Ext.ux.plugins');
   ```

2. Define the `RequiredFieldGlyph` plugin:

   ```
   Ext.ux.plugins.RequiredFieldGlyph = {
       init: function(field) {
           var thisXType = field.getXType();
   ```

3. Inside the plugin's `init()` method, check that the host field is either a `TextArea` or `TextField` instance. Your plugin will only modify these types:

   ```
           // You only want to modify textfield fields.
           if ('textarea' != thisXType && 'textfield' != thisXType)
   return;
           onRender = field.onRender;
   ```

4. Define a rendering function that will execute right after the host field's `onRender()` function:

   ```
           Ext.apply(field, {
               allowBlank: false,
               onRender: onRender.createSequence(function(ct,
               position) {
   ```

5. Inside the rendering function, calculate the position of the glyph and add the glyph to the field:

```
if ('textarea' == thisXType) {
    if (Ext.isGecko) {
        glyphX = this.el.dom.clientLeft + this.
        el.dom.offsetLeft + 2;

        glyphY = this.el.dom.clientTop + this.
        el.dom.offsetTop + 2;
    } else {
        glyphX = this.el.dom.clientLeft + this.
        el.dom.offsetLeft + 1;

        glyphY = this.el.dom.clientTop + this.
        el.dom.offsetTop + 1;
    }
} else {
    // For textfield.
    glyphX = this.el.dom.clientLeft + this.el.dom.
    offsetLeft + 1;

    glyphY = this.el.dom.clientTop + this.el.dom.
    offsetTop + 1;
}
theGlyph = '<img style="position: absolute; width:
5px; height: 5px; left:' + glyphX +
        'px; top:' + glyphY + 'px;" src="img/text-
        bg-reqd.png"/>';
Ext.DomHelper.insertAfter(this.el, theGlyph);
            }) // onRender
        });
    }
}
```

6. Create a form panel with a `TextField` that uses your plugin:

```
Ext.onReady(function() {
    var commentForm = new Ext.FormPanel({
    frame: true,
        renderTo:Ext.getBody(),
        title: 'What is your name?',
        bodyStyle: 'padding:5px',
        width: 450,
        layout: 'form',
        items: [
    { xtype: 'textfield',
```

```
            fieldLabel: 'Name',
            name: 'name',
            anchor: '98%',
            allowBlank:false,
            plugins: [Ext.ux.plugins.RequiredFieldGlyph]

        }, {
            xtype: 'textfield',
            fieldLabel: 'Email',
            name: 'email',
            anchor: '98%',
            vtype:'email'
        }
        ],
            buttons: [{
                text: 'Send'
            }, {
                text: 'Cancel'
            }]
        });
    });
```

How it works...

A plugin is an object that provides custom functionality for its host component. The only requirement for a plugin is that it contains an `init()` method that accepts a reference of the `Ext.Component` type. This reference is assumed to be of the plugin's host.

If any plugins are available when a component is created, the component will call the `init()` method on each plugin and pass a reference to itself. Each plugin can then call methods or respond to events on its host, as needed, to provide its functionality.

Implementing this logic, your plugin's `init()` function will be called during the host component's initialization—an ideal time to add your modifications.

Since this plugin targets `TextField` and `TextArea` instances, the first step is to check whether or not the host field is a `TextField` and `TextArea` instance. This preserves the behavior of other fields if they are accidentally assigned the plugin:

```
// You only want to modify textfield and textarea fields.
 if ('textarea' != thisXType && 'textfield' != thisXType) return;
```

Your plugin will define a new onRender() function, which uses Function. createSequence() to execute code immediately after the host's native onRender() function is called. The plugin's onRender() function calculates the location where the glyph will be inserted, based on the input field's position. Observe that the calculation for text areas takes into account browser differences:

```
if ('textarea' == thisXType) {
            if (Ext.isGecko) {
                glyphX = this.el.dom.clientLeft + this.el.dom.
                offsetLeft + 2;
                glyphY = this.el.dom.clientTop + this.el.dom.
                offsetTop + 2;
            } else {
                glyphX = this.el.dom.clientLeft + this.el.dom.
                offsetLeft + 1;
                glyphY = this.el.dom.clientTop + this.el.dom.
                offsetTop + 1;
            }
        } else {
            // For textfield.
            glyphX = this.el.dom.clientLeft + this.el.dom.
            offsetLeft + 1;
            glyphY = this.el.dom.clientTop + this.el.dom.
            offsetTop + 1;
}
```

The glyph is made up of an absolute positioned image that is inserted with Ext.DomHelper. InsertAfter():

```
theGlyph = '<img style="position: absolute; width: 5px; height: 5px;
left:' + glyphX + 'px; top:' + glyphY + 'px;" src="img/text-bg-reqd.
png"/>';
Ext.DomHelper.insertAfter(this.el, theGlyph);
```

Absolute positioning makes the glyph appear near the upper-left corner of the input field, as seen in the following screenshot:

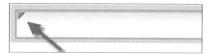

See also...

▶ The *Extending a class* recipe (seen earlier in this chapter) explains how to use class extension to create custom fields

▶ The next recipe, *Building preconfigured classes*, illustrates a useful pattern that consists of creating classes with built-in configuration options

Building preconfigured classes

Preconfigured classes are extensions of the Ext classes with built-in configuration options. This pattern allows you to set up your components to perform specific tasks, without having to pass configuration options through the configuration object.

In this recipe, you will build two portlets; instances of the `Panel` class, preconfigured with fixed dimensions, a choice of tools, and event handlers. The two portlets can be seen below:

How to do it...

1. Create a naming container for your code and define the `Portlet` class as an extension of the `Ext.Panel` class:

```
Ext.ns('Dashboard');
Dashboard.Portlet = Ext.extend(Ext.Panel, {
```

2. Preconfigure the portlet. All instances of this class will use these settings by default:

```
initComponent: function() {
Ext.apply(this, {
            anchor: '100%',
            frame: true,
            collapsible: true,
            draggable: true,
            height: 150,     // Default height and widths.
            width: 200,
            tools: [{
```

```
                    id: 'gear',
                    handler: function() {
                        // Put common handler code here.
                        Ext.Msg.alert('Message', 'The Settings tool
                        was clicked.');
                    }
                }, {
                    id: 'close',
                    handler: function(e, target, panel) {
                        // Put common handler code here.
                        Ext.Msg.alert('Message', 'The Close tool was
                        clicked.');
                    }
                }]
            });
```

3. Call the base class `initComponent()` method:

```
Dashboard.Portlet.superclass.initComponent.apply(this, arguments);
```

4. Now, create a couple of instances of your custom class. You can combine the preconfigured properties with values passed at runtime:

```
Ext.onReady(function() {
    var p1 = new Dashboard.Portlet({
        title: 'Portlet 1',
        renderTo: 'p1',
        html:'A preconfigured panel'
    })
    var p2 = new Dashboard.Portlet({
        title: 'Portlet 2',
        renderTo: 'p2',
        html: 'Another preconfigured panel'
    })
});
```

How it works...

You can create preconfigured classes by extending a base class. In this case, some properties, tools, and event handlers are added to the `Panel` class when `Ext.extend(...)` is called. This is a template you can use for your preconfigured classes:

```
MyPreConfigClass = Ext.extend([BASE CLASS], {
    initComponent: function() {
```

```
        Ext.apply(this, {
            // Preconfigure. Options here cannot be changed from
            outside.
        });
        MyPreConfigClass.superclass.initComponent.apply(this,
        arguments);
        // Install event handlers on rendered components here.
    }
});
```

See also...

▶ The *Extending a class* recipe (seen earlier in this chapter) explains how to use a class extension to create custom fields

▶ The previous recipe, *Augmenting a Class with a plugin*, explains how to change the behavior of the Ext JS components by using plugins

Implementing state preservation with cookies

In this recipe, you will learn to use the state management features in Ext JS for preserving the selected tab in a TabPanel across page loads. Specifically, the selected tab's ID will be saved to and read from a cookie.

A notification of a State Change event will be displayed upon selecting a tab, as shown in the following screenshot:

As seen in the following screenshot, after a page reload, the TabPanel recovers its previous state:

How to do it...

1. Create a naming container for your code:

```
Ext.ns('Example');
```

2. Define the `StatefulTabPanel` class as an extension of `Ext.TabPanel` and configure the state management options:

```
Example.StatefulTabPanel = Ext.extend(Ext.TabPanel, {
    stateEvents: ['tabchange'],
    getState: function() { return { tab: this.getActiveTab().id}
},
    applyState: function(state) { this.setActiveTab(state.tab); }
});
```

3. Define the state provider, a `CookieProvider` instance:

```
Ext.onReady(function() {
var cp = new Ext.state.CookieProvider({
    path: "/",
    expires: new Date(new Date().getTime() + TIME_OFFSET)
});
Ext.state.Manager.setProvider(cp);
```

4. A handler for the state provider's `statechange` event will alert us when a change of state occurs:

```
cp.on('statechange', function(provider, key, value) {
    Ext.Msg.alert('State Change', 'key: ' + key + ', value: ' +
    value);
});
```

5. Lastly, create the `StatefulTabPanel` instance:

```
var tab = new Example.StatefulTabPanel({
        stateful: true,
        stateId:'myTabPanel',
        renderTo: document.body,
        activeTab: 0,
        width: 500,
        height: 250,
        plain: true,
        defaults: { autoScroll: true },
        items: [{
        title: 'First Tab',
            bodyStyle:'padding:5px',
            html: 'Switch tabs and refresh'
```

```
        }, {
            title: 'Second Tab',
            bodyStyle: 'padding:5px',
            html:'Remember me?'
        }, {
            title: 'Third Tab',
            bodyStyle: 'padding:5px',
            html:'I remember'
        }]
    });
});
```

How it works...

Start by creating an extension of the `TabPanel` class with the state management features: `stateEvents`, `getState()`, and `applyState()`.

As you want to save the index of the selected tab, use `tabchange` as the event that triggers the saving of the state. While `getState()` returns the `ID` of the selected tab, `applyState` (state) takes care of selecting the tab that is supplied in the state argument.

State-aware components check the `Ext.state.Manager` singleton—the global state manager—for state information. The global state manager, in turn, needs a state provider in order to route state information to and from the location where it is persisted; for example, a cookie or a database. This is why the next step in the example consists of creating an `Ext.state.CookieProvider` instance that is supplied to the state manager:

```
var cp = new Ext.state.CookieProvider({
    path: "/",
    expires: new Date(new Date().getTime() + TIME_OFFSET)
});
Ext.state.Manager.setProvider(cp);
```

As an alternative, you can pass a custom state provider directly to the `TabPanel`. This is something you can do with any state-aware component.

The last step is creating a handler for the state provider's `statechange` event, so that you can have visual confirmation when the event occurs.

There's more...

Note that you can specify an array of events as the value for the `stateEvents` config option. These events can be of any type supported by the component, including browser and custom events.

Index

S

Safari
detecting, Ext.isSafari2 used 9
scoping variables
preventing 26
preventing steps 26
slider component
configuring, for displaying custom tip 322-324
enhancing, with custom tick marks 324-326
start() method 297
state preservation
implementing, with cookies 354-356
status bar items, custom look
creating 293
strings manipulation
about 20
steps 20, 21
working 22

T

tab activation
handling 254, 255
tabbed GUI 46
tabbed look
using 46
tab data
loading, with Ajax 255-257
table layout
about 51, 53
employing 51, 52
TabPanel
enhancing, with TabCloseMenu plugin 259-261
enhancing, with TabScrollerMenu plugin 261-263
TabPanel class 47
tabs
adding, dynamically 257, 258
creating 46
three-panel application layout
details panel 62
master panel 62
navigation panel 62
panel, reconfiguring 62- 67
with, single line code 61

working 68-72
toolbar
buttons, placing 280
menus, placing 285
tooltips
adding, to grid cells 242-244
tree nodes
populating, with server-side data 264, 265
type-ahead feature, combo box
about 140
data store, creating 141
functions 142
local data, creating 140

U

URL
validating 101, 102
URL data
decoding 16
encoding 16

V

validation errors display location
display locationchanging 94-96
validation strategy
rounding up, with server-side validation 108, 109

W

wait(...) function 296
Windows
detecting, Ext.isWindows used 9
Wizard style UI
about 44
card layout, using 46
wizard cards, creating 44

X

XML data
serving, to form 119-123
XML data, sent by server
displaying 164-166

[PACKT PUBLISHING]

Thank you for buying
Ext JS 3.0 Cookbook

Packt Open Source Project Royalties

When we sell a book written on an Open Source project, we pay a royalty directly to that project. Therefore by purchasing Ext JS 3.0 Cookbook, Packt will have given some of the money received to the Ext JS project.

In the long term, we see ourselves and you—customers and readers of our books—as part of the Open Source ecosystem, providing sustainable revenue for the projects we publish on. Our aim at Packt is to establish publishing royalties as an essential part of the service and support a business model that sustains Open Source.

If you're working with an Open Source project that you would like us to publish on, and subsequently pay royalties to, please get in touch with us.

Writing for Packt

We welcome all inquiries from people who are interested in authoring. Book proposals should be sent to authors@packtpub.com. If your book idea is still at an early stage and you would like to discuss it first before writing a formal book proposal, contact us; one of our commissioning editors will get in touch with you.

We're not just looking for published authors; if you have strong technical skills but no writing experience, our experienced editors can help you develop a writing career, or simply get some additional reward for your expertise.

About Packt Publishing

Packt, pronounced 'packed', published its first book "Mastering phpMyAdmin for Effective MySQL Management" in April 2004 and subsequently continued to specialize in publishing highly focused books on specific technologies and solutions.

Our books and publications share the experiences of your fellow IT professionals in adapting and customizing today's systems, applications, and frameworks. Our solution-based books give you the knowledge and power to customize the software and technologies you're using to get the job done. Packt books are more specific and less general than the IT books you have seen in the past. Our unique business model allows us to bring you more focused information, giving you more of what you need to know, and less of what you don't.

Packt is a modern, yet unique publishing company, which focuses on producing quality, cutting-edge books for communities of developers, administrators, and newbies alike. For more information, please visit our website: www.PacktPub.com.

Learning Ext JS

ISBN: 978-1-847195-14-2   Paperback: 324 pages

Build dynamic, desktop-style user interfaces for your data-driven web applications

1. Learn to build consistent, attractive web interfaces with the framework components.

2. Integrate your existing data and web services with Ext JS data support.

3. Enhance your JavaScript skills by using Ext's DOM and AJAX helpers.

4. Extend Ext JS through custom components.

Learning jQuery 1.3

ISBN: 978-1-847196-70-5   Paperback: 444 pages

Better Interaction Design and Web Development with Simple JavaScript Techniques

1. An introduction to jQuery that requires minimal programming experience

2. Detailed solutions to specific client-side problems

3. For web designers to create interactive elements for their designs

4. For developers to create the best user interface for their web applications

5. Packed with great examples, code, and clear explanations

Please check **www.PacktPub.com** for information on our titles

4057601